LUND STUDIES IN ENGLISH. 32

EDITOR: PROFESSOR OLOF ARNGART

ELIZABETHAN SONNET THEMES AND THE DATING OF SHAKESPEARE'S 'SONNETS'

BY

CLAES SCHAAR

C. W. K. GLEERUP
LUND

EJNAR MUNKSGAARD
COPENHAGEN

The printing has been subsidized by Statens Humanistiska Forskningsråd

LUND
HÅKAN OHLSSONS BOKTRYCKERI
1962

PREFATORY NOTE

On finishing my studies in Renaissance sonneteering, I should like to render my sincere thanks to the friendly and tireless staffs of Lund University Library, the Royal Library of Copenhagen, the British Museum Library, the Bodleian Library, the Library of St. Mark's at Venice, and the National Library of Naples. I am also very grateful to Mr. Edward Carney, Lector in English in the University of Lund, who has been kind and patient enough to read this book in manuscript and to discuss it with me. Finally, my thanks are due to Professor F.Y. St. Clair, of Grand Forks, North Dakota, for kindly answering my questions about his work on the chronology of Shakespeare's sonnets.

The author.

TABLE OF CONTENTS

INTRODUCTION

The dating of Shakespeare's sonnets has long been a problem. No generally acceptable solution has been found, and several critics maintain, perhaps rightly, that none *can* be found, at least as far as all the sonnets are concerned. The discussion of the problem up to the early 1940's was summed up by ROLLINS in his *Variorum* edition of 1944 (II, pp. 53—73). It may be said that attempts to date the sonnets have been based on five main groups of data or pseudo-data: a) assumed allusions to contemporary events (eclipses or political incidents); b) the assumed identity of the recipient of the sonnets or of other people referred to in them (rival poet, dark lady); c) parallel passages in the *Sonnets* and other works by Shakespeare; d) parallel passages in the *Sonnets* and the works of other authors; and e) grammatical and stylistic features of the *Sonnets* compared with similar features in Shakespeare's other works.[1] Some instances of datings based on group a) are DARBY's suggestion[2] that no. XXXV, 3 (*Cloudes and eclipses staine both Moone and Sunne*) alludes to a lunar eclipse followed by a solar one in 1594; KITT-REDGE's,[3] that no. CVII contains references to Queen Elizabeth's death and the accession of James I in 1603; and TYLER's,[4] that nos. CVII and CXXIV allude to the Essex rebellion in 1601. The divergence of opinion has been particularly marked in the case of no. CVII, as appears from ROLLINS's summary (I, pp. 263—270).

The b) group earlier attracted most attention. As is well known, a host of critics believed that the *Sonnets* were addressed to Henry Wriothesley, third Earl of Southampton,[5] another host that the

---

[1] WALSH (*Sonnet* ed. 1908, p. 30) only admitted three possible tests: those based on the a), c), and e) data.

[2] *The Date of Some Shakespeare Sonnets*, SJ LXXV, 1939, pp. 135 ff.

[3] Shakespeare edition, 1936, p. 1491.

[4] *Sonnet* ed. 1890, pp. 22 ff.

[5] One of the most undaunted advocates of this view was J. A. FORT (*The Two Dated*

recipient was William Herbert, third Earl of Pembroke. The former category generally assumed an earlier date than the latter (the early or mid-1590's as against the late 1590's or the turn of the century). Attention was also paid to other possible addressees, and opinion was sharply divided as to the identity of the rival poet and the dark lady. Parallels between the *Sonnets* and other works by Shakespeare (c) were diligently amassed, particularly in the 1880's and at the beginning of this century, the best known investigations being those of ISAAC (1884) and DAVIS (published by ALDEN in 1916; cf. p. 191 below). These parallels were considered to indicate the mid-1590's as the likely period of composition for most sonnets. The d) group was not systematically utilized. Following MALONE, critics generally assumed that the *Sonnets* were inspired by Daniel's *Delia* and could thus be dated after 1592.[6] Influences from Sidney's *Arcadia*, pointed out by MASSEY in the 1860's, indicated a date later than 1590 for certain sonnets. Interest was also focussed on resemblances between the *Sonnets* and the works of Drayton. These parallels were variously interpreted: diametrically opposite conclusions were drawn for example by FLEAY[7] and TYLER.[8] The latter, incidentally, was one of the few to point out the importance of the d) group for purposes of dating. The significance of these clues was also stressed by LEE,[9] who believed that Barnfield had levied loans on the *Sonnets* and that these could thus be considered early. Scholars using the criteria of group e) (EMERSON 1923,[1] MILLER 1930,[2] and others) dealt with rhymes, the use of certain forms, and details of style in the *Sonnets*, and arrived at various dates, from the early 1590's to the early 1600's. It should be added that many attempts were made to rearrange the

---

Sonnets of Shakespeare, Oxford, 1924, *A Time Scheme for Shakespeare's Sonnets*, London, 1929, and *The Order and Chronology of Shakespeare's Sonnets* (RES IX, 1933, pp. 19 ff.)). On slender grounds, FORT read detailed biographical facts into the sonnets.

[6] Many critics regarded Daniel's assumed influence on the *Sonnets* as extensive. One of them, L. E. PEARSON, remarked: "No wonder Shakespeare read them [the sonnets of *Delia*] again and again, and, like a bee, sucked their honey" (*Elizabethan Love Conventions*, Berkeley, Cal., 1933, p. 155).

[7] *Biographical Chronicle* II, 1891, pp. 226 ff. (Shakespeare imitated Drayton).

[8] *Sonnet* ed., pp. 38 ff. (Drayton imitated Shakespeare). The latter view was also put forward by TILLOTSON in 1941 (cf. p. 82 below) in the case of most parallels.

[9] *Sonnet* ed. 1905, pp. 25 ff.

[1] *Shakespeare's Sonneteering*, SP XX, pp. 111 ff.

[2] *The Use of the Third Person Singular of Have and Do in the Works of Shakespeare and Massinger*, PQ IX, pp. 373 ff.

order of the *Sonnets* as given by the Quarto, the best known being that of BRAY in 1925[3] and that in BROOKE's edition of 1936.

The discussion after the early 1940's has mainly followed the same trends as before, except that particular attention has been paid to group a) owing to HOTSON's well-known suggestions in 1949.[4] According to this critic no. CVII, the 'mortal moon' sonnet, alludes to the Spanish Armada, no. CXXIII to obelisks erected in Rome by Pope Sixtus V, and CXXIV to the murder of Henry III. This would assign all three sonnets to 1589. Since moreover HOTSON regarded them as belonging near the end of the 'first series', his conclusion was: "Shakespeare completed this main group of his sonnets by 1589" (p. 33). HOTSON's views were opposed, sometimes violently, by a good many critics who refused to accept his evidence and mostly argued for a later date (SHAPIRO[5] and HARBAGE[6] 1950, BATESON[7] 1951, NOSWORTHY[8] 1952, STONE[9] 1953, and others). Other interpretations of nos. CVII, CXXIII, and CXXIV besides those suggested by HOTSON are doubtless possible, and the early date he proposed raises various difficulties. Earlier on, CHAMBERS[1] had seen reason to date no. CVII as written in 1599 since events that year seemed to him to agree best with the allusions in the sonnet. GITTINGS[2] has recently suggested that the 'mortal moon' may refer to the menace of the Turks, that CXXIV possibly alludes to an attempted assassination of Henry IV of France, while CXXIII admits of various explanations. GITTINGS's suggestions as regards CVII do not seem implausible, though it might have been pointed out that LAWRENCE in 1925 expressed a similar idea.[3]

---

[3] *The Original Order of Shakespeare's Sonnets.*

[4] *Shakespeare's Sonnets Dated.* HOTSON amplified his arguments in *The Date of Shakespeare's Sonnets*, TLS, 1950, p. 348, and in *More Light on Shakespeare's Sonnets*, SQ II, 1951, pp. III ff.

[5] *Dr. Hotson's Arguments*, TLS, p. 245.

[6] *Dating Shakespeare's Sonnets*, SQ I, pp. 57 ff.

[7] *Elementary, My Dear Hotson!* EC I, pp. 81 ff.

[8] *All Too Short A Date: Internal Evidence in Shakespeare's Sonnets*, EC II, pp. 311 ff.

[9] *Shakespeare and the Sad Augurs*, JEGP LII, pp. 457 ff.

[1] *Shakespearean Gleanings*, Oxford, 1944, pp. 130 ff.

[2] *Shakespeare's Rival*, London, 1960, pp. 95 ff.

[3] Cf. ROLLINS I, p. 263. LAWRENCE was a Baconian and the date he proposed for no. CVII (1579) of course quite wrong, but in his suggestions as regards the 'mortal moon' he anticipated GITTINGS's conclusion.

Critics interested in the b) data have carried on the Southampton-Pembroke controversy. Among the Southamptonists we may refer to GRAY, who in 1948 regarded the 'rival poet' sonnets, which in his opinion allude to Spenser, as composed in 1596 or -97.[4] Among the Pembrokists we find LEISHMAN, who suggests that Shakespeare began to compose his sonnets during the same years.[5] LEISHMAN is unperturbed by — or unfamiliar with — an essay by TAYLOR in 1959,[6] in which the author seeks to prove that the Earl of Pembroke "in no way resembled any of the several youths who might be extracted from the sonnets as they were printed in 1609". Southampton and Pembroke, incidentally, are not the only candidates to have been suggested for the 'Friend' of the Sonnets. — The rival poet problem is the main subject of GITTINGS's work: it is suggested that Gervase Markham may possibly be the poet alluded to. This would place the rival poet sonnets in 1597 or -98. There is something to be said for this theory although — as is the case with other rival poet theories — the evidence could have been stronger on various points. On the whole, in the discussion of the b) data, a considerable amount of conjecture rests on rather slender foundations, now as earlier.

The most comprehensive and systematic attempt to date the Sonnets on the basis of parallels between this work and other works by Shakespeare was made by BALDWIN in 1950.[7] According to this scholar, the sonnets were written between 1593 and 1599. — NOSWORTHY tried to refute HOTSON's theories with the aid of vocabulary tests: in this way he arrived at early as well as late dates for a limited number of sonnets.[8]

Group d) has not loomed very large during the last two decades: there are only stray notes and observations. DAVENPORT[9] found parallels to Astrophel and Stella LXIV and CVIII in no. XXIX, and though he did not conclude borrowing on Shakespeare's part, he thought it "certain" that the poet had read Sidney's sonnets. The relationship

---

[4] *Shakespeare's Rival Poet*, JEGP XLVII, pp. 365 ff.
[5] *Themes and Variations in Shakespeare's Sonnets*, London, 1961, pp. 15 ff.
[6] *The Earl of Pembroke and the Youth of Shakespeare's Sonnets: An Essay in Rehabilitation.* SP LVI, pp. 26 ff.
[7] *On the Literary Genetics of Shakspere's Poems & Sonnets.*
[8] *Op. cit., passim.*
[9] *Shakespeare's Sonnets.* NQ CXCVI, 1951, pp. 5 f.

between Shakespeare's sonnets and Drayton's was discussed by, among others, LEISHMAN[1] and ST. CLAIR.[2] DAVENPORT earlier suggested that no. II may have been prompted by certain details in Drayton's second *Eglog* of *The Shepheards Garland* (1593).[3] MC NEAL[4] said that no. CXXVIII is not, as formerly believed, dependent on Jonson's *Every Man Out of His Humour* but that the reverse is probably the case. The same, he thought, is true of no. XXIX. These two sonnets would therefore date before instead of after 1599.

The idea of Daniel's influence on the *Sonnets* has been put forward and elaborated by several critics;[5] the present author has tried to show that there are no sufficient grounds for this view. If anything, there is an influence in the opposite direction.[6]

Stray remarks on the similarities or differences between the style of the *Sonnets* and that of other works by Shakespeare are to be found in books and articles. So far as I can see, however, such features have not been used as evidence for dating the *Sonnets* except in the case of NOSWORTHY's and BATESON's criticism of HOTSON (cf. also pp. 180 f. below). BATESON adduced details which he found indicative of a late rather than an early date. Finally, it should be mentioned that we have not seen the end of the attempts to rearrange Shakespeare's sonnets according to subject-matter or formal characteristics or both. Such an attempt is found in CELLINI's edition of the sonnets in 1943;[7] and STIRLING tried to make one homogeneous group out of eleven sonnets assumed to be scattered in the Quarto.[8] The new order is: C, CI, LXIII—LXVIII, XIX, XXI, CV. Like all other previous rearrangements, both views are in some measure defensible but not really convincing. We shall have reason to analyse some of these suggestions later. Many other works briefly referred to above will also later be discussed in more detail.

*

[1] *Op. cit.*, pp. 85 ff.

[2] *Drayton's First Revision of His Sonnets*, SP XXXVI, 1939, pp. 56 ff. Cf. also below, p. 82, n. 5.

[3] *The Seed of a Shakespeare Sonnet?* NQ CLXXXII, 1942, pp. 242 ff. Cf. p. 78 below.

[4] '*Every Man Out of His Humour*' and Shakespeare's '*Sonnets*', NQ CXCVII, 1952, p. 376.

[5] Cf. for example below, p. 14, note.

[6] *An Elizabethan Sonnet Problem. Shakespeare's Sonnets, Daniel's Delia, and their Literary Background.* Lund, 1960.

[7] *Vita e arte nei sonetti di Shakespeare col testo dei sonetti.*

[8] *A Shakespeare Sonnet Group*, PMLA LXXV, 1960, pp. 340 ff.

In short: a good deal remains to be discussed, even if the research of the last twenty years may be said to have simplified the issue somewhat. Thus the Hotson controversy has amply shown, if this was not apparent before, how idle are the attempts to identify topical allusions in the *Sonnets*: clues seem to be irretrievably lost, suggestions are as numerous as they are unprovable, and no convincing answer to these questions can be found unless entirely new material is brought to light. The same is true of the identity of the people referred to in the *Sonnets*. It is not at all certain that the people who are referred to in Shakespeare's sonnets ever did exist, and it would be quite wrong to base the discussion of date on the axiom that they did.[9] On the other hand we must reckon with the possibility that the characters in the *Sonnets* were real contemporaries of Shakespeare's, even if we cannot now identify them.[1]

As regards what we may call 'intra-Shakespearean' parallels, nobody in the last two decades has been able to controvert the results arrived at by ISAAC and DAVIS, namely, that the bulk of the resemblances between the *Sonnets* and other works by Shakespeare fall within his early period. Even BALDWIN, whose datings do not wholly agree with this, accepts these results. However, it may safely be said that the precise dating of Shakespeare's sonnets is as much of an enigma as before, and it is understandable that many scholars prefer to avoid the whole problem by assuming that the *Sonnets* are likely to have been composed in the heyday of sonnet writing, between 1592 and 1597 or -98.[2] But it is not certain that Shakespeare followed the fashion.

We have seen from our survey that of the five groups of data, a), b), and c) are by far those most extensively utilized, while d)

---

[9] MÖNCH (*Das Sonett*, Heidelberg, 1955, p. 138) points out, which does not seem to have been noticed before, that the story told in the *Sonnets* resembles certain details in the plot of *Euphues*.

[1] Much anachronism has marred the discussion of autobiography in the *Sonnets*. In *Shakespeare, His World and His Work* (London, 1953, p. 415), REESE rightly remarks: "To understand Shakespeare's sonnets it is necessary to read widely among the sonnets written by other men. His plays cannot be judged independently of the drama of his age, and in the same way most of the false assumptions about his sonnets have proceeded from the error of reading them independently of the prolific convention of which they were a part."

[2] Cf. HALLIDAY, *A Shakespeare Companion*, London, 1952, p. 607; earlier PEARSON, *op. cit.*, p. 260, and others.

and e) have not played a very prominent part. The use of e) would *a priori* seem to be somewhat risky since in matters of style the sonnet naturally obeys other laws than those valid for narrative poems and plays (cf. further p. 180 below). Group d), on the other hand, appears to be more useful. If borrowings could be established, the advantages would be considerable. The texts themselves would gain a hearing, and we should have definite *a quo* and *ante quem* limits to work from instead of the vague and approximate datings that emerge from the accumulation of intra-Shakespearean parallels. Again, the dating of one sonnet would help to date sonnets obviously connected with it. However, it is important to observe that a similarity of subject-matter naturally does not in itself indicate a connection in point of time. Special conditions must be fulfilled, to which attention will be drawn in each particular case.[3] Yet in spite of these and other difficulties to be dealt with below, it is tempting to make practical use of Meres's oft-quoted piece of information: Shakespeare's *sugred Sonnets among his priuate friends*. Shakespearean sonnets did circulate, and it is more than likely that some of them fell into the hands of impressionable fellow-poets.[4]

But it may indeed be asked if there is a usable method for dealing with data of the d) type. To examine parallels and to decide which author influenced the other — is not this merely a kind of subjective hocus-pocus, fully comparable with the methods too often applied in the rearrangement of the order of the sonnets?

First of all it is obvious that, as S. B. LILJEGREN[5] has recently pointed-ed out, a distinction must be made between real in f l u e n c e exerted by one poet on another, and i n s p i r a t i o n derived from one by another. Influence appears in close, mostly verbal, similarities of a kind that cannot be explained away as due to common tradition or to chance. It does not follow that the closeness of the similarity consists in the number of words that correspond: a whole line may be entirely conventional (cf. p. 37 ff. below), while a mere couple of words that resemble one another strikingly in two poets

[3] Cf. chapter II, pp. 177 ff.
[4] For the circulation of poems in manuscript in Elizabethan times cf. LEE, ed. 1905, pp. 26 f.
[5] *Archiv für das Studium der neueren Sprachen* CXCVIII, 1961, p. 117.

may be logically and stylistically impeccable in one but not in the other. In many such cases it is reasonable to suppose that they were taken over by the latter poet if the similarity is otherwise unparalleled. The provenance of inspiration, on the other hand, is in most cases impossible to trace objectively, at least in the case of sonnet poetry. Themes and conceits are largely common literary property, the situations described are often similar, vague resemblances are insufficient evidence and leave us in the lurch when we try to tackle the question as to which poet inspired the other. The confusion of these two concepts, influence and inspiration, has rendered a great deal of the discussion of parallels unfruitful. This appears not least from statements on the supposed dependence of the *Sonnets* on Daniel's *Delia*.[6] We also find it amply attested in the discussion of the relationship between Shakespeare's sonnets and those of Drayton and others, and shall have reason to discuss these things closely in the next chapter.

It follows from this that the first thing to be done in an examination of sonnet parallels as evidence of date is to dismiss the vague and general resemblances. The next thing is to investigate the sources if there are any: are the similarities due to a common source? If not, we must examine the background carefully: are the points of similarity commonplaces or not? But what is the background? Formerly, critics often contented themselves with examining Petrarch's *Canzoniere*; later, 16th-century French and Italian poets entered the picture, and the findings and results in this field were aptly summed up by SCOTT in 1929.[7] But there is still a strong tendency to concentrate on the poets who are rated high by modern literary criticism but to neglect those who were fashionable in the 16th century. Thus in his discussion of the handling of various

---

[6] A characteristic statement is found in PRINCE's essay *The Sonnet from Wyatt to Shakespeare* in *Elizabethan Poetry* (Stratford-upon-Avon Studies 2, London, 1960), in which it is declared (p. 24) that the *Delia* sonnet "xxx and the six that follow, of which five form a chain, are unmistakably Shakespeare's inspiration for many of the earlier sonnets in his own book". The author is equally confident when declaring that "there is no doubt that Shakespeare read *Amoretti* at a time when he had discovered his own use for the sonnet, and that much of Spenser's feeling and atmosphere, and some of his phrasing, entered into Shakespeare's creations" (*ibid.*). It is a pity that "it would take more space than I have to substantiate this"; it would have been interesting to get acquainted with the evidence on which PRINCE's confidence is based.

[7] *Les Sonnets Élizabéthains* (Bibliothèque de la revue de littérature comparée, 60).

Shakespearean sonnet-themes in ancient and Renaissance poetry, LEISHMAN limits his discussion of the French and Italian sonneteers to Petrarch, Tasso, Michelangelo, du Bellay, Desportes, and Ronsard, while some other names are mentioned once or twice in passing. He observes on the absence of other Italian poets: "Of Italian poetry and, more particularly, of the Italian sonnet from Petrarch to Tasso, I cannot claim more than a slight and superficial knowledge. The quantity, published and unpublished, must be so vast that there is probably no scholar who has read it all, and certainly no scholar able to remember even what he has read well enough to enable him to make confident generalisations about the presence or absence of significant treatments of particular topics" (p. 53).[8] Yet it can hardly be irrelevant that in this vast quantity we find a large number of poets who are nowadays neglected but who were of great importance for the 16th-century sonneteers of Spain, France, and England. The researches of VIANEY, KASTNER, LAUMONIER, SCOTT, and FUCILLA have been in vain if they have not taught us this. Again, how can we hope to make any generalisations about "the presence or absence of significant treatments of particular topics" — for instance, such generalisations as are made by LEISHMAN himself — unless we try to cover as much of this vast quantity as we can? If we make an attempt we have at least a fair chance, particularly if we take notes in order to remember better; if we give up in advance we have none at all.

Thus we must try to get as adequate an idea as possible of the poetry that was of importance for the Elizabethan sonneteers. Although in Shakespeare's sonnets there is much that is unconventional,[9] it has been shown that he leans heavily on traditional conceits and, to some extent, themes,[1] and as said before, many faulty

---

[8] It is all the more surprising to find the cited declaration in an author who expressly states some of his aims as follows: ... "From Petrarch onwards, I am almost exclusively concerned a) with the appearance of the topic [of Poetry as Immortalisation] in love-poetry and, more particularly, in sonnets, and b) with the contrast between the merely incidental and seldom very serious treatments of it in ancient love-poetry and the importance and centrality it eventually assumes in Shakespeare's Sonnets", etc. (p. 25); or in whom we find the following headline: "Devouring Time and Fading Beauty from the Greek Anthology to Shakespeare". (My emphasis).

[9] Cf. e.g. HUNTER, *The Dramatic Technique of Shakespeare's Sonnets*, EC III, 1953, pp. 152 ff., REES, *Italian and Italianate Poetry*, Stratford-upon-Avon Studies 2, 1960, p. 66, LEISHMAN, *op. cit.*, p. 11, SCHAAR, *op. cit.*, pp. 21 ff.

[1] WOLFF, *Petrarkismus und Antipetrarkismus in Shakespeares Sonetten*, Engl. Studien

interpretations are due to ignorance of this fact. However, I should like to stress the fact that when in the next chapter I refer to numerous poets representing various conventions, I of course do not mean that Shakespeare and his contemporaries had read them all. But it can be taken for granted that the more often a conceit or a theme in the English sonneteers is also found elsewhere, the greater is the chance that it was conventional and common property, whatever the channels through which it may have reached any particular poet. Besides English 16th-century poetry we must try to cover all the relevant French and Italian sonneteering — much of the latter available in contemporary anthologies — with the classical verse that was popular in the Renaissance. Not least, attention must be paid to the Greek Anthology, an inexhaustible source of inspiration, directly or indirectly, for European poets of the 16th century.

In the study of Renaissance poetic conventions, there are various dangers to which I should like to call attention — not because they are particularly remarkable in themselves but because criticism is continually exposed to them. Thus it is often concluded that a conceit or a theme that is observed a number of times in different authors is 'traditional,' although no attempt is made to ascertain its relative frequency. Critical discussion of the procreation theme in Shakespeare's nos. I—XVII, for example, was long led astray by LEE and others who maintained, without modification, that this theme was a commonplace in Renaissance literature.[2] It may well have been common in certain genres, but in sonneteering it is very rare and apparently does not form part of the tradition.[3] It is thus remarkable to find it in a whole cycle of the Shakespearean sonnets. Another error consists in equating this theme with the common *carpe diem* motif: it is conceivable, though not at all likely, that it is a particular form of *carpe diem*,[4] but the difference between it and the ordinary *carpe diem* motif is too obvious to be pointed out.

XLIX, 1915, pp. 161 ff. Though this article is not entirely free from exaggerations and misinterpretations, it affords very valuable information on the traditional elements in Shakespeare's sonnets.

[2] Edition of Shakespeare's sonnets 1905, p. 19. Cf. ROLLINS I, p. 6.

[3] SCOTT (*op. cit.*, pp. 238 ff.) justly objected to some examples adduced by WOLFF which she proved to be specious; for a similar case cf. below, p. 143.

[4] I have suggested this elsewhere (*op. cit.*, p. 22) but I was probably wrong. The theme should rather be considered a member of the *Natura genitrix* motif complex (cf. CURTIUS, *Lateinische Literatur und Europäisches Mittelalter*, Bern, 1946, p. 136).

It is therefore strange to find ISAAC naïvely observing on Daniel's nos. XXXI and XXXII (*But loue whilst that thou maist be lou'd againe*): "Die Gedanken dieser beiden Sonette finden wir nun bei Shakespeare in den Sonetten 1—7 wieder," etc. Other critics have vented similar opinions.[5]

Even more common are of course attempts to connect directly sonnets which merely treat the same conventional theme, such as those on 'eloquent eyes betraying dumb poet's passion', or sonnets which are superficially similar but in reality represent different branches of tradition. Thus comparison has often been made between a Shakespeare sonnet and a Daniel one because both deal with the motif of the 'wrinkled face', the inference being that Shakespeare was here dependent on Daniel. But Shakespeare uses the wrinkles to represent the theme of 'faded beauty', while in *Delia* they illustrate the theme of 'lover's sufferings', and there is no sufficient reason for concluding dependence of one poet on the other.[6] A further source of error lies in regarding a certain poetic convention as more homogeneous than the facts warrant. Thus WYNDHAM observed on Shakespeare's XCIX, blaming various flowers for stealing his friend's beauty, that flower-sonnets were imitated from Petrarch and were commonplace in the poetry of the sixteenth century.[7] But the flower conceits form a large and complex group, of which some members are common and others rare, some stemming possibly from Petrarch and others certainly from elsewhere.[8] In each case we must determine as exactly as we can the place of a given conceit in the whole, and the degree of possible involvement with other related conceits. In the cited case the dependence on tradition cannot prevent us from concluding that no. XCIX is directly connected with a sonnet by another poet. Thus even if two sonnets are found to represent the same *main* convention, this of course does not necessarily preclude a direct influence from one on the other. But we must have strong reasons before establishing a direct connection

[5] *Wie weit geht die Abhängigkeit Shakespeare's von Daniel als Lyriker?* SJ XVII, p. 177; cf. ROLLINS *ibid.* and PRINCE, n. 6 above.

[6] I have earlier given several instances of similar errors (*op. cit.*, pp. 153 ff.) and more will be given below, pp. 75, 98 ff. In spite of the dilettantish character of LEISHMAN's work on Shakespeare's sonnets, this book is an important attempt to keep different conventions and topics apart.

[7] Edition of Shakespeare's *Poems*, 1898, p. 309. Cf. below, p. 85.

[8] Cf. below, pp. 86 ff.

in such cases. As a rule supplementary facts must aid us; examples will be given in chapter I.

It may be tempting to conclude a direct connection when two non-conventional expressions resemble one another closely, particularly if there are also other similarities. But we cannot be sure. As mentioned before, LEE called attention to a number of resemblances between the *Sonnets* and Barnfield's poems. Thus he remarked that Barnfield's no. XII (*Some talke of Ganymede th'Idalian Boy | And some of faire Adonis make their boast*) and no. XVII (*Cherry-lipt Adonis in his snowie shape, | Might not compare with his pure Iuorie white*) "both seem crude echoes" of Shakespeare's no. LIII, particularly ll. 5 ff.: *Describe Adonis and the counterfet, | Is poorely immitated after you*, etc. He also commented on the similarity between expressions in *The Affectionate Shepheard* and in the *Sonnets*: *Amber locks trust vp in golden tramels* which *dangle adowne his louely cheekes*, and *Cut off thy Locke, and sell it for gold wier* (I,II, II,xix) reminded him of Shakespeare's LXVIII, 5 ff.: *Before the goulden tresses of the dead, | The right of sepulchers, were shorne away*, etc. Some other resemblances of the same kind were also quoted, none of them in any way striking. But LEE also pointed out another and more important parallel. The first quatrain of Shakespeare's LXXXV runs:

> *My toung-tide Muse in manners holds her still,*
> *While comments of your praise richly compil'd,*
> *Reserue their Character with goulden quill,*
> *And precious phrase by all the Muses fil'd.*

In Barnfield's *Cassandra*, stanza no. 18, we read:

> *This said: he sweetly doth imbrace his loue,*
> *Yoaking his armes about her Iuory necke;*
> *And calls her wanton Venus milk-white Doue,*
> *Whose ruddie lips the damask roses decke.*
> > *And euer as his tongue compiles her praise,*
> > *Loue daintie Dimples in her cheekes doth raise.*

And three stanzas further on:

> *Scarce were these honywords breath'd from her lips,*
> *But he, supposing that she ment good-faith,*
> *Her filed tongues temptations interceps;*

And (like a Nouice) thus to her he saith:
Ask what thou wilt, and I will giue it thee:
Health, wealth, long life, wit, art, or dignitie.

Each one of the words *tongue, praise, compile, file* is of small interest, and *filed tongue* is a commonplace, but it cannot be denied that the combination of all the four words here is suggestive — "the collocation of the expressions is curious", as LEE says. It might be plausible to argue that Barnfield made use of Shakespeare's quatrain in two different passages, and the conclusion may seem strengthened by the other passages in Barnfield more vaguely reminiscent of Shakespearean sonnets. LEE, concluding a direct connection, remarks: "The likelihood that Shakespeare was the borrower is very small." But what shall we say to this when we read in *The Faerie Qveene*, III,ii,12:

> *But to occasion him to further talke,*
> *To feed her humour with his pleasing stile,*
> *Her list in strifull termes with him to balke,*
> *And thus replide, How euer, Sir, ye file*
> *Your courteous tongue, his prayses to compile,*
> *It ill beseemes a knight of gentle sort,*
> *Such as ye haue him boasted, to beguile*
> *A simple mayd, and worke so haynous tort,*
> *In shame of knighthood, as I largely can report.*

It is possible that the passages in these three authors are somehow interrelated and if they are, the probability is that Spenser's text, which is doubtless earliest, constitutes the base. But whether Barnfield and Shakespeare both drew on Spenser, or whether only Shakespeare did, and Barnfield then drew on Shakespeare, or whether the reverse is true, I find no means of determining: there is nothing to indicate clearly who was indebted to whom, and the less close resemblances of course do not help us. Problems of this kind are unfruitful and will be left aside, and though I think it highly probable that Barnfield did know and utilize Shakespeare's sonnets, I see no practicable way of demonstrating this.

We must also be careful not to conclude mechanically from a very close similarity, indicative of real borrowing, that other less close similarities indicate borrowing too. There are indeed cases where this is a justifiable conclusion (cf. pp. 124 ff. below), but there are those where it is a mere paralogism. In his edition of Shakespeare's sonnets in 1890, TYLER suggested that a sonnet in Drayton's *Idea* is influenced by Shakespeare's no. CXLIV: the similarity is striking and there are various reasons for believing that TYLER was right (cf. pp. 74 ff. below). But he also adduced many other parallels, most of them insignificant, inferring that "Drayton must have had an acquaintance with some portion of Shakespeare's Sonnets" (p. 42). Possible and perhaps probable, but not provable; and in this case the weak parallels cannot derive support from the strong one. On the contrary: if left to themselves they are unable to stand on their own legs and had better be left out of account.

It will appear from these considerations that the material on which my own conclusions are based is fairly restricted, nearly all parallels which I regard as ambiguous or inconclusive being disregarded. This does not always mean that they have been left out of the discussion, but if they are discussed it is only to prove that they are indecisive. It may be thought that I have left out too many, but restrictiveness is the better practice in a study of this kind. I do not think that the parallels I have explained as due to imitation can be easily dismissed as traditional commonplaces. On the other hand I am not under the illusion that I have myself been able to avoid all the pitfalls that I have enumerated, though I have tried to. The subjective element cannot be wholly eliminated, but it can be considerably reduced. The conclusions cannot be mathematically certain, but they can be more reasonable and natural than other conclusions. I may sum up as follows what to my mind are the decisive criteria: If two passages in different poets resemble each other in some striking manner, if this resemblance cannot be explained as due to chance, a common source, or conventional phrasing, and if one of the parallel passages shows notable deviations from the author's usual style and manner, from common rhetorical principles, or from simple logical and psychological norms — then these facts are strongly indicative of imitation on the part of the poet in whom the deviations occur. The likelihood is small that the reverse is true; the probability is that under the impact of his model the imitator swerved from natural norms. Of course the more skilful an imitation the more difficult it is to spot it, in literature as in art (cf.

further p. 78 below). [9] — Special cases are series of such similarities as result from revisions in one text, so that a number of passages in it are brought into closer conformity with another text. Evidence of this kind has a cumulative force that cannot be neglected.

Many of the parallels adduced have not been discussed before; others have, but on a wrong basis. In certain cases, though I agree with the results of previous scholars, my discussion is as detailed as if I had rejected them: it is possible to arrive at right results on the basis of wrong reasoning. To the *arbitri elegantiarum* of to-day my arguments may at times seem circumstantial enough, but it has in many cases been necessary, in the analysis of the background, to trace the history of topics and formulas in some detail in order to present as complete a body of evidence as possible. Furthermore, it is hoped that the distribution of certain themes and formulas as discussed in the following chapter may in itself be of interest to literary critics. Full details have accordingly been given in the discussion of themes less generally known.

*

The first chapter of this study deals, then, with a set of parallel passages which may be seriously suspected of being, in effect, a series of originals and imitations. On the basis of the results arrived at, a number of Shakespeare's sonnets are tentatively dated within certain limits *a quo* and *ante quem*. In the second chapter a series of intra-Shakespearean parallels will be examined in connection with a study of possible objections to the datings made on the basis of parallels between the *Sonnets* and the works of other poets. An attempt is also made to narrow down these datings and at the same time to see whether they can be extended to other sonnets as well,

---

[9] No doubt there are many cases where loosely organized or merely collocated material in one author has been skilfully adapted and fused by another. Suspected instances of this will be regarded as uncertain and will mostly be left out of the discussion unless any of the criteria mentioned above can be applied: if they cannot, the only available arguments are esthetic ones coloured, moreover, by modern evaluations. Theories of imitation based merely on (modern) esthetic arguments and hence unsatisfactory are those of DAVENPORT (cf. further p. 78 below) and of WATKINS (*Shakespeare and Spenser*, Princeton, 1950, pp. 280 ff.), the latter suggesting that Shakespeare's no. LXXIII "may be partially indebted" to a passage in Spenser's *Januarie*.

which may be found to form groups including those already dated. In this chapter an evaluation will further be made of the usefulness of the e) data. It follows from the restrictions I have already referred to that my conclusions are valid only for a limited number of Shakespeare's sonnets. If mention is made of the rest, it is only by way of brief supplementary discussion.

Shakespeare's sonnets are quoted from the *Variorum* text with various minor alterations, which as a rule are not specified in each particular case. Like all writers on the *Sonnets* I draw largely on ROLLINS's (sometimes unreliable) commentary; like some of them, I refer to ROLLINS every time I do so. The other Elizabethan sonneteers are quoted from LEE's 1904 edition except in the case of poets edited separately: Sidney, Watson, Daniel, Spenser, Constable, Drayton. Greville and Barnfield were not edited by LEE. *Parthenophil and Parthenophe* XLIX and *Fidessa* XXVIII and XXIX (pp. 103 and 106) are quoted from the copies in the British Museum and the Bodleian Library, respectively. — With the recent publication of GRUNDY's edition of Constable's poems it has at length become possible to study this poet in a satisfactory way: problems of bibliography have been adequately dealt with by GRUNDY and a reliable corpus has been established. The author(s) of the non-authentic poems in the 1594 *Diana* will be referred to below as Pseudo-Constable. The present study is based on and further develops the conclusions arrived at in my *An Elizabethan Sonnet Problem*. Part of what is said on parallels in that book I have had to repeat in this one; in most cases short accounts, which I now consider insufficient, have been amplified. As in my previous study, what I have to say about the text of *Delia* is largely founded on SPRAGUE's 1930 edition, so the correctness of my version of the text depends on the correctness of SPRAGUE's variant readings. However, I have collated a fair number of passages in the 1592, 1594, and 1601 editions of *Delia* to test the reliability of SPRAGUE's edition, and have not come across any errors in text or variants.

I. PARALLELS BETWEEN THE 'SONNETS' AND NON-SHAKESPEAREAN WORKS

The 'Sonnets' and 'Delia'

We begin our analysis of parallel passages in the *Sonnets* and *Delia* with a small group, of which the passages cited from *Delia* were first printed in 1592. Before we can enter on a discussion of these, however, we shall have to make an excursus on two subjects: a common motif in contemporary poetry, and a particular feature of Daniel's technique.

The motif is that of immortality: the poet promises that he himself and/or the recipient of his poem will be made immortal by his verse,[1] and will continue to live in others' memory. The number of ways in which this motif is expressed in sonneteering are limited, and we may distinguish between certain main types of formulas. One derives from Ovid's *Metamorphoses* xv, 871 f., or Horace's *Odes* III, xxx, 1 ff., or both. In these classical texts, the theme is the poet's certainty that he himself will be immortal thanks to the permanence of his work. Ovid:

> *Iamque opus exegi, quod nec Iouis ira, nec ignis,*
> *Nec poterit ferrum, nec edax abolere vetustas.*

Horace:

> *Exegi monumentum aere perennius*
> *regalique situ pyramidum altius*
> *quod non imber edax, non aquilo inpotens*
> *possit diruere aut innumerabilis*
> *annorum series et fuga temporum.*

---

[1] For critical opinion on this theme in Shakespeare and his predecessors cf. ROLLINS I, pp. 147 ff. A recent treatment of the matter is found in LEISHMAN, *op. cit.*, pp. 27—91.

The classical poet also frequently made room for another's fame besides his own.[2] The same is true, of course, of the Renaissance poet, who was fond of the Ovid-Horace monument imagery in such contexts:

> *Que si en moy le souverain donneur*
> *Pour tel subject heureusement poursuyvre*
> *Eust mis tant d'art, tant de grace & bonheur,*
>
> *Mieux qu'en tableau, en bronze, en marbre, en cuyvre,*
> *Je luy feroy' & à moy un honneur,*
> *Qui elle & moy feroit vivre & revivre.*[3]

Baïf similarly speaks of his verse as a *beau monument qui parlera de nous.*

There is a further "development" in passages which are wholly devoted to the glory of the recipient without mentioning the poet himself. One example among countless others is Ronsard's sonnet *Pour Madame de la Chastre, en faveur d'un livre composé de ses louanges* (no. XLVIII of the *Sonnets divers*):

> *Ces vers gravez icy plus fort que dans le cuivre*
> *Sont plus propres à vous qu'au soleil sa splendeur,*
> *Le pesant à la terre, à la mer sa froideur,*
> *A l'air l'agilité qui le monde fait vivre.*

These lines still retain the *aere perennius* detail. They differ from another type of the immortality motif in which not only is the theme of the poet's own fame omitted, but there is no longer any mention of bronze or marble. Paper and ink themselves assume the rôle of monuments: braving time, making an honoured name resound all over the world:

> *Quel, che con infinito, alto gouerno,*
> *E con immensa prouidentia, & arte,*
> *Sua mirabil virtue à noi comparte,*
> *Santo, saggio, diuin, Motore eterno,*
> *Vi diede à questa età, perche l'interno*
> *Vostro valor, LVCRETIA, in mille carte*

---

[2] Cf. LEISHMAN, *ibid.*
[3] Du Bellay's *Olive* XVIII, 9—14.

Per noi rimbombi, e viua à parte à parte
Tutto quel, ch'è di voi chiaro, e superno.[4]

A combination of paper, ink, and monument is represented by the last tercet of one of Bembo's poems to Vittoria Colonna (no. CXII):

> *Rara pietà, con carte e con inchiostro*
> *Sepolcro far, che'l tempo mai non lime,*
> *La sua fedele al grande Aualo nostro.*

There is yet another related theme, which describes somebody's memory hidden in the poet's or lover's mind. This theme is fairly often fixed in the 'heart-tomb' formula. Thus Barnfield laments the death of Bounty:

> *Therefore as one, whose friend is lately dead,*
> *I will bewaile the death, of my deere frend;*
> *Vppon whose Tombe, ten thousand Teares Ile shead,*
> *Till drearie Death, of mee shall make an end:*
> *Or if she want a Toombe, to her desart,*
> *Oh then, Ile burie her within my hart.*

A poet contributing to *The Phoenix Nest* with *An Epitaph vpon the right Honorable sir Philip Sidney knight,* apostrophized the dead poet in a similar way:

> *In worthy harts sorow hath made thy tombe,*
> *Thy soule and spright enrich the heauens aboue.*[5]

Magno utilized the conceit in the sestet of one of his love-sonnets (ed. Venice, 1600, p. 75):

> *Et, s'allhor gli occhi per piu crudo fato*
> *Chiusi mi fian; così dipinti almeno*
> *Terrogli aperti nel bel viso amato:*
> *Et per sepolcro hauendo il vostro seno,*
> *Felici essequie haurò pianto, e bagnato*
> *De la pietà del ciglio almo, e sereno.*

---

[4] Bernardo Tomitano, Ruscelli's *Fiori* 1558, fol. 47 v.
[5] Ed. ROLLINS, Cambridge, Mass., 1931, p. 10.

Other instances are found in Drayton's *Idea* XLV and in the sixth Canto of his *Barons Warres* (*For thy deare Ashes be my Brest the Urne,* l. 761), in Alexander's *Aurora* LXXXVI, in Annibal Caro,[6] Berardino Rota,[7] Ronsard,[8] and others.[9]

The types illustrated above, then, are the basic ingredients of the immortality theme. We naturally find various combinations and intermediate forms. Thus we have seen immortal verse combined with monuments and heart and mind combined with tombs in the sense 'receptacles enclosing someone's memory'. Certain other combinations, however, are uncommon. Thus so far as I am aware the theme of 'entombment in verse,' as distinct from 'verse-monument', is rare in Renaissance poetry. Isolated instances are Pseudo-Constable VIII, iv:

> *My teares are true, though others be diuine,*
> *and sing of warres, and Troys new-rising frame,*
> *meeting Heroick feete in euery line,*
> *that tread high measures on the Scene of Fame.*
> *And I though disaccustoming my Muse,*
> *to sing but low songs in a humble vaine,*
> *may one day raise my stile as others use,*
> *and turne Elizon to a higher straine.*
> *When reintombing from oblivious ages*
> *in better stanzas her suruiuing wonder,*
> *I may oppos'd against the monster-rages*
> *that part desert, and excellence a sunder:*
> *That shee (though coy) may yet suruiue to see*
> *Her beauties wonder lyues againe in mee,*

the sense being, of course, "hiding away in better stanzas, as in a second tomb, 'her wonder' from the oblivion of future ages". — In *The Legend of Matilda*, Drayton makes the heroine address the "Authours vertuous Mistris":

[6] Ruscelli's *Fiori*, fol. 27 r.
[7] Sonnets *In Morte*, Naples ed. 1726, p. 102.
[8] *Epitaphes de Louyse de Maillay* VI, ed. LAUMONIER X, p. 145.
[9] The formula is found well into the 17th century, and the ways in which it is used become increasingly strange. Thus in Ford's *'Tis Pitty Shee's a Whoore* (published in 1633) Giovanni appears in the last scene with Annabella's heart on his dagger: *'Tis a heart, / A heart, my lords, in which is mine intomb'd* (V, vi, 28 f.). — Cf. also the earlier *Fidessa* passage discussed below, p. 106 f.

> *It shall suffice, if you for me be sorrie,*
> *Reading my Legend, builded by his Verse,*
> *Which must hereafter serve me for a Herse* (19 ff.).

A third example is the first tercet of Guarini's sonnet XC, promising that immortality will be the lot of the recently deceased Duchess of Mantua — her fame will take wing from the urn of the poet's verse:

> *L'urna di sì gran Donna è in queste carte;*
> *non dove estinto il suo mortal si serra,*
> *Mà d'onde s'apre à la sua fama il volo.*

Our second excursus, before we turn to the relationship between the *Sonnets* and *Delia*, deals with a feature that is often characteristic of Daniel's way of imitating other poets. Out of several instances[1] I choose sonnet XII in *Delia*:

> *My spotles loue hoouers with white wings,*
> *About the temple of the proudest frame :*
> *Where blaze those lights fayrest of earthly things,*
> *Which cleere our clouded world with brightest flame.*
> *M'ambitious thoughts confined in her face,*
> *Affect no honour, but what she can giue mee :*
> *My hopes doe rest in limits of her grace,*
> *I weygh no comfort vnlesse she releeue mee.*
> *For she that can my hart imparadize,*
> *Holdes in her fairest hand what deerest is :*
> *My fortunes wheele, the circle of her eyes,*
> *Whose rowling grace deigne once a turne of blis.*
> *All my liues sweete consists in her alone,*
> *So much I loue the most vnlouing one.*

I have elsewhere suggested that Guarini's no. XLIV may colour the first quatrain and Tasso's no. 81 the third; and if I now feel hesitant on the first point I have little doubt about the second. Tasso's sonnet bears the following heading: *Assomiglia a la Fortuna la sua donna, la quale egli aveva veduta co' capegli sparsi su la fronte.* The first part of

---

[1] Cf. SCHAAR, *op. cit.*, pp. 168 ff.

this *argomento* could also be applied not only to the third quatrain of Daniel's poem but to other sonnets as well. But there are certain similarities between Daniel's quatrain and Tasso's poem which cannot reasonably be explained away as due to common tradition:

> *Costei, che su la fronte ha sparsa al vento*
> *L'errante chioma d'òr, Fortuna pare;*
> *Anzi è vera Fortuna, e può beare*
> *E misero può far il piú contento.*
> *Dispensatrice no d'oro o d'argento*
> *O di gemme che mandi estraneo mare,*
> *Ma tesori d'Amor, cose piú care,*
> *Fura, dona, e ritoglie in un momento.*
> *Cieca non già, ma solo a'miei martíri*
> *Par che s'infinga tale, e cieco uom rende*
> *Con due luci serene e sfavillanti.*
> *Chiedi qual sia la rota ove gli amanti*
> *Travolve e'l corso lor ferma e sospende?*
> *La rota fanno or de' begli occhi i giri.*

There is in itself no very striking resemblance between *E misero può far il piú contento* and *For she that can my hart imparadize*, or between *Dispensatrice ... cose piú care ... dona* and *Holdes in her fairest hand what deerest is*. But these resemblances take on a new significance in view of the harsh and surprising transition from *Holdes in her fairest hand what deerest is: | My fortunes wheele* to *the circle of her eyes*. The poet would scarcely have got this idea unless he had read Tasso's poem, imitated the cited details in the quatrains, skipped the continuation in which Tasso develops his thought, and, translating the last line of the Italian poem almost literally, tacked it on abruptly to l. 10 of his own sonnet. In the editions of Tasso's *Rime d'Amore*, only a few poems separate no. 81 from two sonnets to which, as is well known, Daniel was heavily indebted in XXXIII and XXXIV (nos. 77 and 78).

We can now turn to *Delia* and the *Sonnets*. No. XLVI of the former sequence reads:

> *Let others sing of Knights and Palladines,*
> *In aged accents, and vntimely words:*

> *Paint shadowes in imaginary lines,*
> *Which well the reach of their high wits records;*
>   *But I must sing of thee and those faire eyes,*
> *Autentique shall my verse in time to come,*
> *When yet th'vnborne shall say, loe where she lyes,*
> *Whose beautie made him speake that els was dombe.*
>   *These are the Arkes the Tropheis I erect,*
> *That fortifie thy name against old age,*
> *And these thy sacred vertues must protect,*
> *Against the Darke and times consuming rage.*
>   *Though th'error of my youth they shall discouer,*
> *Suffice they shew I liu'd and was thy louer.*

In this poem Daniel thus promises to immortalize Delia, and we recognize the 'verse-monument' theme in the third quatrain. These lines offer no problem, any more than the couplet and the first quatrain do. But the second quatrain is more remarkable. The hapax verb *autentique*, directly adapted from the corresponding adjective, is used with *eyes* as its object, the sense apparently being: 'My verse shall render your eyes true and real to future ages'.[2] This awkward expression of the traditional idea that the lady's beauty will live for ever thanks to the poet's verse, is unexpectedly combined with a striking variant of the uncommon 'entombment in verse' theme. *Loe where (s)he lyes*[3] is a formula used either in real epitaphs and elegies,[4] or else as a conclusion of erotic poems describing the author's untimely death of passion for the hard-hearted lady: the reader is asked to contemplate the epitaph of a victim of love.[5] But in poems announcing the triumphant victory of the

[2] The punctuation of course need not disconcert us: in *Delia*, as in many other Elizabethan texts, a comma often separates verb and object: XIII *I figured on the table of my harte, | The fayrest forme ...*, XXIX *The broken toppes of loftie trees declare, | The fury of a mercy-wanting storme*, etc.

[3] Some readers may possibly think that *Loe where she lyes* alludes to the spot where the lady will be buried, and that ll. 7—8 thus refer to the reflections of someone visiting the lady's real tomb in the future. But this is impossible for a very simple reason: the whole point of the poem is that the poet's verse is her tomb and alone can protect her from oblivion. In addition, 'visit to lady's tomb' is a Romantic rather than a Renaissance *topos*.

[4] Instances, of course, abound; some are found in *Tottel's Miscellany*, pp. 135 (*Vpon sir Iames wilfordes death*), 160 (*A praise of Audley*), 167 (*Of the ladie wentworthes death*); in Greene's *Pandosto*, p. 32 (Bellaria's epitaph), etc.

[5] One out of many instances is the end of *Harpalus complaynt on Phillidaes loue bestowed on Corin* attributed to Surrey and printed in *England's Helicon* (ed. ROLLINS, pp. 40 ff.):

poet's verse, capable of perpetuating beauty and braving time, the formula is to my knowledge avoided. How did Daniel come to use the uncommon theme of 'entombment in verse' expressed in the even more uncommon form *Loe where she lyes*? The answer, it seems, is to be found in the first two quatrains of Shakespeare's sonnet XVII, which resemble Daniel's lines more than any other passage does:

> *Who will beleeue my verse in time to come*
> *If it were fild with your most high deserts?*
> *Though yet heauen knows it is but as a tombe*
> *Which hides your life, and shewes not halfe your parts:*
> *If I could write the beauty of your eyes,*
> *And in fresh numbers number all your graces,*
> *The age to come would say, "This poet lies,*
> *Such heauenly touches nere toucht earthly faces."*

The theme of these lines, where nothing needs explaining, is thus the common one of the poet's inability to praise the friend in adequate terms,[6] combined with the idea that if he could, nobody would believe him. One explanation of the similarities between the *Sonnets* XVII and *Delia* XLVI is that Shakespeare used some rhetorically odd lines in *Delia* in order to express a common idea; another is that Daniel by mere chance happened to combine something rare, something unique, and something closely resembling the passage in Shakespeare. But can we ignore the laws of probability? If we cannot, it is easy to explain the oddities of Daniel's second quatrain by assuming that he had read the Shakespearean poem and remembered it, well in part, vaguely in part. The word-group

> *Heere lyeth vnhappy Harpalus,*
> *by cruell Loue now slaine:*
> *Whom Phillida vniustly thus,*
> *hath murdred with disdaine.*

Watson uses the formula in *Hekatompathia* c, imitated from Parabosco, Lodge in *Strive no more*, printed in *The Phoenix Nest*, Ronsard has it in *Am.* I, LXII (*Cy dessous gist un amant vendomois*), the Italians often have recourse to it (Sasso, Chariteo, Molza, Costanzo, etc.) The prototype of the formula in love-poems is probably Propertius II, xiii, 35 f.:

QUI NVNC IACET HORRIDA PVLVIS,
VNIVS HIC QVONDAM SERVVS AMORIS ERAT.

[6] Cf. SCHAAR, *op. cit.*, p. 21, n. 1. The expressions of this theme were not fixed in a conventional system of formulas, and *tombe* is used in the same way as in LXXXIII,12, *When others would giue life, and bring a tombe.*

my verse in time to come was reproduced bodily; *this poet lies* was transformed, by way of association, into *loe where she lyes* because, psychologically, the theme of the tomb is not far removed from the theme of immortality. And the material derived from Shakespeare was condensed by Daniel in much the same way as that derived from Tasso.[7]

The second parallel also comprises passages dealing with the theme of immortality. In *Delia* xxxvi, the poet tries to reconcile the lady to the thought that he is praising her in his unworthy verse:

> *Thinke not sweete Delia, this shall be thy shame,*
> *My Muse should sound thy praise with mournefull warble:*
> *How many liue, the glory of whose name,*
> *Shall rest in yce, when thine is grau'd in Marble.*
> *Thou maist in after ages liue esteem'd,*
> *Vnburied in these lines reseru'd in purenes;*
> *These shall intombe those eyes, that haue redeem'd*
> *Mee from the vulgar, thee from all obscurenes.*

This time, then, it is the lady's eyes that are praised in terms which we have found to be exceptional, and which, moreover, clash with *vnburied* in the preceding line. 'Sweet honey-dropping Daniel' did not particularly like antithesis, and the harsh instance above is unparalleled in his writings.[8] Again, if the 'entombment in verse' theme is rare enough in 'immortality' contexts, 'entombment of eyes in verse' is unprecedented there. The instances we have of 'entombment of eyes' are found in laments for the death of beauty, as for example in Daniel's *The Complaint of Rosamond*:

> *And you fayre eyes, containers of my blisse,*
> *Motiues of loue, borne to be matched neuer:*
> *Entomb'd in your sweet circles sleepe for euer* (670 ff.),

---

[7] Besides the direct influence from Shakespeare suggested above and affecting certain details, there is an influence from tradition in that the basic theme of the sonnet is the conventional one of 'let others sing of feats and heroes, *my* verse shall praise only you'. This theme derives ultimately from the Anacreontic ode no. 16 (Σὺ μὲν λέγεις τὰ Θήβης), imitated by Ronsard (*L'un dit la prise des murailles | De Thebe & l'autre les batailles* etc.; cf. LAUMONIER, ed. VII, p. 193), and by Belleau (I, p. 25). We can trace the theme in the Pseudo-Constable sonnet cited above; it also occurs in Soowthern's *Pandora* (Odellet), and a Neo-Latin version is found in Johannes Secundus' first elegy. Thus various influences, traditional and direct, seem to merge in Daniel's poem.

[8] Cf. SCHAAR, *op. cit.*, pp. 133 ff.

in a sonnet by Fabio Galeota,

> *In terra copre fredda nebbia oscura*
> *I tuoi begli occhi e'l tuo leggiadro uiso,*[9]

and in another by Jamyn (*Souspirs*, L):

> *Puis que sous le sepulchre est caché ce bel œil*
> *Qui d'amour mutuelle enflamboit mon courage* (7—8).[1]

Daniel was not an original poet, as even his admirers admit; his natural style is not pointed but smooth, allowing no harsh antitheses. How then did he happen to break with tradition and with his usual principles of style — if not by imitating someone else? In sonnet LXXXI Shakespeare contrasts the futility of his own destiny with the immortal fame that his verse shall secure for the friend:

> *Or I shall liue your Epitaph to make,*
> *Or you suruiue when I in earth am rotten,*
> *From hence your memory death cannot take,*
> *Although in me each part will be forgotten.*
> *Your name from hence immortall life shall haue,*
> *Though I (once gone) to all the world must dye,*
> *The earth can yeeld me but a common graue,*
> *When you intombed in mens eyes shall lye,*
> *Your monument shall be my gentle verse,*
> *Which eyes not yet created shall ore-read,* etc.

Is it hard to see a repetition in *Delia* XXXVI of the same mental process that probably took place when Daniel wrote no. XLVI? If he had before him — or, which is more likely — if he remembered Shakespeare's no. LXXXI, he remembered a sustained antithesis (a feature of style that is typical of the Shakespearean sonnets) and a line conspicuously combining *intomb* and *eyes*. The antithesis and the word-group *These shall intombe those eyes* in *Delia* may without greater difficulty be explained as due to these impressions and to Daniel's tendency to condense material from other sources. As to

---

[9] *Rime di diversi* V, 112, Venice, 1552.

[1] Other variations on this theme are found in the monodies by Giacomo Cencio in *Rime di diversi* II, 1547, 55 (*Mentre, che Roma auuolta in panno nero | Al sepolchro portaua i raggi spenti | De piu begliocchi*), and by Antonio Gaggi in *Rime di diversi* IX, 1560, 51 (*E un uiuo marmo copre il morto lume | Ch'era mia luce, quello ardente foco*).

Shakespeare's poem, l. 8 is a variant of a fairly common motif (survival in memory) discussed above on p. 25 (cf. particularly Magno's sonnet). Since the poet's verse will be *your monument*, the friend will be for ever "present to the mind's eye" (POOLER).

*

The other resemblances between the *Sonnets* and *Delia* differ from those now discussed in that the similarities are the result of revisions in the latter work. Thus we have a string of *Delia* passages which are unlike Shakespearean lines in the earlier editions, but resemble them in the later. To these cases we shall add some parallels including Daniel sonnets first printed in later editions of *Delia*.

Occasionally, as is well known, Daniel rewrote the same poem several times, and a series of versions on the same theme has been handed down. Thus sonnet xx reads as follows in 1592:

> *Come death the Anchor-holde of all my thoughtes,*
> *My last Resort whereto my soule appealeth;*
> *For all too long on earth my fancy dotes,*
> *Whilst my best blood my younge desiers sealeth.*
> *   That hart is now the prospectiue of horror,*
> *That honored hath the cruelst faire that lyueth:*
> *The cruelst faire, that sees I languish for her,*
> *Yet neuer mercy to my merit giueth.*
> *   This is her Lawrell and her triumphes prize,*
> *To tread me downe with foote of her disgrace:*
> *Whilst I did builde my fortune in her eyes,*
> *And laide my liues rest on so faire a face;*
> *   That rest I lost, my loue, my life and all,*
> *   So high attempts to lowe disgraces fall.*

In this version (which with trifling alterations is the same as that of 1591) the poet thus beseeches Death to put an end to his sufferings, which are described in detail at the same time as the author accuses the lady. In the 1601 and later editions, the poem was rewritten:

> *Come Tyme the anchor-hold of my desire,*
> *   My last Resort whereto my hopes appeale,*

> *Cause once the date of her disdaine t'expire :*
> *Make her the sentence of her wrath repeale.*
> *Rob her faire Brow, breake in on Beautie, steale*
> *Powre from those eyes, which pittie cannot spare :*
> *Deale with those daintie cheekes as she doth deale*
> *With this poore heart consumed with dispaire.*
> *This heart made now the prospectiue of care,*
> *By louing her, the cruelst Faire that liues*
> *The cruelst Fayre that sees I pine for her,*
> *And neuer mercie to my merit giues.*
> *Let her not still triumph ouer the prize*
> *Of mine affections taken by her eies.*

However, the poet is not content with this version either. In the editions which contain it, we find it immediately followed by a third version in which the author seems a little regretful. The revenge theme is still there, but somewhat toned down; the poet questions time and does not merely urge him on, and the couplet blows a retreat:

> *Tyme, cruell tyme, come and subdue that Brow*
> *Which conquers all but thee, and thee too staies*
> *As if she were exempt from Syeth or Bow,*
> *From loue or yeares vnsubiect to decaies.*
> *Or art thou growne in league with those faire eies*
> *That they may helpe thee to consume our daies?*
> *Or dost thou spare her for her cruelties,*
> *Being merciles like thee that no man weies?*
> *And yet thou seest thy powre she disobaies,*
> *Cares not for thee, but lets thee waste in vaine,*
> *And prodigall of howers and yeares betraies*
> *Beautie and youth t'opinion and disdaine.*
> *Yet spare her Tyme, let her exempted bee,*
> *She may become more kinde to thee or mee.*

But there was more to come. In the *Songs* by Samuel Daniel's brother John, published in 1606, the theme of the couplet spread far into the bulk of the poem, making up eight fresh lines which replace the third quatrain and the couplet. What we now have is a 16-line sonnet running the gamut from desire for revenge through a discussion with Time and a plea for mercy to a complete *volte-face* as compared with version no. 1:

> *Tyme, cruell tyme, canst thou subdue that Brow*
>> *That conquers all but thee, and thee too staies*
>> *As if she were exempt from Syeth or Bow,*
>> *From loue and yeares vnsubiect to decaies.*
> *Or art thou growne in league with those faire eies*
>> *That they might helpe thee to consume our daies?*
>> *Or dost thou loue her for her cruelties,*
>> *Being merciles like thee that no man weies?*
> *Then doe so still although shee makes no steeme,*
>> *Of dayes nor yeares, but lets them run in vaine:*
>> *Hould still thy swift wing'd hours that wondring seeme*
>> *To gase on her, euen to turne back againe.*
> *And doe so still although she nothing cares,*
>> *Doe as I doe, loue her although vnkinde,*
>> *Hould still, yet O I feare at vnawares,*
>> *Thou wilt beguile her though thou seem'st so kinde.*

The question is whether Daniel traversed these stages of increasing lenience (not backed by tradition) owing to a corresponding change of attitude to the woman concerned, or whether acquaintance with some other poem made him alive to the possibility of developing his theme. Anyone willing to admit, a) that *Delia* is more suggestive of literary convention than of experience of real life, and b) that its author did not despise borrowing, is not likely to dismiss a comparison with Shakespeare's no. XIX. The first line of this poem reads, *Deuouring time blunt thou the Lyons pawes*, followed by four lines of a similar content; ll. 6 ff. deal with a contrasting theme:

> *And do what ere thou wilt swift-footed time*
> *To the wide world and all her fading sweets:*
> *But I forbid thee one most hainous crime,*
> *O carue not with thy howers my loues faire brow,*
> *Nor draw noe lines there with thine antique pen,*
> *Him in thy course vntainted doe allow,*
> *For beauties patterne to succeding men.*
>> *Yet doe thy worst ould Time dispight thy wrong,*
>> *My loue shall in my verse euer liue young.*

Thus in the second version of 1601, the *Delia* poem begins to show similarities with Shakespeare's sonnet. Even in the first 1601 version, *Tyme* had been substituted for *death*, but the *anchor-holde* is still there; in the second the *anchor-holde* is gone and we have an apostrophe made up of an adjective+*Tyme*, reminiscent of the introductory line of Shakespeare's no. XIX. In addition, a *yet*-clause in l. 13 is addressed to Time, just as it is in Shakespeare's sonnet. In *Songs*, fresh resemblances are added: there is *thou* in l. 1 and the triple imperative *doe*, there are *thy swift wing'd hours*, which may owe something to *swift-footed time* and *thy howers*;[2] there is the larger space given to the plea for mercy. It should be added that no other contemporary poem yields any parallel.[3]

When *Delia* appeared in 1594, 1595, and 1598, it was prefaced by a sonnet dedicated to the Countess of Pembroke. This sonnet replaced a prose epistle addressed to the same lady and found in both 1592 editions. The sonnet is as follows:

> *Wonder of these, glory of other times,*
> *O thou whom Enuy eu'n is forst t'admyre:*
> *Great Patroness of these my humble Rymes,*
> *Which thou from out thy greatnes doost inspire:*
> *Sith onely thou hast deign'd to rayse them higher,*

[2] This, however, does not mean that the 'winged hours', the *horae*, occur only in the passage in *Delia*, though they are rare enough. Isolated instances are Dekker's *Lust's Dominion* I, i, 180 f., *Old time I'le wait bare-headed at thy heels,* | *And be a foot-boy to thy winged hours*, Rogers's *Celestiall Elegies* XVII, *We that are calde Tymes golden winged Howres*, and Davies's *Orchestra* (p. 169), *Time, whose wingèd howers* | *Going and comming.*

[3] In his review of *An Elizabethan Sonnet Problem* (Stud. Neophilol. XXXIII, 1961, pp. 337 ff.), J. BUXTON raises two objections to my assumption of an influence from Shakespeare on the different versions of *Delia* XX: a) I am led "into occasional error", not observing that the sonnet "also underwent the drastic metrical revision to a Spenserian form"; b) the version found in John Daniel's *Songs* "certainly seems to show some influence from Shakespeare's sonnet XIX, but may not this be due to an adaptation by John Daniel himself of his brother's poem?" My answer is that I am concerned with Shakespeare's, not other poets', influence on no. XX, and influence from more than one poet may be at work in this sonnet. Like many other critics BUXTON overlooks the fact that *Delia* is a highly eclectic piece of work. What prevented Daniel from deriving ideas and phrases from Shakespeare, a metrical scheme from Spenser? As to objection b), the similarities to Shakespeare's XIX as found in the 1606 version of *Delia* XX are only, as I have pointed out, the final stage of a development which brings Daniel's poem gradually closer to Shakespeare's. It is hardly to be expected that John Daniel took over at a point where Samuel had left his sonnet in some measure dependent on the *Sonnets* XIX, and made this dependence even more pronounced.

Vouchsafe now to accept them as thine owne,
Begotten by thy hand, and my desire,
Wherein my Zeale, and thy great might is showne.
And seeing this vnto the world is knowne,
O leaue not, still to grace thy worke in mee :
Let not the quickning seede be ouer-throwne,
Of that which may be borne to honour thee.
Whereof, the trauaile I may challenge mine,
But yet the glory, (Madam) must be thine.

This sonnet paraphrases part of the earlier prose epistle. The couplet, however, is an addition, and LEE observed[4] that it is similar to the couplet of no. XXXVIII of Shakespeare's *Sonnets*:

If my slight Muse doe please these curious daies,
The paine be mine, but thine shal be the praise.

LEE apparently regarded Shakespeare as the borrower, and wrongly gave 1592 as the date of the edition containing Daniel's sonnet. Now there are passages in contemporary and earlier sonnet poetry which are reminiscent of the cited lines and at the same time differ from them. Pseudo-Constable ends one poem (*Diana* VI,i): *Mine be the torment, but the guilt be thine*; similarly Daniel in XV, 14: *The fault is hers, though mine the hurt must bee*. Thus in these cases it is not a matter of the lady's glory and the poet's pain but of the lady's guilt and the poet's suffering, and I have said before that this is "almost invariably" so when we find phrases like these in sonnet poetry. But we may well ask to what extent Daniel and Shakespeare are exceptional. As I feel I have not answered this question properly before,[5] I shall try to do so now.

Constable has one phrase like that in Pseudo-Constable and Daniel: *I haue the payne, beare yow the blame of it* (III, iii, 1, 14). Commenting on this, GRUNDY refers to "Petrarch's much-imitated line, '*Vostro, donna, il peccato, e mio fia 'l danno*' (CCXXIV, 14)". The same reference had already been made by SCOTT in almost the same words (p. 139). There are, in fact, two examples in Petrarch: The

---

[4] *Life of Shakespeare*, 1898, pp. 129 f. WALSH (ed. 1908) repeated the observation without mentioning LEE (p. 268).
[5] *Op. cit.* p. 177.

cited sonnet-ending and the last line of stanza 6 of the *canzone* numbered CCVII: *La colpa è vostra, e mio 'l danno e la pena*. Before we move backwards from Petrarch we must glance at the adaptations in his followers. Only a few Quattrocentists pay attention to the line. Chariteo ends his *strambotto* no. XIII with a rendering that does not keep very close to Petrarch:

> *Ma quanto più di voi serva si mostra*
> *Tanto serrà magior la colpa vostra;*

while a version in Seraphino is more epigrammatic: *Io pato e altrui pecca* (son. VIII, 5). In the early Cinquecentists the formula is also rare. We find it in Olympo da Sassoferrato, who is fairly faithful to Petrarch in the last two lines of a *strambotto* in his *Aurora*:

> *Et se la notte in me doppio e l'affanno,*
> *vostro donna e il peccato e mio fia il danno.*

In the later Cinquecentists the phrase is fairly common and the formulations are mostly suggestive of Petrarch's. Parabosco complains that he must *Lagrimar l'altrui colpa, e 'l mio tormento* (l. 11 of a sonnet in *Rime di div.* I, 305). Some other instances are Gradenico, *Vostro Donna il peccato, e mio fia 'l danno* (*Rime di div.* VI, 248 r.), Varchi, *Mia la pena, | Ma la colpa fia vostra, vostro il danno* (CCCCX, 3—4), Tasso, *Vostra è la colpa e 'l danno è mio* (son. 187,14). Cencio ends a monody in the same way: it is the gods' fault that the survivors mourn — *Fia lor la colpa, come nostro il danno* (*Rime di div.* II, 56). Giraldo Cinthio says he has got used to pain and sorrow, *Ond' è, per colpa altrui, la mia ment' egra* (*Le Fiamme*, 1548, 55 r.). Boscán, the pioneer of Petrarchism in Spain, adopts the formula in a shape closely similar to that in Petrarch's CCVII,6: *La culpa es vuestra y el dolor es mío* (LVII, 14). — The French do not use it often, and also prefer the epigrammatic version: *L'offence en est sur vous, et sur moy le dommage* (Desportes, *Diane* I, viii, 14); similarly Magny, who cleverly adopts the line in a poem describing the horrors of war: *La coulpe vient d'autruy mais nostre est le domage* (*Souspirs* VII, 14). This passage is reminiscent of Piccolomini's sonnet written *l'anno del* XLVIII *ne i pericoli de la guerra in Italia, ch'alhor pendeuano*, of which the last tercet reads:

Miseri noi, che i gran signor trà loro
Giuocansi ognihor le nostre uite, é l'oro:
Lor son le colpe, é nostr'è sempre il danno.[6]

The formula is fairly common in the English poets. In addition to the examples given above, it is found twice in Wyatt: *And yours the losse, and mine the deadly payne*[7] (96, 14), *Yours is the fault, and mine the great annoy* (98,14); and once in Surrey (*The Trammels of Loue*): *The fault is hers, the losse ys myne* (last line but one), which also seems to be imitated from Petrarch. In Greene's *Menaphon*, we find it in the last line but one of Menaphon's ditty to Pesana: *Mine be the paine, but hirs the cruell cause of this strange torment* (ed. COLLINS II, p. 256). In the *Gorgeous Gallery of Gallant Inventions* it occurs, similarly in the last line but one, in a complaint *agaynst the vniust dealing of his Lady beloued: The fault is thine, the payne is mine* (p. 50); in *A Handefull of pleasant Delites* we find it in the last stanza, 1.4, of a similar kind of poem: *The fault is hers the pain is mine* (p. 60). Sir William Alexander uses the formula when blaming Fortune for his sufferings: *That fault was fortunes, though the losse be mine* (*Aurora*, 53).

If we move backwards from Petrarch there are two relevant lines to be considered: *E porto pena de l'altrui peccato* in Guittone d'Arezzo of the 13th century (son. 123),[8] and *Meus er lo danz e vostre er lo pecatz* in Rigaut de Berbezilh of the late 12th and early 13th century (IX,iii).[9] In the first case the line is found in the centre of a sonnet (1.6), in the second at the beginning of a nine-line stanza (1.3). What happened, then, seems clear: the line in Guittone's or Rigaut's poem — probably the latter's — was imitated by Petrarch[1] and moved by him from within his predecessor's poem to the very end of one sonnet and one *canzone* stanza in his own *Canzoniere*. In

---

[6] *Cento Sonetti*, Roma, 1549, no. LXIV.

[7] Because of *losse* I have earlier regarded this as a deviation from the theme, but I now believe with ROLLINS (*Tottel* edition II, p. 197) that the line is a translation of Petrarch's CCXXIV, 14. *Losse* instead of *fault* as in 98 may then be a metonymical rendering of *peccato*: 'loss'='perdition'. Cf. the Varchi line quoted above.

[8] Pointed out in the TASSONI-MUZIO-MURATORI edition of the *Canzoniere* in 1711.

[9] MURATORI and CARDUCCI & FERRARI wrongly ascribe the line to Sordello, misled by the inaccurate ALESSANDRO TASSONI (*Considerazioni sopra le Rime di Petrarca*, 1609). RIGUTINI gives the correct reference, similarly Rigaut's editor, ANGLADE.

[1] For the question of de Berbezilh's influence on Petrarch cf. RIGUTINI's preface (*Petrarca e i Trovatori*), ed., pp. 40 ff.

this position the phrase attracted the attention of Petrarch's imitators and became a fixed formula.

ꞏI am afraid I have been trying the reader's patience a good deal when following the fortunes of the 'poet's-pain-lady's-guilt' formula, and I can only hope I have made my point in so doing. My aim has been to demonstrate that this formulaic pattern constitutes a massive background and that, though variations occur, the pattern is semantically homogeneous. If it nearly always occurs as the last line or at least at the end of poems from Petrarch onwards (the only clear exceptions in sonnets known to me being Varchi's no. CCCCX and, earlier, Seraphino's VIII), it can fairly safely be said practically always to deal with the poet's suffering and the lady's (rarely someone else's) guilt. Against this homogeneous background the deviations stand out conspicuously. In fact, the only deviation known to me similar to that found in Daniel's and Shakespeare's sonnets is met with in son. LXXII of *The Tarantula of Loue* by the Scottish sonneteer, William Fowler: *So sal the prayse be yours and paynes all myne* (l.13). [2] It is not quite clear when the *Tarantula* was composed — possibly around 1590, possibly later — but one thing is certain: as in the case of the other Scottish sonneteers, there is not a single trace of direct influence from Fowler's sonnets on Elizabethan poetry. [3] If anything, the sonnets of the *Tarantula* were inspired, at least in part, by the Elizabethans. There is thus every indication, either that Fowler "invented" the praise-pain variant quite independently of Daniel and Shakespeare, or that he was influenced by the latter's XXXVIII, 14, which is more similar than Daniel's couplet to his own line. The occurrence of the praise-pain formula in Fowler's sonnet, therefore, does not make the relationship between Daniel's introductory sonnet and Shakespeare's XXXVIII more complicated than it would have been if no third example of the formula had existed. In other words, in spite of the line in the *Tarantula* sonnet there is strong reason to connect the passages in *Delia* and the *Sonnets*. I shall here only add that, beyond the above-mentioned unconventional similarity of theme,

[2] Edited by MEIKLE, I, Edinburgh, 1914, p. 209.

[3] For the literary background of the Scottish sonneteers cf. the edition of Fowler, III, pp. 23 ff., KASTNER's edition of Drummond, I, Edinburgh, 1913, pp. xv ff., KASTNER & CHARLTON's edition of Sir William Alexander, II, Edinburgh, 1929, pp. 632 ff. (notes on *Aurora*), and SCOTT, *op. cit.*, pp. 275 ff., 324 ff.

a) these passages are connected by the use of *mine-thine*, b) the passage written by the less original poet is the result of revision, c) in the prose epistle on which the sonnet is based the pronoun of address is *you*, changed everywhere to *thou* in the sonnet. On this point, too, Daniel's poem has thus been brought closer to Shakespeare's XXXVIII, where *thou* is used throughout.[4]

One of the numerous sonnets in *Delia* in which the poet laments his hard fate is no. XXIII. The two 1592 editions read:

> *Looke in my griefes, and blame me not to morne,*
> *From care to care that leades a life so bad;*
> *Th'Orphan of fortune, borne to be her scorne,*
> *Whose clouded brow dooth make my daies so sad.*
> *Long are their nights whose cares doe neuer sleepe*
> *Loathsome their daies, whome no sunne euer ioyde:*
> *Her fairest eyes doe penetrate so deepe,*
> *That thus I liue booth day and night annoyde.*
> *But since the sweetest roote doth yeeld thus much,*
> *Her praise from my complaint I may not part:*
> *I loue th'effect for that the cause is such,*
> *Ile praise her face, and blame her flintie hart.*
> *Whilst that wee make the world admire at vs,*
> *Her for disdaine, and me for louing thus.*

The third quatrain thus introduces a contrast motif of a kind common in sonnet poetry. But we are hardly prepared for the form in which this contrast motif appears in the revised version of the 1601 and subsequent editions:

> *But since the sweetest roote yeelds frute so sowre,*
> *Her praise from my complaint I may not part:*
> *I loue th'effect the cause being of this powre,*
> *Ile praise her face, and blame her flintie hart.*

This of course is less consistent since l. 9, as it now stands, is an objection to the statement made in l. 10 rather than a reason for it. The sense therefore requires the very opposite of *since*, and we should have expected: *But though the sweetest roote* (her face)

---

[4] *You* in *Delia* is otherwise changed to *thou* only in the revision of no. XXIX.

yeelds frute so sowre (the poet's suffering) | *Her praise from my complaint I may not part.* However, l. 9 in its new form comes closer to Shakespeare's causal clause *For sweetest things turne sowrest by their deedes* in XCIV, 13 than to any other contemporary or earlier passage. It is likely that the poet, if he borrowed at all, borrowed from Shakespeare's sonnet. If so, he forgot to substitute *though* for *since* in the new version of l. 9. It is hard to see why he should rewrite l. 9 the way he did unless induced to do so by external influence.

When the fourth edition of *Delia* appeared in 1594, the poet added a sonnet (no. XVI A) the first two quatrains of which were filled with bitter rhetorical questions. These questions are to the same effect: Why strive to eternize such a cruel creature? In the third quatrain the poet toys with a less melancholy idea:

> *If her defects haue purchast her this fame,*
> *What should her vertues doe, her smiles, her loue?*
> *If this her worst, how should her best inflame?*
> *What passions would her milder fauours moue?*
> *Fauours (I thinke) would sence quite ouer-come,*
> *And that makes happy Louers euer dombe.*

Shakespeare's no. XCVI, as pointed out by ISAAC,[5] expresses the same idea in a manner suggestive of Daniel's poem, though the verbal resemblances are not striking:

> *Thou makst faults graces, that to thee resort:*
> *As on the finger of a throned Queene,*
> *The basest Iewell wil be well esteem'd:*
> *So are those errors that in thee are seene,*
> *To truths translated, and for true things deem'd.*
> *How many Lambs might the sterne Wolfe betray,*
> *If like a Lambe he could his lookes translate.*
> *How many gazers mighst thou lead away,*
> *If thou wouldst vse the strength of all thy state?* (ll. 4—12).

These passages are interesting for two reasons. First, as I have earlier tried to show,[6] it is to the intensifying structure as such (if A

---

[5] *Op. cit.*, p. 174.
[6] *Op. cit.*, p. 163.

when B, how much more so when C) that we find parallels in other poetry rather than to the actual idea expressed in *Delia* and the *Sonnets*. To the instances I have quoted before I might add an Italian couplet cited by Melin de St. Gelais and rendered by him into French (II, p. 28):

> *S'el bel ch'in voi si scorge ogni altro eccede,*
> *Quanto deve esser quel che non si vede,*

and

> *S'el bel ch'in voi si vede il cor mi strugge,*
> *Quanto potrebbe quell' che gli occhi fugge.*

But the idea expressed in these couplets is different from that in *Delia* and the *Sonnets*, to which I still do not know any striking parallel. Ovid's *Amores* III, xi, 41 ff. I have mentioned elsewhere as providing a vague similarity; there is also a faint resemblance by implication in an epigram by Johannes Secundus (*In Neæram*): *Lumina mi atque animum cepit tua candida forma; | Moribus offendor, torva Neæra, tuis*, etc., but it does not really help us any more than Ovid's poem does.

Secondly, there is something unusual about Daniel's choice of words: *defect* and *worst*. When describing the lady's faults, Daniel invariably uses traditional terms in the earlier *Delia* editions. Thus she is of course *cruell* (10), *vnkinde* (9), *proud* (1), *merciles* (2), a *tyrant* (2), a *sweet foe* (1); she shows *pride* (3), *disdaine* (21), *crueltie* (4); has *faults* (2); *frowns* (1) and *scorns* (5); is *made of flint* (6); has a *hard hart* (6). But *defect* and *worst* are words used to suggest depravity, an irrelevant theme in this context: Daniel objects to the lady's unresponsiveness, not to her immorality. They also remind us of the words with which Shakespeare blames the recipient of *his* sonnets for blemishes of character. It may be added that in the few other cases in *Delia* where Daniel uses similar words we have to do with revision work and additional poems. Thus the couplet of XXVI A (first printed in the second ed. of 1592) reads:

> *Then iudge who sinnes the greater of vs twaine:*
> *I in my loue, or thou in thy disdaine,*

a passage which, in fact, was compared by ISAAC with the *Sonnets* CXLII, 1 ff.:

> *Loue is my sinne, and thy deare vertue hate,*
> *Hate of my sinne, grounded on sinfull louing;*
> *O, but with mine, compare thou thine owne state,*
> *And thou shalt finde it merits not reproouing.*

I have earlier dismissed this parallel as one of small interest (*op. cit.*, pp. 163 f.), but I did not then consider the importance of the vocabulary (cf. also p. 63 below, on no. CXLII). — Again in no. XXVI D in *Delia* (second ed. 1592) we find *Ile hide her sinne, and say it was my lot* (changed from *fault* in ed. 1591). In no. XLVI A, finally, added in 1594, Daniel laments the strange case

> *That errours should be grac'd that merrite shame,*
> *And sinne of frownes bring honor to the face* (11—12),

a pair of lines that bears some resemblance to our starting-point, the latter part of XVI A. It is not surprising, on the other hand, that Shakespeare's sonnets to the faithless friend and the dark lady are conspicuous for making a restricted use of the traditional 'disdain' vocabulary. A bare survey shows the tendencies: *unkind* in relevant contexts 2, *disdain* 2, *cruel* 4, *proud* 2,[7] *frown* 3, *fault* 6, *scorn* 1; the other words and phrases used in *Delia* do not occur in similar contexts in the *Sonnets*. With this we may compare, in relevant contexts, *sin* 4, *hate* 8, *error* 2, *shame* 4, *vice* 2, *defect* 2, *worst* 2. Thus in the *Sonnets* there is little difference between the two groups, in the unrevised *Delia* the former group is practically the only one used. Of course we must not make too much of this — not least because the vocabulary of the *Sonnets* XCVI is not identical with that of *Delia* XVI A. But it is at least noteworthy that Daniel's way of characterizing Delia in the revised editions becomes more like Shakespeare's way of characterizing the friend and the dark lady.

In other comparable English poems reproaching the hard-hearted lady, the vocabulary conforms to that of the unrevised *Delia*. The commonest word is *disdain*, and the lady is also *unkind*, *ruthless*, *stern*, *obdurate*, *remorseless*, *flinty*, *unrelenting*, *cruel*, *scornful*, *proud*, *niggard of her grace*, *unmerciful*, *pitiless;* has a *hard heart* or a *heart of flint*, *marble*, or *stone*, and a *mind of adamant*. She shows *rigour*,

---

[7] *Pride* in a comparable context is only used *sensu obsceno* (in CXLIV).

44

contempt, fury, strangeness; is a *tyrant,* a *stock,* a *block,* a *stone (Fidessa);* is comparable to a *tiger,* a *wolf,* a *panther,* a *griffon,* a *savage Moor,* and a *scorpion. Hate* is much less common than *disdain, cruelty,* and *flinty hearts* (instances in Barnes, Ma. vi, *El.* xii and xviii, *Licia,* An Ode, *Diana* VII, x, *Diella* xxvii, *Laura* I, x). *Coy* is found a few times. *Sin, error, defect, worst, vice,* do not seem used at all in descriptions of the unkind lady. Wyatt sometimes speaks of the lady's infidelity: *dowblenes* (v), *vnfaithfulnes* (vi), *bering in hand* (xiv), *thyn hert mutable* (xix).[8] — This vocabulary reflects the usage of the Continental poets.

We have just referred to the ending of no. xxvi A; a few words may also be said about its beginning. The poem, as appears from the cited couplet, is one of the numerous variations on the theme of poet's suffering and lady's cruelty, and the first two quatrains run:

> *Still in the trace of my tormented thought,*
> *My ceaselesse cares must martch on to my death:*
> *Thy least regarde too deerely haue I bought,*
> *Who to my comfort neuer deign'st a breath.*
> *Why should'st thou stop thine eares now to my cryes,*
> *Whose eyes were open ready to oppresse me?*
> *Why shutt'st thou not the cause whence all did rise,*
> *Or heare me now, and seeke how to redresse me.*

The poet then goes on to assure the lady that his love is nevertheless unchanged, and that he is even prepared to *blame my selfe for to excuse thy hart.*

In 1601 Daniel prints another version of ll. 1—8:

> *Still in the trace of one perplexed thought,*
> *My ceaselesse cares continually run on:*
> *Seeking in vaine what I haue euer sought,*
> *One in my loue, and her hard hart still one.*
> *I who did neuer ioy in other Sun,*
> *And haue no stars but those, that must fulfill*
> *The worke of rigor, fatally begun*
> *Vpon this hart, whom crueltie will kill.*

---

[8] Ed. MUIR, London, 1949.

Thus the poet slightly changes his subject: in the first version he emphasizes his suffering and beseeches the lady to put an end to it; in the second he lays more stress on his fidelity and the lady's stubborn coldness. This is in itself quite natural. But the vocabulary of l. 4 in its new version is remarkable: *one* first indicates constancy and then unresponsiveness, first something positive and then something negative. This way of expressing both matters is unique in *Delia*, though the second *one* is much more remarkable than the first. There are many variations in *Delia* on the theme of the lady's chronic unresponsiveness: *her sleeping pittie* (II), *I pray in vaine, a merciles to moue* (XI), *her pride is so innated ... all this will not moue her* (XVII), *The cruelst faire ... neuer mercy to my merit giueth* (XX), *no comfort would her brow reueale mee* (XXVI), etc. But the phrase *still one* used about this lamentable attitude on the part of the lady is something out of the ordinary: not unnaturally this equivalent of *semper eadem*, Queen Elizabeth's well-known motto, normally denotes a commendable quality. *Semper idem, semper eadem*, as BALDWIN has observed (*Genetics*, pp. 161 ff.), had religious implications, being derived via Cicero's *Tusculan Questions* from the Platonic 'Unchanging Same' in *Timaeus*. It could be added that Socrates is described in similar terms in one of the most popular books in the Renaissance, Xenophon's *Memorabilia* (IV, iv, 6). In Shakespeare's age, Spenser in *The Faerie Qveene* (VII, vii, 51,2) says that the planet Mercury — personified in the context — seems to be *alwayes as one*; and Sir John Davies winds up his praise of the Queen's moderation by alluding to her motto:

> In her *one* temper *still* is seene,
> No libertee claimes she as Queene,
> And showes no alteration.[9]

The religious connotations of the phrase are in Daniel's mind when, in *Cleopatra*, he makes the queen apostrophize the holy serpent:

> *Well did our Priests discerne something diuine*
> *Shadow'd in thee ...*
> *Comparing thy swift motion to the Sunne,*
> *That mou'st without the instruments that moue:*

---

[9] *Hymne* XXV, ed. GROSART I, London, 1876, p. 153. My emphasis.

And neuer waxing old, but alwayes one,
Doost sure thy strange diuinitie approue (1537 ff.).

In Daniel's *The Qveenes Arcadia* the phrase also occurs in a 'sublime' context: the pure and happy inhabitants of Arcadia, far from the tumult and incessant change of the rest of the world, have *continued still the same and one | In all successions from antiquitie* (2207 f.).[1] — In view of the cited uses of the phrase, it is not surprising that it should occur in descriptions of faithful and constant love. Thus in sonnet LXXVI, 5, Shakespeare says that he writes *still all one, euer the same*; and in no. CV, in a passage which concerns us nearly here, he intensifies the phrase:

> *Let not my loue be cal'd Idolatrie,*
> *Nor my beloued as an Idoll show,*
> *Since all alike my songs and praises be*
> *To one, of one, still such,[2] and euer so.*
> *Kinde is my loue to day, to morrow kinde,*
> *Still constant in a wondrous excellence* (1—6).

Thus Daniel's new version of XXVI A, 4 gives a reading which comes close to Shakespeare's CV, 4—5: it includes *still* and the double *one* of l. 4, with the *epanalepsis* of l. 5, condensing these features in one line, and the pattern *one in my loue* resembles *Kinde is my loue*. As we have seen, the use of *one* is partly odd in *Delia*, but wholly natural in the *Sonnets*. We may even ask ourselves whether Daniel's way of using this equivalent of the solemn *semper eadem* in his 1601 version of XXVI A does not result in the "vicious speech" called *acyron* by the rhetoricians, the words used being opposite in sense to what the author would express. As may be expected, no other son-neteer uses *still one* to describe the lady's permanent coldness. When Wyatt in X, 10 f. says *Still after oon rate ... kepe ye in the same state*, he is begging his lady to be always merciful; he ends the poem by

---

[1] For the kind of concepts with which the phrase is normally associated cf. also Daniel's *Musophilus*, 307 ff.:

> *Either truth, goodnes, vertue are not still*
> *The selfe same which they are, and alwaies one,*
> *But alter to the proiect of our will,*
> *Or we our actions make them waite vpon*, etc.

[2] In his notes to no. CV TUCKER points out that "'still such' should be taken as referring to 'one' rather than to 'my songs and praises.'"

promising, like Shakespeare, that he himself will be *alwaies oon*, always the same, always true and faithful. Similar assertions are of course common; in his *Stanses*, Desportes assures his lady, *Vostre amour est à moy toute une mesme chose* (l. 36). When poets lament the fact that a lady is permanently hard-hearted they use various other expressions: *Hard is thine heart, and never will repent* (*Parthenophil* xxviii), *Though She still rest pitiless* (ibid. Ma. 8), *Whiles she as steel and flint doth still remain* (*Amoretti* xviii), *She'll never yield* (*Fidessa* vii), *Thou constant art | My daily grief and anguish to increase* (*Chloris* xxviii), *Nor I ... Could euer thy obdurate beuty moue* (Barnfield, son. xix), etc. The Continental sonneteers use similar phrases.

In a sonnet numbered xiv in 1591, xv in 1592 and later, the poet bitterly complains that all his fidelity has not been able to move the lady. This is the third quatrain and the couplet of 1591:

> *If I haue wept the day, and sigthd the night,*
> *Whilst thrice the Sun approcht this northern bound :*
> *If such a faith hath euer wrought aright,*
> *And well deserud, and yet no fauour found :*
> *Let this suffice, the wholeworld it may see ;*
> *The fault is hers, though mine the most hurt be.*

In the 1592 and later editions, the third quatrain was entirely rewritten, the couplet partly altered, and some trifling details changed in the remainder of the sonnet. This is the new version of ll. 9—14:

> *If I haue doone due homage to her eyes,*
> *And had my sighes styll tending on her name :*
> *If on her loue my life and honour lyes ;*
> *And she th'vnkindest maide still scornes the same.*
> *Let this suffice, the world yet may see ;*
> *The fault is hers, though mine the hurt must bee.*

Ll. 11 and 12 are an obvious improvement on the somewhat laborious version of 1591, l. 11 establishing, as it does, a fitting *auxesis*. Similar ideas as that expressed in l. 11 are naturally common with the sonneteers: *Divine fleur où ma vie demeure* (Ronsard, *Am.* I, lxxvii), *S'il vit, je vy, s'il meurt, je ne suis riens* (clxi), *Thou, that anchor art and root to me* (*Diella* xx, 1596), *O fairest Fair! on whom depends my life* (*Chloris* ii, 1596). The prototype may have been formed by the Provençal poets: *En vos es ma mortz e ma vida*, and there are countless Italian examples. The closest and most interesting parallel, however, is Shakespeare's sonnet XCII, 1—10:

> *But doe thy worst to steale thy selfe away,*
> *For tearme of life thou art assured mine,*
> *And life no longer then thy loue will stay,*
> *For it depends vpon that loue of thine.*
> *Then need I not to feare the worst of wrongs,*
> *When in the least of them my life hath end,*
> *I see, a better state to me belongs*
> *Then that, which on thy humor doth depend.*
> *Thou canst not vex me with inconstant minde,*
> *Since that my life on thy reuolt doth lie,* etc.

Thus Daniel's revision has made one line in his poem similar to two in Shakespeare's. The main point, however, is that *lie on*= 'depend on' occurs in four other Shakespearean passages but nowhere else, to the best of my knowledge, in Daniel's works. The expressions invariably used in the Daniel texts are *stand on*, *depend on*, and *lie in*. The least common equivalent is *rest in*, which has a sense sometimes bordering on 'depend on'.

There is another set of parallels which, like the pair discussed above, is in the nature of 'point' resemblances. Thus in *Delia* XXXVII there are two interesting details which result from the revision of 1601. The first half of this poem deals with the transience of monuments and the immortality of well-earned fame. The third quatrain and the couplet draw the conclusions:

> *Why then though Delia fade let that not moue her,*
> *Though time do spoyle her of the fairest vaile*
> *That euer yet mortallitie did couer;*
> *Which shall instarre the needle and the trayle.*
> > *That grace, that vertue, all that seru'd t'in-woman;*
> > *Dooth her vnto eternitie assommon.*

This is, with minor alterations, the reading of the editions between 1592 and 1598. But in 1601 and subsequent editions we find the following version:

> And therefore grieue not if thy beauties die,
> Though time do spoyle thee of the fairest vaile
> That euer yet couered mortalitie
> And must instarre the Needle, and the Raile.
>   That Grace which doth more then in woman thee,
>   Liues in my lines, and must eternall bee.

We have here another resemblance brought about by revision, since the last line of the *Delia* couplet in 1601 reads like a condensed version of the end of Shakespeare's XVIII, but cannot be closely paralleled elsewhere:

> Nor shall death brag thou wandr'st in his shade,
> When in eternall lines to time thou grow'st,
>   So long as men can breath or eyes can see,
>   So long liues this, and this giues life to thee.

Among the *Delia* sonnets written on the model of Tasso's *Rime d'Amore* we find two (XXXIII and XXXIV) which are linked together by the common figure of *anadiplosis*. The couplet of one and the first two lines of the other read as follows in 1592:

> Thou maist repent, that thou hast scorn'd my teares,
> When Winter snowes vppon thy golden heares.

> When Winter snowes vpon thy golden heares,
> And frost of age hath nipt thy flowers neere, etc.

In 1601 we find *sable* instead of *golden* in both places, and *flowers* replaced by *beauties*. As to this latter word, except at l. 9 of the revised no. XXXVII we have just discussed, it is not used for physical charms in *Delia*, nor does it occur in *Rosamond*, written at about the same time. The only other instance in Daniel is found in a later work, *The Qveenes Arcadia* I, i, 49, with a plural possessive: *Their beauties* (i.e. of the nymphs). Again, *frost hath nipt thy flowers* is naturally a much commoner expression than *frost hath nipt thy beauties;* cf. e.g. Campion's *Booke of Ayres*, II, *Know buds are soonest nipt with frost; Emaricdulfe* XI:

> Thrise had the Sunne the world encompassed,
> Before this blossome with deaths winter nipt, etc.,

and many parallels in French and Italian sonnets, some of which I have adduced elsewhere.[3] Daniel, in other words, has broken up a fixed image by substituting *beauties* for *flowers*. But a similar deviation from the norm is found in Shakespeare, who often departs from convention in his sonnets, when in no. v, 7 f. he speaks of

> *Sap checkt with frost and lustie leau's quite gon,*
> *Beautie ore-snow'd and barenes euery where.*

I have earlier shown that this belongs to a different image-group from that represented by the passage in *Delia*,[4] but I did not then pay sufficient attention to the fact that when writing *beauties* Daniel was revising his text and that he otherwise avoids the plural *beauties* in his early poetry except in another revised line. Naturally an image may absorb details from another image of a different type, and doubtless xxxiv, 2 in 1601 has moved closer to Shakespeare's v, 8. If *beautie* was derived from Shakespeare's sonnet, the plural form would seem prompted by the plural of the original word, *flowers*. As regards *sable* for *golden*, it has actually been suggested earlier that the revision may be due to influence from a Shakespeare sonnet. Thus GUGGENHEIM, though believing that *Delia* influenced the *Sonnets*, asked himself: "Sollte hier vielleicht Daniel seinerseits von Shakespere beeinflusst sein?";[5] and BRADY, who otherwise shared the belief in Shakespeare's indebtedness, expressed the same idea.[6] Obviously taking for granted the identity of Delia with the Countess of Pembroke, CROW suggested that Daniel's radical change of the colour of the lady's hair was due to his desire to "shield her personality from too blunt a guess".[7] But apart from the fact that it was rather late to be so tactful nine years after the first appearance of 'the golden hairs', we do not know at all if Delia really stands for Mary of Pembroke. As a matter of fact, it is well known that 'golden hair' is one of the most solid conventions of sonnet poetry, and the Tasso poem to which Daniel is indebted here begins,

---

[3] *Op. cit.*, pp. 155 ff. Incidentally, *beauties* in *Rosamond* 135 means 'beautiful women' (cf. p. 64 below).

[4] *Ibid.*

[5] *Quellenstudien zu Samuel Daniels Sonettencyklus 'Delia'*, Berlin, 1898, p. 12.

[6] *Samuel Daniel. A Critical Study*, Urbana, 1923, p. 6.

[7] *Elizabethan Sonnet-Cycles* II, London, 1896, p. 10.

Quando avran queste luci e queste chiome
Perduto l'oro e le faville ardenti,

whereas dark hair is far less common.[8] The Shakespearean lines that
GUGGENHEIM and BRADY had in mind are XII, 3—4:

When I behold the violet past prime,
And sable curls all siluer'd ore with white.

Besides departing from the main current of tradition, *sable* in
Shakespeare's poem forms an antithesis with *siluer'd ore with white*.
The same effect is obtained in the *Delia* line of 1601, which is thus
made more pointed than before, and in this shape is not typical of
Daniel's manner.

I have earlier[9] discussed the old theory that there is an influence
from *the table of my harte* in Daniel's 'Pygmalion' sonnet, no. XIII
(found as early as 1591) on a corresponding expression in Shakespeare's no. XXIV. The relevant passage in Daniel's sonnet reads as
follows in the 1591 edition:

For haples loe euen with mine owne desires,
I figured on the table of my hart
The goodliest shape that the worlds eye admires,
And so did perish by my proper arte (4—8).

This is the version of the 1592 edition:

For haples loe euen with mine owne desires,
I figured on the table of my harte,

---

[8] Although it is quite wrong to believe, as some critics seem to do, that dark hair only
occurs in vituperative contexts (cf. p. 111 below). — BUXTON (*op. cit.*, p. 340) objects to
my interpretation of Daniel's change from *golden* to *sable* by pointing out that in no. XV
(the correct number is XIV) Daniel revised "amber locks" to "snary locks" (in 1594).
"Such revisions about the colour or texture of Delia's hair", he says, "may be due to
something more personal than a phrase in another poet's sonnet" (*ibid.*). BUXTON is thus
unfamiliar with the well-known fact that a change from *amber* to *snary* means a conven-
tionalization of the phrase, locks snaring the poet being one of the most widespread of all
commonplaces in sonneteering. A change of *golden* to *sable*, on the contrary, means a
deviation from convention. It is more surprising, however, that the reviewer does not
see why Daniel changed *amber* to *snary*: in this way the adjective was brought into accordance with the first two lines of the sonnet, which read in 1592: *Those amber locks, are*
those same nets my deere, | Wherewith my libertie thou didst surprize. To believe, moreover,
that there is anything "personal" about 16th-century sonneteers' descriptions of ladies'
hair is always a potential source of error.
[9] *Op. cit.*, pp. 159 ff.

The fayrest forme, the worldes eye admires,
And so did perish by my proper arte.

The Shakespearean quatrain with which this has often been compared (by critics believing in Shakespeare's indebtedness) is as
follows, with CAPELL's *stell'd* for Q *steeld*:

Mine eye hath play'd the painter and hath stell'd
Thy beauties forme in table of my heart,
My body is the frame wherein ti's held,
And perspectiue it is best Painter's art.

Now the 'picture in the heart' is a motif characteristic of a very
large group of conceits: we find the beloved's picture engraved,
imprinted, or painted in the poet's heart. The prototype would
seem to be an epigram by Paulus Silentiarius (*Anth.Gr.* v, 274).
But the 'table of the heart' is a rare member of the group,[1] though
what may appear to be several instances can be adduced. TUCKER
cites an example in *Euphues*, MALONE another in *All's Well*, and I
have elsewhere given instances from *Parthenophil*, *Zepheria*, Ronsard, and Tansillo. It may be added that the 'table of the heart'
is also found in Daniel's *Hymens Triumph*, I, i, 127 ff.:

Should I another loue, then must I haue,
Another heart, for this is full of her,
And euermore shall be: here is she drawne
At length, and whole, and more, this table is
A story, and is all of her.

Similarly Baïf says (*Amours de Meline*, pp. 66 f.),

O graces, ô beautez saintes
Que i'emprain dans ce Fouteau,
Vous estes bien mieux empraintes
Dans vn bien autre tableau,
Tableau de mon ferme cœur,
Dont Amour fut le graueur.

We also find the conceit twice in Sir John Davies (*Of the Soule*
of Man, GROSART I, p. 94, and *Minor Poems*, II, p. 79). It is even used

---

[1] It is unlikely that this variant owes anything to Plato's famous 'waxen tablet' in
Theaetetus (191).

by Heywood in *A Woman Kilde with Kindnesse* (ed. 1874, II, p. 112), where Wendoll speaks of what he has *recorded | Within the red-leau'd Table of my heart*, and by Ford in *Love's Sacrifice*, II, iv, 84 f. (*I'll write | This loue within the tables of my heart*). Instances, however, are not so common as it may seem from this (possibly not exhaustive) survey, since other members of the 'picture-in-the-heart' group are extremely frequent. In fact, the 'table' variant can be calculated at only 3 per cent, approximately, of a very large English and Continental material of the whole group. There are thus certain possibilities of a direct connection between the passages in *Delia* and the *Sonnets*, particularly since there are other signs of such a connection. In favour of the theory that Shakespeare is the debtor it might be pointed out that the 'table' in *Delia* is found as early as the 1591 edition and that the alteration *goodliest shape>fayrest forme* is after all too trivial to be necessarily inspired by the *Sonnets*, but that the *forme* may easily have been borrowed by Shakespeare at the same time as the *table*. On the other hand since we do not know when Shakespeare's sonnet was written, the argument based on chronology is a circular one. Furthermore, as pointed out by TUCKER, there is some probability that Shakespeare is indebted to Lyly for the 'table', and, as I have shown, Daniel's sonnet bears obvious traces of having been pieced together by details imitated from other poets.[2] Even if we cannot exclude the possibility that Shakespeare's lines may be inspired by Daniel's this is not capable of proof, and it is not impossible that the reverse is true or that both wrote independently of each other. In view of all this it seems safest to regard the instances of the 'table-in-the-heart' conceit in *Delia* and the *Sonnets* as analogues, not as original+imitation.

Among the revisions in the *Delia* of 1601 we find a parallel to a Shakespeare sonnet which was noted as early as 1790 by MALONE. The relevant passage is to be found in no. XLII, 9—12, on the transitoriness of the lady's beauty:

> *When thou surcharg'd with burthen of thy yeeres,*
> *Shalt bend thy wrinkles homeward to the earth :*

[2] SCHAAR, *op. cit., ibid.*

When tyme hath made a pasport for thy feares,
Dated in age the Kalends of our death.

The editions from 1592 to 1598 have this reading. In 1601 the quatrain was changed to

When thou surcharg'd with burthen of thy yeeres,
Shalt bend thy wrinkles homeward to the earth:
And that in Beauties lease expir'd, appeares
The date of age the Kalends of our death.

The phrase in Shakespeare with which MALONE compared this detail is l. 5 of no. XIII, one of the procreation sonnets:

So should that beauty which you hold in lease
Find no determination, then you were
You selfe again after you selfes decease.

The fact that the expression 'beauties lease' in *Delia* is due to revision escaped MALONE, for his comment on the phrase, in a note to Shakespeare's no. XIII, is as follows: "So Daniel, in one of his sonnets, 1592"+quotation (p. 202). To the expression *beauty-lease* I can find no parallel elsewhere, and it is doubtful whether Daniel invented this striking combination himself. Legal terminology is rare in *Delia* while it is a well-known feature of the *Sonnets*.

A more far-reaching revision of *Delia* affected no. XXXI, first printed in 1592. This is a sonnet on the *carpe diem* motif, though the traditional exhortation to love before youth is gone is postponed till the couplet. The main part of the poem deals with the transitoriness of beauty described, in the first two quatrains, as a fading rose:

Looke Delia how wee steeme the half-blowne Rose,
The image of thy blush and Summers honor:
Whilst in her tender greene she doth inclose
That pure sweete beautie, Time bestowes vppon her.
No sooner spreades her glorie in the ayre,
But straight her ful-blowne pride is in declyning;
She then is scorn'd that late adorn'd the fayre:
So clowdes thy beautie, after fayrest shining.

But this would not do in 1601. Various alterations were made in the whole poem, and this is the new version of ll. 1—8:

> *Looke Delia how w'esteem the half-blowne Rose,*
> *The image of thy blush and Summers honor:*
> *Whilst yet her tender bud doth vndisclose*
> *That full of beautie, Time bestowes vppon her.*
> *No sooner spreades her glorie in the ayre,*
> *But straight her wide blowne pomp comes to decline;*
> *She then is scorn'd that late adorn'd the fayre:*
> *So fade the Roses of those cheeks of thine.*

To begin with l. 3, the alteration is noteworthy in two respects. *Undisclose* is otherwise only used as a perfect participle (this particular instance is the only exception given by the NED, and I can add no other). Surely *undisclose* is an odd substitution for the straightforward *inclose*. Secondly the thought, which is clear and simple in the earlier version, becomes more involved in the later. The original sense is simply that the flower is the *pure sweete beautie*, which is at its best when not fully developed but still hidden by the *tender greene*. The corresponding line in the *Gerusalemme Liberata* XVI, 14 — the source of the poem[3] — reads, *quanto si mostra men, tanto è più bella*. In 1601 it is the bud itself that hides away *that full of beautie, Time bestowes vppon her*. Thus the graphic image of 1592 has been replaced by a more artificial phrase which is a less adequate expression of the fundamental idea: we now have an example of *periergia*, when "ye ouerlabour your selfe in your businesse" (Puttenham).[4] Thirdly, *full* as a substantive does not elsewhere occur in any edition of *Delia* (or *Rosamond*). In these poems, Daniel is invariably in the habit of resorting to superlatives or the like in relevant contexts.

As to the alteration *fade the Roses* in the second quatrain I shall only observe that the poet here concentrates the description upon the lady's cheeks while otherwise, also in this line before 1601, the poem deals with her beauty in general.

What we find in 1601 is thus a series of alterations stylistically and rhetorically different from the original reading. On one

---

[3] KASTNER, *The Italian Sources of Daniel's Delia*, MLR VII, 1912, p. 155.
[4] Ed. WILLCOCK & WALKER, Cambridge, 1936, p. 258.

point we also find a deviation from the poet's normal usage. If we look for some outward stimulus which may have induced Daniel to give up his original version, there is one Shakespearean sonnet which we cannot pass by: no. LIV, particularly quatrains 2 and 3:

> The Canker bloomes haue full as deepe a die,
> As the perfumed tincture of the Roses,
> Hang on such thornes, and play as wantonly,
> When sommers breath their masked buds discloses:
> But for their virtue only is their show,
> They liue vnwoo'd, and vnrespected fade,
> Die to themselues. Sweet Roses doe not so, etc.

It is not a matter of extensive similarities, and the content of Shakespeare's poem is quite different from that of Daniel's. But it is a matter of definite resemblances on certain points: *Full of beautie — full as deepe a die, tender bud ... vndisclose — masked buds discloses,*[5] *fade the Roses — fade ... sweet Roses.* It is a set of correspondences which suggest vague reminiscences rather than conscious imitation, induced association rather than deliberate adoption. *Full as deepe a die* would thus have led to the use of *full* in *Delia*, and *inclose* being the necessary concept in l.3, the impact of Shakespeare's *disclose* would yield *vndisclose.* As the result of a different train of associations, 'fade'+'roses' would lead the poet's thoughts to 'cheeks', which would accordingly find a place in his poem although they did not form part of the Shakespearean lines he remembered. There is no similarly close parallel to Daniel's poem, and his alterations are not backed by tradition.

In *Delia* XLI, the dejected poet asks a series of questions and answers the last one in the couplet:

> How long shall I in mine affliction morne,
> A burthen to my selfe, distress'd in minde:
> When shall my interdicted hopes returne,
> From out despayre wherein they liue confin'd.

---

[5] On the use of *disclose* here BEECHING remarks: "The word 'disclose' would seem here to be suggested by the epithet; the wind's opening the rose being compared to a rough lover's pulling off a lady's visor" (ed. 1904, p. 95).

> *When shall her troubled browe charg'd with disdaine,*
> *Reueale the treasure which her smyles impart :*
> *When shall my faith the happinesse attaine,*
> *To breake the yce that hath congeald her hart.*
> *Vnto her selfe, her selfe my loue dooth sommon,*
> *If loue in her hath any powre to moue :*
> *And let her tell me as she is a woman,*
> *Whether my faith hath not deseru'd her loue.*
> *I knowe she cannot but must needes confesse it,*
> *Yet deignes not with one simple signe t'expresse it.*

This is what becomes of the couplet in the 1601 and later editions:

> *I know her hart cannot but iudge with mee,*
> *Although her eyes my aduersaries bee.*

The antithesis has thus been sharpened: from being merely indifferent in l. 14, the lady here becomes openly hostile. This is perhaps not in itself remarkable. As it happens, however, 'eyes-adversaries' is not the usual way of describing an attitude of coldness or animosity on the part of the lady. Generally in such cases we find the characterizations referred to on p. 44 f. above, and eyes are not very often mentioned. When they are, poets mostly use what we may call the 'eclipse' metaphor: *Dark disdayne eclipsed hath my sun* (*Tears of Fancie* LII), *Her eyes eclipse him of his blisse* (*Licia* XXIII), *Misty aspects will cloud your sun-bright eye* (*Diella* XII). Frowns are naturally common, either with or without the 'eclipse' detail: *My cruel fortunes, clouded with a frown* (*Fidessa* XLIX), *What time, with brow, the Loveliest 'gins to scowl; | Shewing disdain and fury in her face; | Methinks I see the clouds wax dark and foule* (*Laura* I, xx); *Cruell disdaine, reflecting from her brow* (*Diana* 1594, VII, iv). These are commonplaces. The Italians often elaborate the 'eclipse' metaphor in the same way as Tofte does in *Laura*; thus Amaltheo complains (*Rime di div.* III, 1550, 92 v.),

> *Se de begli occhi 'l Sole*
> *La dolce mia guerrera*
> *Non m'ascondesse con nebbie di sdegno,*
> *I formerei parole*
> *Con la mente si altera, etc.*

Variations on this theme are also found in *Delia*, and the poet regularly speaks of *brow* and *frowns*: *Her brow shades frownes* (VI), *If Beautie thus be clouded with a frowne ... And vapors of disdaine so ouergrowne* (XIX), *clouded brow* XXIII), *troubled browe* (XLI). It is the rule in the sonneteers, however, when 'hostile eyes' are mentioned, that emphasis is not laid on the lady's disdain and the poet's dejection but on her threat to his peace of mind and on his infatuation: her eyes kindle his passion. This is the well-known classic description of the *innamoramento*. This, as the context clearly shows, is not the theme of the revised l. 14 of *Delia* XLI: this line is a parallel to l. 5, describing a sign of the lady's disdain. In by far the greatest number of passages on 'hostile eyes', the 'hostility' is illustrated in a concrete way by descriptions of flames spurting from the lady's eyes or darts shot from them. Such accounts of the conquest of the poet-lover's heart are commonplaces in classical, medieval, and Renaissance poetry, and have been illustrated most fully by OGLE (Greek, Roman, Romance, and English material).[6] Other comments on the use of the conceit have been made by JOHN[7] and others. OGLE quotes such instances as Petrarch, *Dagli occhi vostri uscío 'l colpo mortale* (CXXXIII), Baïf, *Les beaux yeux, qui au cœur me blesserent* (p. 116), and Watson's more elaborate *Cupido ... shotte a shaft throughout her cristall eyes | Wherewith he cleft in twaine my yeelding heart* (*Hek.* XXIV). A typical example of this use of 'hostile eyes' is also *Phillis* XIX, *Those assaulting eyes, | That are the lamps which lighten my desire*. Shakespeare in *Romeo and Juliet* (I, i, 219) makes Romeo express his fears that the lady he loves will not *bide the encounter of assailing eyes*. Eyes are described as 'enemies' for instance in *England's Helicon*, where an anonymous poet exclaims, *Ah wanton eyes, my friendly foes, | And cause of woes* (p. 150). In Barnes's sonnet C in *Parthenophil* the infatuated poet is "pleading for pity" to the lady's eyes, complaining of his "hid flames, and secret smarts", and the lady replies that *Her eyes were never made man's enemies*. *Murthering eyes* is a fairly common description of the source of the lover's passion; Daniel uses the phrase in *Delia* XXIX and again in *A Description of Beauty*, st. 6, imitated from Marino.[8] In a madrigal

---

[6] *The Classical Origin and Tradition of Literary Conceits*, AJPh XXXIV, 1913, pp. 133—146.

[7] *The Elizabethan Sonnet Sequences*, New York, 1938, pp. 60 ff.

[8] GROSART's edition I, p. 264.

assigned to Francis Davison in *A Poetical Rhapsody* the poet addresses the *Fayre, yet murdring eies, | Starres of my miseries* (p. 267); another instance is found in Drayton's *Ideas Mirrour*, 40. Rota speaks of the *foco micidal di due begli occhi* (ed. 1726, p. 52), many sonneteers make comparisons with the *basilisco* killing its victim. — The prototype of the whole group of 'hostile eyes' conceits is found in classical Greek poetry.

Thus the last line of the revised no. XLI in *Delia* contains an exceptional detail. I know no closer parallel to this detail than a line in Shakespeare's no. CXXXIX:

> *O call not me to iustifie the wrong,*
> *That thy vnkindnesse layes vpon my heart,*
> *Wound me not with thine eye but with thy toung,*
> *Vse power with power, and slay me not by Art,*
> *Tell me thou lou'st else-where; but in my sight,*
> *Deare heart forbeare to glance thine eye aside,*
> *What needst thou wound with cunning when thy might*
> *Is more then my ore-prest defence can bide?*
> *Let me excuse thee, ah my loue well knowes,*
> *Her prettie lookes haue beene mine enemies,*
> *And therefore from my face she turnes my foes,*
> *That they else-where might dart their iniuries:*
> > *Yet do not so, but since I am neere slaine,*
> > *Kill me out-right with lookes, and rid my paine.*

We here recognize two details similar to those introduced into the revised *Delia* couplet and absent in the first version: the heart and the 'hostile eyes'. As regards the latter detail, the poet resorts to the traditional *innamoramento* conceit of darting glances (ll. 10—12) in order to excuse the lady: her 'glancing aside' is interpreted as an act of mercy since her eyes can kill (a similar idea occurs in *Amoretti* XLIX and in Sylvester's sonnet XV). But while Shakespeare does not depart from tradition in l. 10, Daniel does in l. 14. The reason for this may be that, if he was influenced by the *Sonnets* CXXXIX, he was also impressed by the fact that the main part of this poem does in fact deal with the lady's indifference towards the poet. This impression would then colour his use of the 'hostile eyes' conceit.

I shall finally call attention to an instance of a word that is unusual in *Delia*. In no. xx the poet as we have seen invokes *Death*, praying him to put an end to the lover's miseries:

> *For all too long on earth my fancy dotes,*
> *Whilst my best blood my younge desiers sealeth* (3—4).

This is the reading of 1592. In 1594 the last line was changed to *Whilst age vpon my wasted body steales*. There is only one more inst-ance of *steale* in *Delia*, and this case, too, is due to revision (xx A, 5 f.: *Steale / Powre from those eyes*, etc.). It might be pointed out that *steale* is a fairly common word in the *Sonnets* and that the new ver-sion of xx, 4 has become more similar to lxxv, 6 *Doubting the filching age will steale his treasure*, and to civ, 9 f. *Ah yet doth beauty like a Dyall hand, / Steale from his figure*, than to any other earlier or contemporary passage.[9]

The 'Sonnets' and 'The Complaint of Rosamond'

Daniel's *Complaint of Rosamond* was published along with *Delia* in 1592 (twice), 1594, 1595, 1598, 1601, 1602, 1611, and 1623; in addition it appeared in 1599 (*Poeticall Essayes*), 1605 (*Certaine Small Poems*), and 1607 (*Certaine Small Workes*). While *The Complaint of Rosamond* was highly appreciated by Daniel's contemporaries,[1] less attention is paid to it nowadays, though recent critics are more appreciative than those of the early years of the century and the 'twenties. The following estimates are characteristic: '*The Complaint* ... is remarkable for little beyond the polished purity of its English" (COURTHOPE, *History of English Poetry* III, 1911, p. 17); "There is no need to dwell on 'The Complaint of Rosamond', an easy, ambling poem, well turned, in six-line stanzas" (BULLEN, *Elizabethans*, 1924, p. 33). On the other hand TILLOTSON (Drayton edition v, p. 102) says that *Rosamond* is "one of the most successful of Elizabethan

---

[9] MILLER (*Samuel Daniel's Revisions in 'Delia'*, JEGP LIII, 1954, p. 62) thinks that Daniel's 1594 version of l. 4 "reflects the consciousness of maturity, not of youth which, in its blissful embrace of death, refuses to think of the ravages of age". This would mean that the poet, still youthful at the age of thirty, had at thirty-two matured enough to "think of the ravages of age". The reader must judge for himself whether this is a likely explanation or not.

[1] Cf. HELTZEL, *Fair Rosamond* (Northwestern Univ. Stud. in the Hum. 16, 1947, pp. 19 ff.).

narrative poems" and HELTZEL, in his monograph of the legend of Fair Rosamond, remarks that although action and drama are meagre, "Daniel's dignified poem is conceived on the highest level, artistic and moral".[2] Whatever view we take of the merits or demerits of *Rosamond*, the poem is of importance in a discussion of certain Shakespearean sonnets.[3]

Daniel seems to have composed *Rosamond* in intervals of sonnet writing, as indicated by the joint publication of *Delia* and *Rosamond* in the first editions and by several resemblances of phrasing: *Ros.* 44 *And offer vp her sigh among the rest* — D. XVI A, 3 f. *Why should I offer vp vnto her name, | The sweetest sacrifice, etc.; Ros.* 121 f. *Sweet silent rethorique of perswading eyes: | Dombe eloquence, whose powre doth moue the blood* — D. VIII, 6 *Mine eyes ... Told the dumbe message of my hidden griefe; Ros.* 239 *Thou must not thinke thy flowre can alwayes florish* — D. XXXII, 11 *And thinke the same becomes thy fading best*, D. XXXVI, 5 *Thinke not sweete Delia, this shall be thy shame; Ros.* 246 *Reade in my face the ruines of my youth* — D. XXIX, 9 *Then leaue your glasse, and gaze your selfe on mee, | That Mirrour shewes what powre is in your face.* As in the case of *Delia*, several revisions were made in the various editions of the poem, particularly in 1594 and later, when no less than 161 new lines were added after l. 595. In this additional piece there is one passage of particular interest.

The added part contains a moralizing soliloquy, in which Rosamond meditates on her fall and the reasons for it, and begs others to be warned by her example. This part of Rosamond's speech ends with fulminations against *Bed-brokers vncleane, | (The Monsters of our sexe)*, who *betray our cause, our shame, our youth, | To lust, to follie, and to mens vntruth.* Their destructive influence is described in ll. 120—126:

> *You in the habite of a graue aspect,*
> *(In credite by the trust of yeeres,) can shoe*

---

[2] *Op. cit.*, p. 17.

[3] EWIG (cf. below, n. 5), ANDERS (*Shakespeare's Books*, Berlin, 1904, pp. 85 ff.), and THALER (*Shakspere, Daniel, and Everyman*, PQ XV, 1936, pp. 217 f.), who all discussed the possible influence of *Rosamond* on Shakespeare's early work, did not mention the *Sonnets*. A good deal of attention, however, has been paid to the assumed influence of *Rosamond* on *Lucrece* (cf. ROLLINS's edition of Shakespeare's *Poems*, pp. 425 ff.). In the present study I am not concerned with this dependence, which seems to me to have been overestimated, but a few comments will be given below.

> *The cunning wayes of lust, and can direct*
> *The fayre and wilie wantons how to goe:*
> *Hauing (your lothsome selues) your youth spent so.*
> *And in vncleanes, euer haue beene fed,*
> *By the reuenue of a wanton bed.*

The last line contains a striking metaphor, which at once suggests a line in a well-known sonnet of Shakespeare's (no. CXLII, the parallel indicated by LEE, cf. ROLLINS I, 364):

> *Loue is my sinne, and thy deare vertue hate,*
> *Hate of my sinne, grounded on sinfull louing,*
> *O but with mine, compare thou thine owne state,*
> *And thou shalt finde it merrits not reproouing,*
> *Or if it do, not from those lips of thine,*
> *That haue prophan'd their scarlet ornaments,*
> *And seald false bonds of loue as oft as mine,*
> *Robd others beds reuenues of their rents* (1—8).

To my knowledge, no third instance of this image exists. What is remarkable is that the two poets use the phrase in different ways. Shakespeare's is the more consequential: his line fits in with his usual way of employing legal terminology in the *Sonnets*, and it carries on the legal imagery of l. 7: *And seald false bonds of loue as oft as mine.* In *Rosamond*, on the contrary, the image has no similar connection with the context, and Daniel uses metaphors of this type even more rarely in *Rosamond* than he does in *Delia*.[4] Imagery in *Rosamond* is chiefly drawn from the spheres of nature, the Bible, astronomy, mythology, military life, and hunting. There is probably a connection between the line in *Rosamond* and that in no. CXLII, a sonnet which we have had reason to mention once before in our discussion of *Delia* XXVI A (cf. p. 43). The most natural interpretation of the parallel in *Rosamond* would seem to be that Daniel utilized the 'bed-revenue' metaphor in order to provide some variation for a thought that he had already touched on in the original part of the poem: *Feele the warmth of an vnlawfull bed* (l. 326).[5]

---

[4] Cf. SCHAAR, *op. cit.*, p. 72.
[5] Among the numerous parallels collected by EWIG (*Shakespeare's 'Lucrece'*, Anglia XXII, 1899, pp. 436 ff.) in support of the old theory that *Rosamond* influenced *Lucrece*, we also find *Rosamond* 126, discussed above, compared with *Lucrece* 1619 f.: *Dear husband,*

The other parallel, which seems to have passed unnoticed, is more important since the *Rosamond* passage is found as early as the first version of 1592. In the stanzas between ll. 99 and 154 Rosamond describes herself as she was when she came "from Country to Court, from calme to stormes, from shore into the deepes" — young, beautiful, and innocent, and powerful because of her fresh and natural beauty:

> *Such one was I, my beautie was mine owne,*
> *No borrowed blush which banck-rot beauties seeke:*
> *The new-found shame, a sinne to vs vnknowne,*
> *Th'adulterate beauty of a falsed cheeke:*
> *Vild staine to honor and to women eeke,*
> > *Seeing that time our fading must detect,*
> > *Thus with defect to couer our defect* (134—140).

Again a striking and very unusual image: *banck-rot beauties*, derived, as we have seen, from a sphere which is rare in Daniel's poems. The strongly condemnatory language of the stanza is also remarkable. There is an undeniable resemblance to a passage in Shakespeare's no. LXVII:

> *Ah wherefore with infection should he liue,*
> *And with his presence grace impietie,*
> *That sinne by him aduantage should atchiue,*
> *And lace it selfe with his societie?*
> *Why should false painting immitate his cheeke,*
> *And steale dead seeing of his liuing hew?*

in the interest of thy bed | A stranger came. Many of Ewig's parallels are no more striking than this one: some are superficial verbal similarities, others commonplace phrases (*There might I[you] see* (R. 386 and L. 1380), *Night (mother of sleepe and feare) | Who with her sable mantle* (R. 432) — *Sable Night mother of Dread and Fear* (L. 117), etc. Again, a number of the resemblances in *Rosamond* are found in the additions and may thus even be later than *Lucrece*. Finally, Ewig and his followers do not pay enough attention to the fact that the situations described in *Rosamond* and *Lucrece* are *a priori* very much alike: in both poems a girl laments the loss of her honour. The first to conclude a dependence of *Lucrece* on *Rosamond* on the basis of various parallels was Malone in 1780. — It cannot be denied, however, that a certain amount of influence is probable (form of stanza, certain episodes, a limited number of details, etc.). This would mean that the two poets influenced one another and that they probably knew each other, which in itself of course seems likely enough in the small world of literary London in the 1590's. Incidentally, the recent discussion of the relationship between Daniel's *Cleopatra* and *Antony and Cleopatra* seems to show that there is a reciprocal influence in these works.

Why should poore beautie indirectly seeke,
Roses of shaddow, since his Rose is true?
Why should he liue, now nature b anckrout is,
beggerd of blood to blush through liuely vaines,
For she hath no exchecker now but his,
And proud of many, liues vpon his gaines.
O him she stores, to show what welth she had,
In daies long since, before these last so bad.

What we have here is one main idea worked out in a set of antithetic questions and wound up, before the answer in the couplet, by a coherent image filling the whole of the third quatrain.[6] The similarities to the *Rosamond* stanza are apparent at first sight: *Shame, sinne — impietie, sinne; Th'adulterate beauty of a falsed cheeke — false painting ... his cheeke; borrowed blush which banck-rot beauties seeke — poore beautie ... seeke, Roses of shaddow ... banckrout.* Add to this the fourfold *b*-alliteration in both cases and the uniqueness of the combination *beautie seeke borrowed blush* (*Roses of shaddow*). The probability is infinitesimal that such a set of correspondences is due to chance. If not, who is the debtor? A study of the way in which 'bankrupt' is used indicates the answer. In Shakespeare's works the word is found several times (among these instances there are three in other poems than the *Sonnets*). In no. LXVII, furthermore, it is the cornerstone of a carefully constructed 4-line image: Nature is bankrupt, 'unable to supply genuine life-blood' (TUCKER), and the only available fund is provided by the friend on whose means Nature is nowadays compelled to live. In *Rosamond*, 'bankrupt' — which otherwise occurs only once in Daniel[7] — is not similarly integrated in the whole. Furthermore, the forcible words used by Shakespeare have a natural motivation in the fact that he is through-

---

[6] The antithetic character of the poem strongly supports RIDLEY's (palæographically easy) emendation *'priu'd* at l. 12, *'priu'd of many* affording a reason for *liues vpon his gaines.*

[7] In *The Civil Wars* III, 89, in its literal sense: *He* [Richard II] *was not found a Bankrupt in his chests.* Elsewhere, Daniel invariably uses synonymous words and expressions. Curiously enough, he avoids *bankrupt* even in such a work as *The History of England,* where he has ample opportunities of using it. He is here in the habit of preferring such expressions as *naked* ('destitute'), *exhausted his treasure, had utterly consumed his estate, all was vented, were despoiled of their fortune,* etc. *Bankrupt* is used by Drayton in *Idea* III, 14 (*And I a Bankrupt, quite undone by Thee*) and by Sidney in *Astrophel* XVIII, 3 (*And by such counts my selfe a Banckerowt know | Of all those goods which heaven to me hath lent*). Both passages thus occur in contexts quite different from that in *Delia* and the *Sonnets.*

out contrasting a depraved, sinful, and artificial world with the pure, artless and genuine beauty of the friend. *Infection, impietie, sinne* do not merely indicate the use of rouge and powder, but obviously refer back to the evils described in no. LXVI:[8]

> *Tyr'd with all these for restfull death I cry,*
> *As to behold desert a begger borne,*
> *And needie Nothing trimd in iollitie,*
> *And purest faith vnhappily forsworne,*
> *And gilded honor shamefully misplast,*
> *And maiden vertue rudely strumpeted,*
> *And right perfection wrongfully disgrac'd,*
> *And strength by limping sway disabled,*
> *And arte made tung-tide by authoritie,*
> *And Folly (Doctor-like) controuling skill,*
> *And simple Truth miscalde Simplicitie,*
> *And captiue Good attending Captaine ill.*
> > *Tyr'd with all these, from these would I be gone,*
> > *Saue that to dye, I leaue my loue alone.*

There is no similar justification for *sinne* and *vild staine to honor* in Daniel's passage on cosmetics, lamentable though the use of these may be. True, false beauty is contrasted with a young woman's *happy blooming flowre | Whilst nature decks her with her proper fayre* (131 f.), and it is not in itself remarkable that the poet criticizes it; what is striking is that he does it in these very terms and thus so strongly. The words used by Rosamond would be more suitable in a denouncement of grave immorality. Again, *Seeing that time our fading must detect* is of course no sufficient reason for such execrations. The most natural explanation of the whole stanza is that phrases and image fragments were borrowed from Shakespeare's

---

[8] Commentators generally assume a connection between LXVI and LXVII, but BEECHING (p. 99) does not see any worse blot in the 'evil times' than a "superficial fault, namely, the use of cosmetics and false hair, which ... seems to have been especially repugnant to Shakespeare". In this context BEECHING refers to *Tw. N.* I, v, 256, *Ham.* III, i, 150, *Mer. V* III, ii, 92, *Tim. Ath.* IV, iii, 144. The language of these passages, however, is far less strong than that in no. LXVII. The same is true of CXXVII, 6 (*Arts faulse borrow'd face*) and *LLL*, IV, iii, 250 ff, with which the latter sonnet is often compared (*Fie, painted rhetoric ... That painting and usurping hair | Should ravish doters with a false aspect*). 'False', 'borrowed' etc. are natural in condemnations of cosmetics only; 'impiety', 'sin' are not, unless there is a particular motivation.

sonnet and condensed in the *Rosamond* passage according to a pattern we have illustrated earlier in the discussion of *Delia*[9].

Impressions of Shakespeare's LXVII would then also seem to have launched Daniel on the further fulminations against artificial beauty which make up the subsequent stanza:

> *Impiety of times, chastities abator,*
> *Falshod, wherein thy selfe, thy selfe deniest:*
> *Treason, to counterfeit the seale of nature,*
> *The stampe of heauen, impressed by the hiest.*
> *Disgrace vnto the world, to whom thou lyest,*
> > *Idol vnto thy selfe, shame to the wise,*
> > *And all that honors thee idolatrise.*

This stanza and the preceding one make up an unexpected deviation from the story.[1]

In the succeeding stanza (the last one containing Rosamond's comments and reflexions before the narrative of the poem is resumed) Rosamond makes some fairly remarkable statements (ll. 148—154):

> *Farre was that sinne from vs whose age was pure,*
> *When simple beautie was accounted best,*
> *The time when women had no other lure*
> *But modestie, pure cheekes, a vertuous brest:*
> *This was the pompe wherewith my youth was blest;*
> > *These were the weapons which mine honour wunne*
> > *In all the conflicts that mine eyes begunne.*

This purports to be a girl's description of the innocent age when she was still unacquainted with counterfeit beauty (not with the depravity of the court, as we should perhaps expect when reading

---

[9] Cf. particularly pp. 28 and 32.

[1] It is not surprising that the brief chronicle accounts that make up the source material (Giraldus Cambrensis, Higden, Holinshed, Stow, etc.) and Deloney's short account in his ballad on *The Imprisonment of Queene Elenor* (ed. MANN, p. 398) do not refer to the 'artificial beauty' theme. It is more interesting that the detailed stories in Warner's *Albions England* (VIII, xli, 1592, probably independent of Daniel's poem, cf. HELTZEL, p. 18), Deloney's *Mournfull Dittie, on the death of Rosamond* (MANN, pp. 297 ff.), and Drayton's *The Epistle of Rosamond to King Henry the Second* (ed. HEBEL II, pp. 133 ff.) also omit the theme. Yet on many points Daniel's *Rosamond* was the model for Drayton's poem (cf. TILLOTSON in Drayton ed. v, 1941, p. 102). The 'false beauty' theme is Daniel's addition to the story, and it is probable enough that it struck Drayton as being out of place.

that sinne). It does not matter that the girl is dead and that her ghost is speaking; what matters is: why does this person refer to her earlier years in the words of someone praising the conditions of 'the Golden Age'? While there is nothing remarkable about the first line, there is something strange about the second, and something quite extraordinary about the third and the fourth: is it natural for somebody describing a phase of her own life to speak of 'the time when *women had* no other lure but modesty, pure cheeks, a virtuous breast'? At least surely the present tense is the only natural one in such a context ('the age of innocence, when *women have* no attraction but modesty', etc.). Could it be that the general statement in the past tense, as well as the *when*-clause in the second line, have some connection with Shakespeare's no. LXVIII, which continues the theme of LXVII and regards the friend's beauty as an incarnation of the unadulterated beauty of times past, in contrast to the sham beauty of his own days:

> *Thus is his cheeke the map of daies out-worne,*
> *When beauty liu'd and dy'ed as flowers do now,*
> *Before these bastard signes of faire were borne,*
> *Or durst inhabit on a liuing brow :*
> *Before the goulden tresses of the dead,*
> *The right of sepulchers, were shorne away,*
> *To liue a second life on second head,*
> *Ere beauties dead fleece made another gay :*
> *In him those holy antique howers are seene,*
> *Without all ornament, it selfe and true,*
> *Making no summer of an others greene,*
> *Robbing no ould to dresse his beauty new,*
> > *And him as for a map doth Nature store,*
> > *To shew faulse Art what beauty was of yore.*

Thus the topic of ll. 2—9 is 'the Golden Age,' the ideal past — *those holy antique howers*[2] —, and the contrast between counterfeit and genuine beauty seems to have become a conventional element in detailed versions of this topic in English Renaissance texts.[3]

---

[2] In the description of the Golden Age in the Prologue to Bk. v of *The Faerie Qveene* (iii, 5), Spenser speaks of *the antique vse, which was of yore.*

[3] The theme is found e.g. in Drayton's description of the Golden Age in *Pastorals*, Fourth Eglogue, ll. 77 f.:

But as observed before, the Golden Age is not the subject of Daniel's lines. Therefore the general statements in the past tense are not natural in the context in *Rosamond*. Similar details in Shakespeare's sonnet, however, with the reference to *daies out-worne*, form organic parts of the theme of the poem.[4] The suggested explanation is perhaps all the more natural if we take the interpretation of *Rosamond* 148—154 in conjunction with that of the preceding stanzas, particularly ll. 134 ff.

*

Although in many cases I have put off the discussion as to how these parallels should be interpreted, some of my remarks will have been indicative. In my opinion the bulk of the material reviewed points to an influence from Shakespeare on Daniel. But is this a necessary conclusion? Cannot Daniel have made such changes as *Beauties lease, frute so sowre, reuenue of a wanton bed* quite independently of similar turns of phrase in Shakespeare's sonnets? Could not Daniel have altered his vocabulary unaided? Could not

> *And Beauties selfe by her selfe beautified,*
> *Scorn'd Paintings Pergit, and the borrowed Haire,*

in Greville's Golden Age sonnet (*Caelica* XLIV):

> *Desire was free, and Beauties first-begotten;*
> *Beauty then neither net, nor made by art,*

and in Nicholas Breton's version of the same topic (*Madcaps Oh the merrie time*, ll. 36 f.):

> *When Mistris Fubs that Fiddle faddle fusse,*
> *No colours knew to mend her coorse complexion.*

Gascoigne had earlier found room for the theme when describing an ideal world in *The Steel Glas*:

> *When Lays lives, not like a ladies peare,*
> *Nor useth art, in dying of hir heare.*

This contrast between natural fairness and beauty brought about by cosmetics seems to be rarer in Continental variations on the Golden Age motif. At least it does not occur in the description of *la bella età d'oro* in Tasso's *Aminta* (I, ii), translated by Daniel (*A Pastorall*, GROSART I, pp. 260 ff.), nor in Guarini's *Il Pastor Fido* (end of Act IV, also modelled on Tasso). It may be added that there are no very striking examples of the 'false beauty' theme in the numerous descriptions of the Golden Age in classical texts. A comparable passage is found in Seneca, *Ep.* XC, 45, *Nondum uestis illis erat picta, nondum texebatur aurum.*

[4] Examples of *when*-clauses of the same type as that in Shakespeare's LXVIII and in Nicholas Breton's lines occur for instance in the allusions to the Golden Age in Lodge's *Phœbes Sonnet*, 1 ff., the anonymous *A Nimphs disdaine of Loue*, 17 ff. (*England's Helicon* pp. 60, 121), Greville's XLIV, the Prologue to *The Faerie Qveene* V, iii, 6 ff., Daniel's *Hymens Trivmph*, 512 ff., etc. Naturally such clauses express a fundamental idea in 'Golden Age' contexts: 'When warriors were brave, craftsmen skilful, merchants honest, women beautiful without cosmetics', etc.

such things as *Loe where she lyes, intombe those eyes*, and the 'glory —
pain' formula be his own inventions? It need hardly be pointed out
that isolated parallels in themselves do not mean a thing. But we
cannot ignore the following facts: a) The resemblances are no isolated phenomena since there is a series of nearly twenty parallels.
b) A substantial number of the passages resembling each other
cannot be paralleled elsewhere; at other times, though we may speak
of 'parallels' in other texts, there are no close ones. c) In some cases
passages are not only unparalleled, but deviate in a noteworthy way
from tradition. d) In the majority of cases the 'suspect' passages in
Delia and *Rosamond* are remarkable also in another respect: we find
words, expressions, and figures which the author otherwise avoids
or at least does not favour, or logical inconsistencies difficult to
account for unless external influence is assumed. e) On some important points we find in Daniel a passage resembling one in
Shakespeare though being more concentrated, sometimes too much
so, and reminiscent of cases where it is practically certain that
Daniel has condensed borrowed material. f) Above all, the similarity between the passages in *Delia* and those in the *Sonnets* is
mostly, in *Rosamond* partly, a consequence of Daniel's revisions.
This in itself constitutes a strong probability that, if we agree that
borrowing is likely, *Delia* and the relevant stanzas in *Rosamond* were
influenced by the *Sonnets* and not the reverse, particularly since g)
Daniel is known to have borrowed from others to an extent that
attracted attention even in an age unscrupulous in such matters.
The anonymous *Return from Parnassus* (ed. SMEATON, London, 1905)
includes a section in which fifteen authors are satirized; out of these,
Daniel is the only one to be blamed for imitation:

> *Sweet honey dropping Daniel doth wage*
> *War with the proudest big Italian,*
> *That melts his heart in sugared sonneting.*
> *Only let him more sparingly make use*
> *Of others' wit, and use his own the more;*
> *That well may scorn base imitation* (I, ii, 125 ff.).

One of Harington's epigrams was entitled, *Of honest Theft, to my
good friend Master Samuel Daniel.*[5]

[5] Cf. WHITE, *Plagiarism and Imitation during the English Renaissance*, Cambridge, Mass.,
1935, pp. 76, 167.

Nevertheless, I have naturally paid attention to the possibility that the resemblances may after all be due to chance. If, for example, we should find that the revisions in *Delia* make passages *less* similar to Shakespeare's sonnets as often as they make them *more* similar, our conclusions as regards Daniel's dependence would of course be practically invalid. However, if we test the *Delia* revisions from this point of view, it turns out that there are only a few cases of the former type, and these are of a trivial and superficial kind. Thus in *Delia* XVII, 8 1592 *So true and loyall loue* is a change from 1591 *So long and pure a faith*, and thus moves away from Shakespeare's LXVI, 4 *And purest faith vnhappily forsworne*, just as XXVII, 10 1601 *No pittying eye lookes backe vppon my feares* is a change from 1592 *No pittying eye lookes backe vppon my mourning* and thus becomes less similar to Shakespeare's CXXXII *Thine eies I loue, and they, as pittying me, ... | Haue put on black and louing mourners bee*. In the same way XXX, 6 1592 *Whose glorious blaze the world dooth so admire* is a change from 1591 *Whose glorious blaze the worlds eie doth admire*, and thus is less like Shakespeare's LXIX, 1 *Those parts of thee that the worlds eye doth view*. These are random phenomena in no way comparable to the parallels we have discussed in the sections above, and there is no reason to assume an earlier connection between *Delia* and the *Sonnets* here. It should be added that I have omitted several details in *Delia* brought closer to the *Sonnets* by revision, cases which are too trivial to be of any importance. Instances are *Delia* XXXVII, 2, 1592 *Those walles the which ambition reared*, 1601 *Those walles which proud ambition reared* — *Son.* XXV, 2 *Of publike honour and proud titles bost; Delia* XXVII, 7, 1594 *Which now are melted by that glorious Sunne*, 1601 *Which now are melted by thine eies bright sun* — *Son.* I, 5 *But thou, contracted to thine owne bright eyes; Delia* XXVI D, 3, 1591 *Thou my worldly light*, 1592 *my deerest comforts light* — *Son.* XLVIII, 6—7 *Most worthy comfort ... Thou best of deerest*, and a good many others. Such resemblances are quite superficial and prove nothing. I have also omitted such a case as Daniel's XXVI, in which l. 3, *She there in that sweete sanctuary slew it* (1591—1598) is changed in 1601 to *Thy rigor in that sanctuary slew*, and thus has been made more similar to *Son.* CXXXIII, 12 *Thou canst not then vse rigor in my Iaile*. Though 'rigor in my gaol' — 'rigor in that sanctuary' are unique combinations, though the revision in *Delia* involves the breaking up of a sustained parallelism, and though — as far as I can see — there is only one more instance in the Daniel corpus of *pro concreto* use of *rigor* (*Civ. W.* VII, 39), the evidence is not sufficient for assuming imitation on Daniel's part here. Such inconclusive details as these, however, are of importance in showing us that also one or two of the 'suspect' *Delia* passages may have moved towards the *Sonnets* by mere chance. I have actually concluded as much in the case of the 'table-in-the-heart' sonnets in *Delia* XIII and the *Sonnets* XXIV (cf. p. 54).

The possibility of a real connection, and not a coincidence, is of course greater when points of style, logic, and poetic convention are clearly involved in the resemblance. We have found various degrees of such involvement in practically all the passages where an influence from the *Sonnets* on *Delia* may be seriously suspected. Thus the cumulative evidence referred to under a) above does not mean that certain passages are regarded as borrowings merely because other passages are regarded as such, and that we have thus been arguing in a circle. On the contrary I have tried to show that each one of the parallels discussed is in fact capable of being interpreted as 'original+imitation' quite irrespective of the others. Many such parallels naturally support one another strongly. To sum up: even if one or other of the resemblances analysed on pp. 28 ff. of this chapter should be due to coincidence (for instance, such a comparatively weak case as *seale*>*steale* in no. XX), it seems hard to doubt that the vast majority are due to the fact that Daniel borrowed from Shakespeare's sonnets, just as he borrowed from many other poets' works. Conversely, there does not seem to be anything that unmistakably indicates an influence from *Delia* on Shakespeare's sonnets. There *may* of course be an influence in this direction as well, but I have not been able to trace one by the methods I have applied.[6] I have tried to show elsewhere that several similarities

[6] In the review article by BUXTON to which I have referred earlier it is maintained that my "assessment of the frequency of feminine endings in *Delia* is misleading, for Daniel made a point of removing many of these ... on revision". So "the contrast between the two poets here is false, for if Shakespeare was influenced at all by *Delia*, there is no reason to suppose that he was influenced only by the earliest editions" (p. 338). There is no reason to suppose that he was influenced by the later editions either. The point is — as appears from BROOKE's figures, to which I have referred in my book, p. 147 — that Shakespeare sided with many other Elizabethan poets (Sidney, Spenser, Fletcher, Rogers, Smith, Linche, Tofte, Drayton, and Barnes in his Petrarchan sonnets) in making a restrict-

earlier regarded as evidence that *Delia* influenced the *Sonnets* are merely due to common tradition. Some isolated resemblances not brought about by revision are probably indicative of a direct connection, though it is impossible to determine the direction of influence.[7]

Probably the thesis that Daniel influenced the *Sonnets* arose as follows: MALONE noticed that there were points of resemblance between Shakespeare's sonnets and *Delia*. Being unfamiliar with the textual history of the latter work and with the sonnet convention,[8] and being also biased by his belief that "the applause bestowed on *The Rosamond* ... gave birth" to *Lucrece*, he concluded that Shakespeare was the borrower — a natural thing for MALONE to do since his real interest was in the plays and he regarded the sonnets as much less original and less important work.[9] Others, however, added to his casual remarks, asserting that the *Sonnets* resembled *Delia* not only in certain passages but in the general style as well, and nobody took the trouble to see if this was really true.

ed use of feminine rhymes (less than two double-ending lines to the sonnet). BUXTON seems to be unfamiliar with this fact. There is thus no reason to assume that Shakespeare's usage on this point had any connection with that in the later editions of *Delia*. It is far more probable that both poets followed a general trend, but while Shakespeare did this spontaneously, Daniel did it so to speak on reflection. BUXTON further observes that in his *Defence of Ryme* Daniel gave his reasons for removing feminine rhymes, "and it could be argued, though not very convincingly, that Shakespeare, in avoiding feminine rhyme, was aware of the arguments that had convinced Daniel to abandon it" (*ibid.*). If the meaning of this obscure statement is that Shakespeare the sonneteer may have read *The Defence of Ryme*, the theory is all the less convincing as this treatise was not published until 1603, a fact not mentioned by BUXTON. — Incidentally, feminine rhymes are only a minor point in my discussion of metre in *Delia* and the *Sonnets*. As to the other metrical features examined by me we find no changes at all, or negligible ones, in the later editions of *Delia*.

[7] Cf. *op. cit.*, pp. 153 ff., 158, 161.

[8] "Of Petrarch (Whose works I have never read) I cannot speak" (ed. 1780, p. 684).

[9] MALONE's views on Shakespeare's *Sonnets* can be studied in the curious dialogue carried on between him and STEEVENS in the notes to no. CXXVII (ed. 1780, pp. 682 ff., ed. 1790, pp. 293 ff.). STEEVENS characterized Shakespeare's sonnets as "A stated number of lines composed in the highest strain of affectation, pedantry, circumlocution, and nonsense." MALONE's defence of the sonnets against this attack is lame in the extreme: "I do not feel any great propensity to stand forth as the champion of these compositions. However, as it appears to me that they have been somewhat under-rated, I think it incumbent on me to do them that justice to which they seem entitled ... When they are described as a mass of affectation, pedantry, circumlocution, and nonsense, the picture appears to me overcharged. Their great defects seem to be a want of variety, and the majority of them not being directed to a female ... It cannot be denied too that they contain some far-fetched conceits; but are our author's plays entirely free from them?" STEEVENS's reply to this is not surprising: "The case of these Sonnets is certainly bad, when so little can be advanced in support of them."

The 'Sonnets' and 'Idea'

There are not very many poems in Drayton's *Idea* that can be seriously connected with sonnets by Shakespeare. As I have observed in the introduction, several critics nowadays hold that Drayton is the debtor. But many of the parallels adduced as proof of this are merely due to common tradition, not to speak of the trivial and insignificant similarities that formed the main part of FLEAY's material.

As the first parallel pair that is clearly indicative of a direct connection between the *Sonnets* and *Idea* I quote Shakespeare's no. CXLIV and *Idea* XXII (1599). The latter poem reads:

> *An evill spirit your beautie haunts Me still,*
> *Where with (alas) I have beene long possest,*
> *Which ceaseth not to tempt Me to each Ill,*
> *Nor gives Me once, but one poore minutes rest:*
> *In Me it speakes, whether I Sleepe or Wake,*
> *And when by Meanes, to drive it out I try,*
> *With greater Torments, then it Me doth take,*
> *And tortures Me in most extremity;*
> *Before my Face, it layes downe my Despaires,*
> *And hastes Me on unto a sudden Death;*
> *Now tempting Me, to drowne my Selfe in teares,*
> *And then in sighing, to give up by breath;*
>   *Thus am I still provok'd, to every Evill,*
>   *By this good wicked Spirit, sweet Angell Devill.*

This poem is remarkable — where else do we find a poet's passion roused by an evil spirit 'tempting him to each ill' and torturing him 'in most extremity', by a *good wicked Spirit, sweet Angell Devill?* When forcible language is used about the lady in Petrarchan poetry we have either the common assortment of terms describing her hardness and mentioned in the chapter on *Delia* (p. 44 f. above): flint, marble, adamant, a tiger's heart, a lioness's mind, Medusa's face, etc. Or else, when the poet blames her falseness or lewdness, we get Shakespeare's 'dark lady' sonnets, Sannazaro's *cieco abisso di vizj empj, e rei, ... le macchie, ... tua colpa* (LVI), Guarini's *luci perverse, | Mentiti sguardi, e di Sirena accenti; | Falsi nunzi del cor* (XLVIII), and Tasso's

74

Ecco, i' rimovo le mentite larve :
Or ne le proprie tue sembianze omai
Ti veggia il mondo e ti contempli e pregi (108).

Jodelle in particular does not mince his words: *Fay—moy vomir*
contre vne,[1] *telle ordure, | Qui plus en cache & en l'ame, & au corps*
(*Contr' Amours* II, 13 f.), *Pute, traitresse, fiere, horrible, & charmeresse*
(V, 13), not to speak of his *Sonnet svr les beavtez d'vne garse.* These
pieces, brimming with hatred and disgust, may at first seem suggestive of Drayton's sonnet. Yet this poem is of a different kind, being
really a description of the lady's complete power, of the poet's
desperation *and* fascination. (SCOTT over-simplifies or rather mis-
judges the matter when observing that Drayton "ne fait que
répéter dans un moment de découragement de conventionnelles
paroles d'injures à sa dame" (p. 256).) How this fascination is mostly
expressed we have already seen in the discussion of the 'eye' metaphors (p. 59). To these could be added Petrarch's *la dolce et acerba*
mia nemica (XXIII, 69), the common *fera gentil, bella guerriera,* and
sweete foe, etc. Classical poets, indeed, may speak of the magic
art by which the lover is irresistibly conquered, as does Propertius
in III, vi, 25 ff.:

Non me moribus illa, sed herbis improba uicit :
staminea rhombi ducitur ille rota, etc.

But striking parallels to Drayton's XXII, 14 are hard to find; so far
as I can see we have to go back to Guittone d'Arezzo's antithesis
dragone — angelo in no. XXXVI and, in a later poet, to Amaltheo's
d'Angela beltà di tigre il core (*Rime di div.* III, 172 r.). These formula-
tions seem to be fairly isolated phenomena. Nor do we find any
forcible language like that in *Idea* in Italian contrasts of *amore ra-*
zionale to *amore sensuale,* at least not in poetry. However, as STEAD-
MAN has recently pointed out,[2] the opposition 'Angel — devil'
has a background in the Ficinian idea of the *gemini amores :* a *bonus*
daemon striving to "elevate the soul towards celestial objects",
a *malus daemon* striving to "degrade it *ad inferna*". It is also pointed
out that Robert Burton interprets this idea in a more Christian sense.

[1] 'Vne' is a noun here, = 'a woman'.
[2] '*Like Two Spirits' : Shakespeare and Ficino,* SQ x, 1959, pp. 244 ff.

Now this kind of dualism is not present in Drayton's sonnet: the lady does not represent the *gemini amores* any more than Petrarch's *dolce nemica* does. Even more striking is *ceaseth not to tempt Me to each Ill* and *Thus am I still provok'd, to every Evill*. What a fatal woman does in sonnets is to exercise her power without reprieve, day and night — a common theme; and to drive the lover to endless tears, sighs, despair, and death — an equally common theme. These things may well be described as torments, even as the poet-lover being tortured *in most extremity*, but we do not normally find *tempt me to each Ill* and *provok'd to every Evill;* nor is the fruitless attempt to exorcise evil spirits (l.6) a natural theme in this context. The demon-and-evil motif, in short, is suspect. It is comprehensible that the poem was long ago compared with Shakespeare's sonnet CXLIV:[3]

> Two loues I haue of comfort and dispaire,
> Which like two spirits do sugiest me still,
> The better angell is a man right faire:
> The worser spirit a woman collour'd il.
> To win me soone to hell my female euill,
> Tempteth my better angel from my sight,
> And would corrupt my saint to be a diuel:
> Wooing his purity with her fowle pride.
> And whether that my angel be turn'd feend,
> Suspect I may, yet not directly tell,
> But being both from me both to each friend,
> I gesse one angel in an others hel.
>   Yet this shal I nere know but liue in doubt,
>   Till my bad angel fire my good one out.

It is well known that this poem was also printed in *The Passionate Pilgrim* (1599), from which version I adopt, with editors, the reading 'fiend' in l. 9. Other variants also found in the *Passionate Pilgrim* version can be disregarded here. Of earlier critics who have commented on the likeness of the two poems — as appears from ROLLINS's notes on the Shakespeare text in 1, 369 f. — FLEAY and LEE believed that Shakespeare was the debtor, while TYLER, WYND-

---

[3] The first to do this seems to have been DOWDEN in his edition of Shakespeare's *Sonnets* in 1881.

HAM, BEECHING, PORTER, REED, and BROOKE held the opposite view. It could be added that ALDEN in his *Variorum* edition (1916) was sceptical and would "desiderate a grain of proof that either sonnet must have been suggested by the other" (p. 347), while SCOTT believed in Shakespeare's influence (p. 256) and PEARSON left the matter open (*op. cit.*, p. 196). Somewhat surprisingly, a more recent authority on Drayton shares ALDEN's scepticism: in her notes on *Idea*, TILLOTSON says that there is "some verbal closeness" but that "the conceits are quite distinct", and concludes that "the likeness has been overstated".[4] I think not. As I have tried to show, Drayton's imagery and phraseology fall outside the convention. A closer parallel than Shakespeare's sonnet is not to be found. Furthermore, the phrases and images in CXLIV are more integral to the subject of that poem as a whole: the *worser spirit a woman collour'd il*, my *female euill*, her *fowle pride*, my *bad angel* are things written in a spirit akin to that found in the Sannazaro and Jodelle passages. The theme also clearly fits in with the background indicated by STEADMAN: as in Ficino and Burton, the two *daemones* appear in no. CXLIV, contending for the poet's soul. The eccentricities of Drayton's sonnet are easily explained on the assumption that he was the imitator. Catching echoes from Shakespeare's sonnet, Drayton may easily have produced such details — otherwise difficult to explain — as *Evill spirit, tempt ... to each Ill, tempting Me, provok'd, to every Evill*, and not least the harsh double antithesis of the last line, reminiscent of *my bad angel ... my good one*. In Shakespeare this of course is no oxymoron — two contrasting characters being the theme of the poem —, but the use of that figure in Drayton may have been facilitated by the current use of the *sweete foe* oxymoron. All in all, it is hard to avoid concluding that Drayton was acquainted with Shakespeare's CXLIV by 1599, when his own sonnet was first printed. As regards previous criticism of the parallels I think we may safely agree with WYNDHAM's verdict (quoted by ROLLINS, *ibid*): "The likeness is but of phrasing ... Drayton's sonnet seems ... a superficial plagiarism". Nobody denies the fact pointed out by TILLOTSON that "the conceits are quite distinct" (ALDEN made the same comment: "Surely the subjects are distinct"), but this is not the point: a poet may borrow

---

[4] *Op. cit.*, p. 140. TILLOTSON's comment is recorded by ROLLINS, *ibid*.

from another and make an entirely different use of what he borrows. In this case, it is the manner in which Drayton utilizes the borrowed matter that gives him away.

So far as I can see, this is the only case where it is possible to demonstrate a clear influence from Shakespeare on an entire sonnet in Drayton's *Idea*.[5] What remains is a series of limited resemblances only some of which, in my opinion, are indicative of indebtedness on Drayton's part. One is to be found in *Idea* XLIII (1599), which according to TILLOTSON contains "some obvious verbal reminiscences" of Shakespeare's LXXXI.[6] TILLOTSON is apparently referring to the entombment theme which we have discussed in connection with *Delia*. The relevant lines in LXXXI are 5 ff.:

> *Your name from hence immortall life shall haue,*
> *Though I (once gone) to all the world must dye,*
> *The earth can yeeld me but a common graue,*
> *When you intombed in mens eyes shall lye,*
> *Your monument shall be my gentle verse, etc.*

In Drayton's XLIII, the last quatrain reads:

> *And though in youth, my Youth untimely perish,*
> *To keepe Thee from Oblivion and the Grave,*
> *Ensuing Ages yet my Rimes shall cherish,*
> *Where I intomb'd, my better part shall save.*

In Shakespeare's lines, the antithesis is between the poet's insignificance and the friend's glory, between his own fate, oblivion, and the friend's, immortality. The context is quite clear, and the conventional character of this theme we have discussed before. In

---

[5] In *The Seed of a Shakespeare Sonnet?*, as pointed out in the Introduction, DAVENPORT hesitantly suggests that a group of images in the second *Eglog* of Drayton's *The Shepheards Garland* (1593) may have had a certain influence on Shakespeare's no. II (*When fortie Winters shall beseige thy brow*). It is quite possible that this is so, but the evidence does not seem convincing, and the images, as DAVENPORT admits, are commonplaces. "The echoing, if any, is unconscious: Drayton's lines are no more the "source" of the sonnet than the travel-books which Coleridge had read were the "sources" of 'The Ancient Mariner' and 'Kubla Khan'", is the author's description of the nature of the suspected influence. But these words also indicate the analyst's difficulties: how is it possible to trace, with any amount of certainty or even probability, an influence of this elusive kind?

[6] First pointed out by TYLER in the preface to his edition of Shakespeare's sonnets (pp. 40 f.).

Drayton we find the same theme though expressed in an awkward construction. Ll. 11—12 of the quatrain in *Idea* mean: 'Posterity will cherish my verse, where I shall preserve the better part of myself though the rest of me will be dead and buried.' *Intomb'd* is thus strongly elliptical, with a concessive force, and forms an antithesis to the rest of the line. The ellipsis is so harsh that the unwary reader, instead of interpreting, 'where I, intomb'd', may easily run these words together and construe them with *my Rimes*. Such ellipses, of course, are not unparalleled in Elizabethan English. The present instance, however, is unusually harsh, and I cannot find that Drayton otherwise favours similar elliptical constructions. On the contrary as regards *Idea* in general, as TILLOTSON points out (p. 137), "the grammar is made clearer and the structure more logical" as compared with earlier versions. But the peculiarities of no. XLIII may be explained without too much difficulty. It would seem that Drayton reproduced the *though*-clause in Shakespeare's LXXXI, 6 as well as *graue* in the following line, but transformed *When you intombed* to *Where I intomb'd*,[7] producing at the same time the combination *Where I intomb'd, my better part shall save*, the latter words perhaps a reminiscence of *the better part of me* in Shakespeare's XXXIX or in Golding's *Ovid* xv, 989.[8] We have earlier found Daniel probably imitating the same lines of Shakespeare's LXXXI and swerving away into the periphery of tradition.

Other parallels may be reviewed more summarily, others again I pass by, the alleged resemblances being too faint or even imperceptible. The 'tenth Muse' sonnets (Sh. XXXVIII, D. XVIII)[9] have been shown to have a traditional background, the earliest instances being found in the Greek Anthology.[1] SCOTT refers to G.A. v, 70 and 95, but the real prototype is IX, 506 ('Εννέα τὰς Μούσας). As other representatives of the theme SCOTT mentions Minturno and Rota; Marullus, Ricci, and many others could be added.[2] A direct

---

[7] In the 1600 and subsequent editions, *Where* was changed to *When*, bringing the line into closer accordance with Shakespeare's.

[8] For this phrase cf. LEISHMAN, p. 33.

[9] The first to connect these two sonnets seems to have been HALL in 1884 (*A Literary Craze*, NQ, 6th series, x, p. 62).

[1] SCOTT, pp. 146 ff., 317.

[2] Cf. further HUTTON, *The Greek Anthology in Italy*, Ithaca, 1935, pp. 559 ff., *The Greek*

connection between Shakespeare's and Drayton's 'tenth Muse' sonnets might of course have been suggested if there had been close verbal parallels. But this is not so, and the differences are conspicuous.

It is strange that *Ideas Mirrour* 14, *Looking into the glasse of my youths miseries | I see the ugly face of my deformed cares* should ever have been directly connected with Shakespeare's XXII, *My glasse shall not perswade me I am ould, | So long as youth and thou are of one date*, the ideas in the two sonnets being different and looking into mirrors found in many other sonneteers. According to ALDEN the prototype is Petrarch's CCCLXI, but there is also the *Anacreontics*, ode XI.[3] — As to the 'eye-heart' conceits of the *Sonnets* XXIV and *Idea* XXXIII, the motif was common and the latter sonnet is much less like Shakespeare's poem than is *Diana* I, i, 3, about which more on p. 92 below. The similarity is greater between the *Sonnets* XLVI and *Idea* XXXIII (*Mine eye and heart are at a mortall warre, | How to deuide the conquest of thy sight* — *Whilst yet mine Eyes doe surfet with Delight, | My wofull Heart, imprison'd in my Brest*, etc.), but not great enough to make a real influence probable. *Idea* XXXIII was first printed in *Ideas Mirrour* and later revised, but the revisions do not make it really similar to Shakespeare's poem.

Idea XLIII has been compared not only to Shakespeare's LXXXI but, with less justification, to LV and LXIII and, with more, to

---

Anthology in France, Ithaca, 1946, pp. 714 ff. Another English poet using the theme is Grimald (*A trueloue*, l. 17, *Tottel's Miscellany*, no. 128).

[3]

> Λέγουσιν αἱ γυναῖκες.
> Ἀνακρέων, γέρων εἶ,
> λαβὼν ἔσοπτρον ἄθρει
> κόμας μὲν οὐκέτ᾽ οὔσας, etc.

(BERGK, *Lyrici Graeci*, Lipsiae 1882, p. 301.) "The girls tell me: 'Anacreon, you are old! Just take a mirror and see how your hair is gone.'" Some Italian post-Petrarch instances of the theme, chosen at random, are Philoxeno's

> Me uegio in questo fonte come a un spechio,
> o quanto e trasmutato il mio colore
> che igran fastidi fan presto lhō uecchio,

(*Sylve*, 1516), and Gradenico's

> Quando talhor mi guardo ne lo specchio,
> Veggendo si cangiata mia figura,
> Pietà viemmi di me stesso, e paura,
> Che sia in poch'anni fatto quasi vecchio.

(Atanagi II, 1565, 101 r.).

LXVIII. To LV because it is an eternizing sonnet — like countless others; to LXIII because Shakespeare says, *Houres haue ... fild his brow | With lines and wrincles*, and Drayton, *Age rules my Lines with Wrinkles in my Face* — as if sonnet wrinkles could not be counted by the thousand. It is perhaps somewhat more likely that when Drayton in no. XLIII, after the line with the wrinkles and the face, wrote,

> *Where, in the Map of all my Miserie,*
> *Is model'd out the World of my Disgrace,*

he was thinking of Shakespeare's LXVIII, 1 :[4]

Thus is his cheeke the map of daies out-worne, and developed or doubled the image, or perhaps that he was drawing on *Lucrece* 1712 f., *The face, that map which deepe impression beares | Of hard misfortune*. On the other hand the 'face-map' formula was not uncommon. Drayton uses it several other times, for instance twice in *Matilda* (121, 379). In *The Spanish Tragedy* III, x, 91 Balthazar calls Bel-imperia's *iuorie front* his *sorrowes map*, and to *Fidessa* XI, 2 *Vpon my face (the map of discontent)* referred to by ROLLINS (I, 179) could be added Lodge's *Rosalynde* (p. 1), *The map of age was figured on his forehead*, and Daniel's *Philotas* 495 f. *I view within his face | The map of change and innouation*.

As for other resemblances, TILLOTSON is inclined to connect *Idea* LI (1605),

> *Calling to minde since first my Love begun,*
> *Th'incertaine Times oft varying in their Course,*
> *How Things still unexpectedly have runne,*
> *As't please the Fates, by their resistlesse force:*
> *Lastly, mine Eyes amazedly have seene*
> *Essex great fall, Tyrone his Peace to gaine,*
> *The quiet end of that Long-living Queene,*
> *This Kings faire Entrance, and our Peace with Spaine,*
> *We and the Dutch at length our Selves to sever;*
> *Thus the World doth, and evermore shall Reele;*
> *Yet to my Goddesse am I constant ever;*
> *How e're blind Fortune turne her giddie Wheele:*

---

[4] The first to compare these two sonnets seems to have been FLEAY (II, p. 227), though he regarded Shakespeare as the borrower.

> *Though Heaven and Earth, prove both to me untrue,*
> *Yet am I still inviolate to You,*

with Shakespeare's well-known CVII (*Not mine owne feares, nor the prophetick soule*). "The theme is unusual in sonnet-sequences", she says, "and it seems likely that D had seen Shakespeare's sonnet and had it in mind". LEISHMAN holds a similar view (p. 110). This is conceivable but difficult to prove since there are no resemblances of detail. Drayton might equally well have been inspired by Sidney's *Astrophel* no. XXX (*Whether the Turkish new Moone minded be*, etc.), though this poem is somewhat different.

Finally Shakespeare's no. CXVI, in which the poet speaks of love as

> *an euer fixed marke*
> *That lookes on tempests and is neuer shaken;*
> *It is the star to euery wandring barke,*
> *Whose worths vnknowne, although his higth be taken,*

has also been compared (by WYNDHAM) with *Idea* XLIII (1605), in which the lady's reluctance to look at the poet is contrasted with her gracious glances bestowed 'on ev'ry vulgar Spirit', who like the ploughman gazes at 'the wand'ring Starre', contented with its light but unfamiliar with the astronomical constellation *Beyond the bent of his unknowing Sight*. WYNDHAM said that this poem "seems suggested by" Shakespeare's sonnet. Quite possible, but the similarities are so limited and the differences so marked that one must agree with SCOTT: "A notre avis, il est impossible de tirer une conclusion définitive quant à la dette réciproque des poètes" (p. 255).

As a summary I should say that in a few cases there seem to be definite traces of the *Sonnets* in *Idea*, but that other alleged similarities are much too uncertain to be seriously regarded as indicative of an influence from one poet on the other.[5] TILLOTSON's statement that "Shakespeare had a strong general influence on D." (p. 138) is too vague to carry weight, as is also her remark that "The 1605 group is peculiarly Shakespearean" (p. 139). Similarly vague are

---

[5] Cf. also ST. CLAIR, *Drayton's First Revision of His Sonnets*, SP XXXVI, 1939, pp. 56 f. ST. CLAIR expresses some scepticism, but at the same time admits that though "the trail is indistinct and the scent poor ... there is enough of each to encourage us in the pursuit" (p. 57). He also thinks that some light may be shed on the chronology of Shakespeare's sonnets by an examination of the relationship between them and Drayton's (n. 37).

LEISHMAN's arguments for connecting certain Drayton sonnets with Shakespeare's (pp. 85 ff., 110 f.). LEISHMAN also pays insufficient attention to parallels in other poets. It is naturally possible that some of the *Idea* sonnets he refers to may have been suggested by the *Sonnets* or the reverse, but the evidence is altogether inadequate. In some features Drayton's temperament seems to have resembled Shakespeare's; this may account for a certain general similarity. A limited influence only can be ascertained. On the other hand I can find no clear trace of an influence exerted *by* Drayton *on* Shakespeare.[6]

The 'Sonnets' and 'Diana'

We now come to what is in a sense the most interesting set of parallels to be discussed: the resemblances between Shakespeare's sonnets and Constable's *Diana*. We shall first deal with the most conspicuous of these similarities,[7] that between the *Sonnets* XCIX and *Diana* I, iii, 1 (first printed in 1592). It is convenient first to discuss those features in the two sonnets that are similar and those that are different, then those among the former that are also found elsewhere and may be considered common property, then to concentrate on such as cannot be explained in this way, and finally to consider the permissible conclusions.

Shakespeare's fifteen-line XCIX reads:

> *The forward violet thus did I chide,*
> *Sweet theefe whence didst thou steale thy sweet that smels,*
> *If not from my loues breath? The purple pride,*
> *Which on thy soft cheeke for complexion dwells*
> *In my loues veines thou hast too grosely died.*
> *The Lillie I condemned for thy hand,*

---

[6] LEISHMAN (p. 86 f.) suggests that *Ideas Mirrour* 7, in which Time is invited to see in 'this Celestiall glasse' of the poet's sonnet 'worlds Beautie in her infancie' and then tell posterity about it, may "at least partly" have inspired Shakespeare to such sonnets as LIX and CVI ("all beauty described by earlier poets was a prophecy of his friend's"), LXVII, LXVIII ("in a declining age his friend is a reminder of what beauty once was"), and XXX, XXXI ("all those whom he had supposed lost live again in his friend"). Only CVI bears a certain similarity to *I.M.* 7, and LEISHMAN is unaware of the striking resemblance between this sonnet and a poem in *Diana* (cf. p. 91 below). If Shakespeare's idea in CVI was suggested by anything, it was certainly by *Diana* I, iii, 4.

[7] First pointed out by MASSEY in 1872 (cf. ROLLINS I, p. 245).

And buds of marierom had stolne thy haire;
The Roses fearefully on thornes did stand,
One blushing shame, an other white dispaire;
A third nor red, nor white, had stolne of both,
And to his robbry had annext thy breath,
But for his theft in pride of all his growth
A vengfull canker eate him vp to death.
  More flowers I noted, yet I none could see,
  But sweet, or culler it had stolne from thee.

This is the parallel sonnet in Constable's *Diana*:

My Ladies presence makes the roses red
Because to see her lips they blush for shame
The lilies leaues for envy pale became
And her white hands in them this envy bred

The marygold abroad the leaues did spread
Because the suns and her power is the same
The violet of purple coloure came
Dy'd with the bloud she made my heart to shed

In briefe all flowers from her theyre vertue take
From her sweet breath theyre sweet smells doe proceed
The liuing heate which her eybeames doe make
Warmeth the ground and quickneth the seede
  The rayne wherewith she watereth these flowers
  Falls from myne eyes which she dissolues in shewers.

The general resemblance between these poems is obvious: the lady endows various flowers with her beauty. As to the details, GRUNDY makes the following summary: "Constable mentions the rose, lily, marigold, and violet; Shakespeare the violet, lily, marjoram, and rose. Constable's roses blush for shame; so do Shakespeare's. In each poem the lily is less white than the loved one's hand; in each the purple violet has been dyed in blood — the lover's blood, according to Constable, the loved one's according to Shakespeare. In each the flowers are said to be perfumed by the beloved's breath, although Shakespeare limits this theft to the violet, while Constable extends it to all flowers and indeed does not see it as a theft at all, but simply as a natural process" (p. 61). It could be added that the third quatrain and the couplet of the two poems steer different courses: Constable's quatrain lacks the canker motif; Shakespeare's the heat-and-rain motif. To what extent are these things traditional?

WYNDHAM (ed., p. 309, quoted by ROLLINS *ibid.*) said that "these flower-sonnets are in a mode imitated from Petrarch, which overran Europe in the sixteenth century". BALDWIN: "While such flower-sonnets were conventional, I believe the coincidence here is sufficient to make it clear that Shakspere has borrowed, and by consequence that Sonnet XCIX is later than 1592."[8] The latest commentator, GRUNDY: "The idea itself is a commonplace and at least as old as Persius's second Satire. If any connexion between Shakespeare's sonnet and Constable's is to be established, it must be in the details introduced in the working-out of the conceit ... These conceits too, taken separately, are either commonplace in themselves or a natural development of other commonplaces. It is only their numerical strength that makes a borrowing on Shakespeare's part seem likely" (p. 61). GRUNDY goes on to say that this likelihood is increased in view of other resemblances between the *Sonnets* and *Diana*. These we shall discuss later.

Such statements as these are not very satisfactory. For one thing, as said before, the flower topic is not homogeneous but made up of several different types of different frequency. Second, how 'commonplace' are the conceits referred to, and how important is 'their numerical strength'? The handful of other passages, English and Continental, relevant and irrelevant, that are given in GRUNDY's commentary (p. 227 f.) do not answer these questions.

To begin with, there are at least five main types of flower imagery illustrating the lady's beauty in Renaissance poetry (I do not here differentiate between formal and material categories): a) the metaphor type (*Du thym, du lis, de la rose | Parmy ses lévres desclose, | Fleurante en toutes saisons*, Ronsard *Odes* II, vii), b) the simile type (*Her Cheeks to damask roses sweet, | In scent and colour were so like*, Barnes, *Parthenophil*, Ode 16), c) the 'more-than' type (*Melinelle plus douillette, | Que la rose vermeillette, | Qu'vn Zephire vigoureux, | Hors du bouton éclos pousse*, Baïf, *Amours de Meline* II,

---

[8] *The Literary Genetics*, p. 303.

p. 79), d) the ' charms-borrowed-from-flowers' type (*But lovely Graces, in memorial, | Let both the Rose and Lily's colour fall | Within her cheeks, which, to be foremost hasten*, Barnes, *Parthenophil* Ma. 24), e) the 'charms-lent-to-flowers' type (*O gorge, albastre, où sa blancheur a prise | Le Lys royal*, Jamyn, sonnet no. LXXII). Of course these types are often combined in various ways, particularly a), b), and c), yet are easily distinguishable. It is type e), then, with which we are most nearly concerned. While type a) yields 35, b) 25, c) 21, and d) 4 per cent as calculated on a representative material of English, French, Italian, and classical poetry, type e) covers 15 per cent. But the 'charms-lent-to-flowers' type in its turn consists of several formulas. One of these I have illustrated above, others are: the lady's breath engenders flower-strewn meadows; the lady's tears make the earth fertile; wherever the lady turns her glance the grass becomes lush, the flowers fresh; the lady has an effect like that of the sun; as soon as she appears, trees and flowers rejoice; flowers grow up in her footsteps. The last-mentioned formula, which GRUNDY illustrates from Persius (II, 38, *quidquid calcaverit hic, rosa fiat*) constitutes about 7 per cent of the 'charms-lent-to-flowers' group, but it is *not* found in *Diana* I, iii, 1 and the *Sonnets* XCIX. GRUNDY says (p. 227) that it "probably derives ultimately from Persius"; in reality it is found in several classical poets.[9] Incidentally, its origin is a primitive myth spread all over the world,[1] while the other variants of the 'charms-lent-to-flowers' group have a wholly literary background but, so far as I can see, are practically non-existent in classical Greek and Latin poetry. There is some indication that they derive from Arabic literature.[2] The 'footstep' formula is twice as frequent in the Italian as in the French poets;[3] the other formulas of the 'charms-lent-to-flowers' group are found

---

[9] The oldest instance seems to be Hesiod's Theogony 195 ('grass sprouts under Venus's light feet'), probably imitated by Lucretius in I, 7 f. We also find the footstep formula in Claudian's *Carm. min.* XXIX, 89 f, and even Gregory of Nazianzus adopts it (MIGNE P. G. XXXVII, 1538).

[1] Cf. e.g. *Historische Quellenschriften zum Studium der Anthropophyteia* V, Leipzig, 1909, pp. 17 f. LEISHMAN is thus quite right when, referring to the Hesiod passage, he suggests that perhaps it should be regarded as a "piece of folklore" (p. 166, n.). LEISHMAN also mentions the passage in Lucretius.

[2] Cf. NYKL, *Hispano-Arabic Poetry*, Baltimore, 1946, pp. 39, 43, 63.

[3] One of the best French instances is found in Ronsard's *Regrets* to Mary Queen of Scots (BLANCHEMAIN VI, p. 23): *Tousjours dessous ses pieds la terre se peindra | D'un beau tapis de fleurs.*

equally often. Curiously enough, the 'footsteps' are comparatively rare in English poetry, particularly in the sonnet-sequences. The absence of the formula in Constable's and Shakespeare's sonnets thus agrees with a vernacular convention. One of the few English instances is found in Barnes's *Parthenophil*, Ode IX, 4[4].

Thus the probably Oriental 'charms-lent-to-flowers' theme as represented by Shakespeare's and Constable's sonnets comprises about 8 per cent of the whole group. In other words, its traditional background can be narrowed down, while a direct connection between the two poems becomes increasingly possible. Furthermore, though there are other examples of extended flower series like those found in Shakespeare and Constable,[5] it is true that they are comparatively uncommon and different in various respects from the series in the *Sonnets* and *Diana*. However, there is of course no point in GRUNDY's remark that it is only the "numerical strength" of the conceits that indicates a borrowing on Shakespeare's part. The numerical strength tells us nothing about the question of borrower and debtor, nor does the similarity of some lines in Shakespeare's XCVIII (a sonnet obviously connected with XCIX): 11—12,

> *They weare but sweet, but figures of delight:*
> *Drawne after you, you patterne of all those,*

to another sonnet in *Diana* (I, iii, 4). Both resemblances merely indicate a probable connection, and on such evidence alone Constable may equally well be the borrower. Nor can we point to the early date of Constable's sonnet and use it, as GRUNDY does, as an argument for Shakespeare's indebtedness (p. 62); this is merely begging the question. What settles the matter is something else: the relationship of the two passages to convention. The commonest themes are those in ll. 1, 2, 10, and 11 f. ('lady's presence makes roses red', 'blush-shame' theme, 'breath-scent' theme, 'eye-beams quicken vegetation').[6] The lilies that grow pale for envy represent a com-

---

[4] The formula is satirized in Ben Jonson's *The Sad Shepherd* (1640 fol.):
> *And where she went, the Flowers tooke thickest root,*
> *As she had sow'd 'hem with her odorous foot* (I, i, 8 f.).

[5] Similar extended enumerations are to be found for example in Tomitano (Ruscelli's *Fiori*, 47 v.), Ronsard's *Amours* II, xlii, Baïf, *Amours de Meline*, p. 56, and Barnes's *Parthenophil*, XCVI.

[6] I briefly refer to the following select parallels: theme a) Cino da Pistoia (*Scelta* I, 34),

bination of two motifs that are generally kept apart in tradition but each of which is quite common: *Là de ton teint se pallissoient les fleurs* (Ronsard, *Am.* I, XXXVI); *Le rose in lei ch'invidia il maggio* (Tasso, son. 211).[7] As to Constable's couplet ('lover's tears quickening vegetation'), tears which have this effect are traditionally the lady's (as in *Astrophel and Stella* no. C, Collalto (*Parnaso It.* XXXI, 96), and Costanzo no. CXI), yet the theme in *Diana* is also found elsewhere.[8] A smaller number of details are not similarly conventional, such as the violet *Dy'd with the bloud she made my heart to shed*: GRUNDY observes that violets, though common in poems of this type, are not otherwise dyed in the lover's blood (p. 228). One detail, again, appears to be directly borrowed: the sun making the marigold open its petals seems derived from Watson's *Hekatompathia* IX (*The Marigold so likes the louely Sunne*), a parallel pointed out by GRUNDY (*ibid.*). What is however throughout traditional, finally, is the fact that all the details making up the 'charms-lent-to-flowers' conceit in *Diana* are parts of a description.

If we compare Shakespeare's no. XCIX with this account of Constable's imagery, it is at once apparent that while the poet retains the traditional flowers — violet, lily, rose; and alludes to the 'breath-scent' and the 'blush-shame' themes — he also agrees with Constable on the quite untraditional 'violet-dyed-in-blood' point.[9] This fact, in addition to those mentioned above, makes a direct connection certain. The main point, however, is that Shakespeare entirely changes the setting of the conceit. What is traditionally

Guinizelli (*Poeti di Duecento* II, 454), Sasso CCLXX, Capilupi (*Rime di div.* III, 110), Guidiccioni LX, Amaltheo (*Rime di div.* III, 93); b) *Arcadia* I, 90 (GRUNDY), Lodge, *Phillis* IX, Melin de St. Gelais I, son. XII, Baïf, *Am. de Meline* p. 54, Jodelle, *Am.* V, Camillo (*Rime di div.* I, 67); c) Poliziano's *In Violas* (GRUNDY), di Tieno (*Scelta* II, 158), Tansillo CXV, Rinieri (*Rime di div.* II, 19), Ronsard, *Am.* II, chanson, Belleau II, 289, Baïf, *Am. de Meline* p. 31, Tyard, *Vers liriques* p. 144; d) Desportes, *Cartels et Masquarades* I, Lorenzo de' Medici LXXXVIII (GRUNDY), Bojardo (*Scelta* I, 167), Sannazaro, *Canz.* VIII, Bembo son. LXXXV, Capilupi (*Rime di div.* II, 119), Tasso, son. 3 and 11.

[7] First theme for instance in the *Arcadia* passage noted above, in Melin de St. Gelais I, p. 197, and in *Parthenophil*, Sestine I; second theme in Dolce (*Rime di div.* I, 309), Fletcher's *Licia* XXX, and many others (cf. further below, p. 98). A combination of the themes like that in Constable and Sidney is found e.g. in Caccianimici (*Rime*, Bologna, 1608, p. 46).

[8] Cf. *The Phoenix Nest* p. 44, *Mine eyes are dimd ... Their lids were shut amids the lingring nights: | Their yeelding fountaines watring of the ground;* Philoxeno, *Sylve, La tua radice ho qui bagnato tanto | chel tronco tuo sublime ... | crescera sopra gli altri;* and Capilupi, *Sol questa Riva, che'l mio pianto bagna | Produca fior* (*Rime di div.* III, 109).

[9] Cf. GRUNDY, *ibid.*

descriptive is here dramatic, and where else do we find the 'charms-lent-to-flowers' theme expressed in the shape of accusations brought against the flowers for stealing the charms of the recipient of the poem? It is surely obvious that Shakespeare imitates the more conventional Constable and that he gives the conceit he finds in *Diana* an unexpected and unconventional twist. Similarly in the last quatrain he departs from tradition as handed down by his model and winds up with a particularly Shakespearean motif — the consuming canker. It is also clear that no. xcviii is equally dependent on the *Diana* poem, for the lines in xcviii are a condensation of the theme as found in Constable. — The contrast is obvious between Shakespeare's renderings and two other probable imitations of *Diana* I, iii, 1: *Emaricdulfe* xiv (1595) and Craig's *To Lithocardia* (*Amorose Songs*, 1606), pointed out by GRUNDY (pp. 63 f.). In both these cases the tradition is strictly adhered to, and the descriptive setting is retained.

Thus a comparison between the *Diana* sonnet and Shakespeare's xcix shows the same process as that we have already studied when analysing the relationship of Daniel's and Drayton's sonnets to Shakespeare's: the shift from the conventional to the unconventional. The difference is that while Shakespeare in no. xcix gives us something lively and dramatic, the imitation of the other two poets often results in awkwardness and inconsistency.

In this connection another Shakespearean passage should be mentioned. It is well known that in Shakespeare's *Lucrece*, 477 ff., there is a stanza closely resembling some details in no. xcix and in *Diana* I, iii, 1. This stanza contains Tarquin's answer to Lucretia's questions and entreaties:

> *Thus he replies, the colour in thy face,*
> *That euen for anger makes the Lilly pale,*
> *And the red rose blush at her owne disgrace,*
> *Shall plead for me and tell my louing tale.*
> *Vnder that colour am I come to scale*
>> *Thy neuer conquered Fort, the fault is thine,*
>> *For those thine eyes betray thee vnto mine.*

In his discussion of the passages in *Lucrece*, the *Sonnets*, and *Diana*, BALDWIN remarks that the *Lucrece* stanza shows dependence on

Constable's sonnet but that he can see "nothing about the passages ... to determine whether Sonnet XCIX is earlier or later than the passage in *Lucrece*".[1] With this I think we can safely agree, and the only permissible conclusion would seem to be that sonnets XCVIII and XCIX were written at about the same time as the stanza in *Lucrece*, a time when impressions of Constable's sonnet were fresh in Shakespeare's mind. *Lucrece* was entered for publication in May, 1594 and was probably written in 1593 and early in 1594.[2]

Analysis of another parallel pair in the *Sonnets* and *Diana* is less laborious. The Shakespeare sonnet is no. CVI:

> *When in the Chronicle of wasted time,*
> *I see discriptions of the fairest wights,*
> *And beautie making beautifull old rime,*
> *In praise of Ladies dead, and louely Knights,*
> *Then in the blazon of sweet beauties best,*
> *Of hand, of foote, of lip, of eye, of brow,*
> *I see their antique Pen would haue exprest,*
> *Euen such a beauty as you maister now.*
> *So all their praises are but prophecies*
> *Of this our time, all you prefiguring,*
> *And for they look'd but with deuining eyes,*
> *They had not still enough your worth to sing:*
> > *For we which now behold these present dayes,*
> > *Haue eyes to wonder, but lack toungs to praise.*

As far back as 1880 the similarity of this poem to *Diana* I, iii, 4 was pointed out by MAIN:[3]

> *Miracle of the world I neuer will denye*
> *That former poets prayse the beautie of theyre dayes*
> *But all those beauties were but figures of thy prayse*
> *And all those poets did of thee but prophecye.*
>
> *Thy coming to the world hath taught vs to descrie*
> *What Petrarchs Laura meant (for truth the lips bewrayes)*

---

[1] *The Literary Genetics*, p. 303. The first to notice the resemblance was EWIG in 1899, as appears from ROLLINS's *Variorum* edition of Shakespeare's *Poems* (p. 160).

[2] Cf. ROLLINS, *op. cit.*, p. 414.

[3] Cf. ROLLINS I, p. 261.

Loe why th'Italians yet which never saw thy rayes
To find oute Petrarchs sense such forged glosses trye

The beauties which he in a vayle enclosd beheld
But revelations were within his secreat heart
By which in parables thy coming he foretold
His songes were hymnes of thee which only now before
  Thy image should be sunge for thow that goddesse art
  Which onlye we withoute idolatrye adore.

The resemblance is obvious at first sight: not only are the conceits
— 'descriptions of fairness in ancient poetry prophesy friend's and
lady's beauty' — identical, but *So all their praises are but prophecies |
Of this our time, all you prefiguring* is strikingly similar to *But all those
beauties were but figures of thy prayse | And all those poets did of thee
but prophecye.* GRUNDY rightly calls attention to the novelty of the
idea in the sonnets and the closeness of the resemblance (p. 62) —
neither can in fact be paralleled elsewhere. When other poets,
contemporary and earlier, refer to the art of bygone times in their
praise of beauty, the context is almost invariably a different one.
Tebaldeo says that "the two Tuscans" would be unable to describe
the lady (LXXXIII) and Zeuxis and Apelles to paint her (XCI);
Mozzarello that it would need the powers of a Homer to praise her
charms (*Rime di div.* I, 72), and Martelli that Lisippos, Apelles, and
Homer could only have described her outward beauty, not her in-
ward value (*Fiori* 277). Apelles recurs in a Rinieri sonnet (*Rime di
div.* II, 26): he would be unable to paint her without using the light
of sun, stars, and sky. Petrarch assures us that if Virgil and Homer
had seen Laura, they would have abandoned their work and praised
her instead (CLXXXVI). Du Bellay imitates Mozzarello (XX); Tyard,
Martelli (I, LXVII). Watson in *Hekatompathia* XXIX and Barnes in
Parthenophil Ma. 4 have similar conceits.[4] Nowhere is there a trace
of prediction of beauty, let alone of anything similar to the details
in Constable's ll. 3—4 and Shakespeare's 9—10. Convention then
does not help us; both poets are equally far from it. How then are
we to decide which poet is the borrower? In a very simple way —
by reading the title of Constable's sonnet: *To his Mistrisse vpon*

---

[4] The conceit is also adopted by Marlowe in *2 Tamburlaine the Great*, II, iv, 91 ff.

occasion of a Petrarch he gaue her, shewing her the reason why the Italian Commenters dissent so much in the exposition thereof. I do not know any reason to doubt that this title quite accurately describes the circumstance which suggested to the poet the conceit he used, and that the gift of an abundantly annotated volume of Petrarch's *Canzoniere*[5] gave him an opportunity of showing off his wit in praising his lady. Thus Shakespeare is the imitator, and a small detail in his poem strengthens this conclusion. *Prefigure* (preceded by *praise*) is a word that does not occur elsewhere in the Shakespeare canon, and it was probably suggested by Constable's *figures of thy prayse* combined with the idea of prophecy and prediction.

As GRUNDY points out, Constable's sonnet is only preserved in the Todd MS., which represents a collection completed by 1591 when the poet left England. Her suggestion that Shakespeare had seen Constable's work in manuscript seems then unavoidable at least as far as *Diana* I, iii, 4 is concerned.

But it does not follow from this that he had seen the whole of the collection represented by the Todd MS. or even that he had seen the original MS. itself. Copies were often made of single sonnets or groups of sonnets in MSS. or books and passed around, and if Shakespeare had seen I, iii, 4 in a partial copy of the MS., he may have been ignorant of the rest of the content. Full proof must therefore still be required of any further influence of Constable's MS. Such proof seems to me to be lacking in the case of the assumed connection of Constable's I, i, 3 (*Thyne eye the glasse*) with Shakespeare's XXIV, XLVI and XLVII, all of which are instances of the common 'eye-heart' conceit. We can safely agree with GRUNDY here: "This type of conceit goes back so far and is so frequently encountered in Renaissance literature that we must resist the temptation to trace any particular use of it to any particular source" (p. 62) — not least because there are no details in these sonnets that indicate a possible relationship between debtor and borrower. One doubtful case will be discussed more fully below, p. 97 ff. As regards another parallel pair, on the contrary, we do seem able to trace an influence, and the direction in which it moves, though the task is not easy. The relevant sonnets are Shakespeare's no. XXXI and the introduc-

[5] Cf. GRUNDY's comment, p. 230.

tory sonnet to *Diana*. The resemblance has been pointed out by GRUNDY (p. 62). Shakespeare's XXXI reads:

> *Thy bosome is indeared with all hearts,*
> *Which I by lacking haue supposed dead,*
> *And there raignes Loue and all Loues louing parts,*
> *And all those friends which I thought buried.*
> *How many a holy and obsequious teare*
> *Hath deare religious loue stolne from mine eye,*
> *As interest of the dead, which now appeare,*
> *But things remou'd that hidden in thee lie.*
> *Thou art the graue where buried loue doth liue,*
> *Hung with the tropheis of my louers gon,*
> *Who all their parts of me to thee did giue,*
> *That due of many, now is thine alone.*
> > *Their images I lou'd, I view in thee,*
> > *And thou (all they) hast all the all of me.*

Constable's introductory sonnet to the collection of the Todd MS. is as follows:

> *Grace full of grace though in these verses heere*
> *My loue complaynes of others then of thee*
> *Yet thee alone I lou'd and they by mee*
> *(Thow yet vnknowne) only mistaken were*
> *Like him which feeles a heate now heere now there*
> *Blames now this cause now that vntill he see*
> *The fire indeed from whence they caused bee*
> *Which fire I now doe knowe is yow my deare*
> *Thus diverse loues dispersed in my verse*
> *In thee alone for ever I vnite*
> *But follie vnto thee more to rehearse*
> *To him I flye for grace that rules aboue*
> *That by my Grace I may liue in delight*
> *Or by his grace I never more may loue.*

According to GRUNDY (p. 219), Constable's sonnet is an expression of Neo-Platonic sentiments, and SIMPSON[6] and WYNDHAM[7] held

---

[6] *An Introduction to the Philosophy of Shakespeare's Sonnets*, London, 1868, p. 34.
[7] *Sonnet* ed., p. CXVIII. Cf. ALDEN, *op. cit.*, p. 86.

that the Platonic view of love is the theme of Shakespeare's no. XXXI. In the case of the latter sonnet and other Shakespearean sonnets on similar themes, however, LEISHMAN has pointed out that we have not to do with genuinely Platonic ideas. 'Platonic' love-poetry describes the beloved as an incarnation of ideal, transcendent beauty and goodness; it is by the love for him or her that the lover is guided towards the Absolute. But in such sonnets as Shakespeare's XXXI or LIII the recipient of the verse is himself the archetype, embodying all those that were loved by the poet, all that which is beautiful. As LEISHMAN says: "The friend is represented as transcending all other objects of desire or ambition or contemplation, but never … because of the immanence within him of that which transcends him even as he himself transcends. Indeed, he is sometimes explicitly described, not as *a type* of beauty and excellence, but as *the archetype* of all other beauty and excellence" (*op. cit.*, p. 151). It is well known that sonnets on the Platonic theme of immanent ideal beauty are common enough in Petrarchistic poets. Typical examples are Guidiccioni's XXXIV:

> *La bella e pura luce che'n voi splende,*
> *quasi imagin di Dio, nel sen mi desta*
> *fermo pensier di sprezzar ciò che'n questa*
> *vita più piace a chi men vede e 'ntende;*
> *e si soavemente alluma e'ncende*
> *l'alma, cui più non è cura molesta,*
> *ch'ella corre al bel lume ardita e presta,*
> *senza cui il viver suo teme e riprende;*

and Molza's LXXXV, 12 ff.:

> *Fedele esempio, e specchio unico e puro,*
> *De l'eterna sembianza, ch'in voi splende;*
> *Certo cosa mortal non vi somiglia.*

The last line of Molza's poem is thus the exact opposite of what Shakespeare says. But if the theme as treated by Shakespeare is not Platonic, what is its origin, and how is it related to that of Constable's poem? BALDWIN regards the theme in Shakespeare as an echo of the Plotinian doctrine of the soul.[8] In the Enneads IV, ii, 1,

---

[8] *Op. cit.*, pp. 157 ff.

the soul is described as being 'all in all, and all in every part',[9] a tenet taken over by the Schoolmen and passed on to popular text-books; in fact, the saying became a current formula. BALDWIN finds it in *2 Hen. IV*, in *The Phoenix Nest*, in Drayton, and in other contemporary authors, and very likely it has coloured such a widespread love-doctrine as 'the identity or exchange of hearts.' It is also likely, as BALDWIN says (pp. 165, 168 f.), that it is echoed in such sonnets as nos. xx and liii. The former speaks of

> *A man in hew all Hews in his controwling,*
> *Which steales mens eyes and womens soules amaseth* (8—9);

the latter of the friend's beauty as present in all beautiful shapes and things, which are 'imitations' and 'shadows' of it: *And you but one, can euery shaddow lend* (l. 4), *And you in euery blessed shape we know* (l. 12). These passages show affinities with the Plotinian doctrine: just as the soul is all in all and all in every part, so is the man 'in hew' present in 'all Hews' and controlling them as the soul controls the limbs, and the friend is present in every shadow and every blessed part. This we might call the centrifugal idea: a force spreading from a centre towards the periphery.[1] BALDWIN also considers no. xxxi to deal with this theme, but overlooks an important difference. In no. xxxi the friend does not 'expand' into all other lovable beings or is 'all in every part'; on the contrary the dead friends, the buried loves, are summed up in the friend, are 'things remov'd that hidden in thee lie'.[2] Similarly in the friend's bosom reigns love, and 'all love's loving parts', and all buried friends; he is the grave where 'buried love doth live', who 'all their parts of me to thee did give', consequently: *That due of many, now is thine alone.* This is then a movement from the periphery to the centre, a centripetal movement. But such a theme has nothing to do with the Plotinian doctrine, or if it has, it is merely an incidental association.

---

[9] Plotinus' words are: ὅλη ἐν πᾶσι, καὶ ἐν ὁτῳοῦν αὐτοῦ ὅλη (BALDWIN, p. 158).

[1] Plotinus says explicitly (IV, ii, 1, 25) that the Soul is like the centre of a circle from which lines are drawn, terminating in the circumference (κέντρον ἐν κύκλῳ, ἀφ' οὗ πᾶσαι αἱ πρὸς τὴν περιφέρειαν γραμμαὶ ἐξημμέναι) and never disturbing the centre. From this, however, they all proceed.

[2] *Remov'd:* "They had but gone to take up their abode in his friend's breast" (TYLER), "moved from their former place" (TUCKER), "as having only changed their place" (SCHMIDT).

Constable's sonnet helps us to explain this particular theme in Shakespeare's XXXI. As GRUNDY points out (p. 219), the *Diana* poem particularly resembles some stanzas in Lorenzo de' Medici's *Selve d'Amore* I, 24—28. The lover is here described as finding his way to the beloved with the aid of various signs and indications of beauty, just as hounds find their way to the quarry by observing the tracks it has left on the ground. Lorenzo describes the birth of love in unequivocal Platonic terms:

> *Varie bellezze in varie cose sparte*
> *dà al mondo il fonte vivo d'ogni bene,*
> *e quel che mostran l'altre cose in parte,*
> *in lui tutto e perfetto si contiene* (27).

It is clear that similar Platonic ideas are in Constable's mind: instead of using Lorenzo's hunting image, however, he centres his sonnet on the image of the heat by which he is gradually led to the fire that causes it: *Which fire I now doe knowe is yow my deare.*[3] In the same way although in his verse he 'complains' of many, *Yet thee alone I lou'd*, and in his beloved alone unites the 'diverse loves dispersed' in his verse. Thus in these lines Constable uses the Platonic theme as an *image:* the beloved is compared to the divine to which man is led by manifestations of beauty. Ll. 12—14, however, are a direct and non-metaphorical expression of the Neo-Platonic view of love, describing as they do how through his beloved (*my Grace*) the poet is led to the life in God:

> *To him I flye for grace that rules aboue*
> *That by my Grace I may liue in delight*
> *Or by his grace I never more may loue.*

Thus Constable keeps close to the Platonic tradition, as close as Lorenzo, Guidiccioni, and Molza in the examples cited. There are fairly close resemblances of detail between Shakespeare's XXXI and the *Diana* poem: XXXI *How many a holy and obsequious teare | Hath deare religious loue stolne from mine eye, | As interest of the dead, which*

---

[3] This image is somewhat reminiscent of a passage in Rabanus Maurus, who speaks of heat as a manifestation of the [fire of the] Holy Ghost: *Calor est fervor sancti Spiritus, ut in psalmo:* 'Non est qui se abscondat a calore ejus, quod unicuique datur manifestatio Spiritus ad mensuram' (*Alleg. in sacram Scripturam*, MIGNE CXII, 879). I do not know how widespread this symbol was in Platonic or Christian literature.

now appeare, | But things remou'd that hidden in thee lie — Diana
*though in these verses heere | My loue complaynes of others then of thee
| Yet thee alone I lou'd;* XXXI ... *my louers gon, | Who all their parts
of me to thee did giue | That due of many, now is thine alone* — Diana
Thus diverse loues dispersed in my verse | In thee alone for ever I vnite;
and no two poems on similar themes resemble each other more than
Shakespeare's XXXI and the introductory *Diana* sonnet. This similarity alone points to a direct connection between the two. But the
question still remains as to the direction in which the influence has
moved. It is here that the difference between the sonnets comes in.
Shakespeare's deviates from Constable's in that the idea of the beloved as a manifestation of the ideal-divine is no longer present.
This difference indicates that XXXI is modelled on the *Diana* sonnet
and not the reverse, since the poem founded on accepted tradition
is likely to be the basis of the poem that strongly resembles it though
being at the same time untraditional. The reverse process is rather
less natural. What Shakespeare retains is Constable's conceit of
'many summed up in one'; this yields the similarities of detail.
What he discards is its Platonic setting. In this way we get a poem
on a theme that resembles both the Platonic and the Plotinian motifs
and yet is not identical with either.

If it is thus highly probable that Shakespeare owes the conceit of
no. XXXI to Constable's *Grace full of grace*, it is far less likely that
there is a direct connection between Shakespeare's CXXVIII and
Diana I, ii, 4.[4] No. CXXVIII reads:

> *How oft when thou my musike musike playst,*
> *Vpon that blessed wood whose motion sounds*
> *With thy sweet fingers when thou gently swayst,*
> *The wiry concord that mine eare confounds,*
> *Do I enuie those Iackes that nimble leape,*
> *To kisse the tender inward of thy hand,*
> *Whilst my poore lips which should that haruest reape,*
> *At the woods bouldnes by thee blushing stand.*
> *To be so tikled they would change their state,*

---

[4] The comparison seems first to have been made by SARRAZIN in 1897 (*William Shakespeares Lehrjahre*, p. 153).

And situation with those dancing chips,
Ore whome their fingers walke with gentle gate,
Making dead wood more blest then liuing lips,
Since saucie Iackes so happy are in this,
Giue them their fingers, me thy lips to kisse.

In *Diana* I, ii, 4 (only found in the Todd MS.) we read:

Not that thy hand is soft is sweete is white
Thy lipps sweete roses, breast sweet lilye is
That loue esteemes these three the chiefest blisse
Which nature euer made for lipps delight

But when these three to shew theyre heauenly might
Such wonders doe, devotion then for this
Commandeth vs, with humble zeale to kisse
Such thinges as worke miracles in oure sight

A lute of senselesse wood by nature dumbe
Toucht by thy hand doth speake devinelye well
And from thy lips and breast sweet tunes doe come
To my dead hearte the which new life doe giue
Of greater wonders heard we neuer tell
Then for the dumbe to speake the dead to liue.

First the motifs. On the face of it they seem identical, both sonnets dealing with a charming woman playing an instrument. But fundamentally the themes are different. The conceit in Shakespeare is an instance of what may be called the 'envy-theme', of which there are innumerable examples. Ovid (*Amores* II, xv, 7 ff.) envies the ring he has just given to the lady:

Felix, a domina tractaberis, anule, nostra;
invideo donis iam miser ipse meis.

An anonymous poet in the Greek Anthology wishes he were the wind blowing around the lady's breast or a rose given by her hand to her snow-white bosom (v, 83, 84). There are several other instances in the Greek Anthology: Leontinus envies a cup touching the lady's lip (v, 295), Strato a booklet handled by a beautiful boy (XII, 208), Theophanes a white lily plucked by the beloved (xv, 35).

Scève (CCCXLVII) and Desportes (*Diane* I, li) use the same theme as Ovid; Baïf (*Am. de Meline* p. 39 f.) the same as Leontinus. Other objects envied by the poet because of their intimate contact with the lady are her chemise (Sassoferato, Tebaldeo CXII), her mirror, perfume, ribbon, etc. (Ronsard, BLANCHEMAIN II, p. 287), her glove (Melin de St. Gelais II, p. 56, Shakespeare in *RJ* II, ii, 23 ff.), her sparrow (Sidney *A. & S* LXXXIII), her lap-dog (Sasso CLXXXIV, Ronsard, BLANCH. VII, p. 156, Melin de St. Gelais I, p. 97, Sidney *A. & S.* LIX, Craig, p. 97), a letter addressed to her (Baïf p. 349), book-pages, lines and rhymes (Spenser *Amoretti* I). Belleau (I, p. 27) has a poem on the theme: *Qu'il se voudroit voir transformé en tout ce qui touche sa maistresse*, which greatly resembles Ronsard's in BLANCH. II, p. 287. Watson in *Hekatompathia* also varies this theme. The passage in *Every Man Out of His Humour* (III, ix) to which MCNEAL refers in his discussion of Shakespeare's sonnet CXXVIII,[5] says that the lover envies the viola da gamba played by the lady. This is just another instance of the motif, and there is no need to assume a direct connection with Shakespeare's sonnet. Barnes makes an enumeration in *Parthenophil* LXIII, in which he says he envies the lady's glove, her necklace, her belt, even the wine she drinks. Another type of the envy-theme, more palatable to a modern reader, is the pastoral one found for example in Gradenico (*Rime di div.* VI, 248): the poet envies the valley, the plains, the mountains, the nymphs who are often allowed to see the lady. Similar passages occur in du Bellay (II, p. 172): grass, flowers, river, woods; earlier in Trissino (*Scelta* I, 296): valley, earth, leaves, rivulet. Earlier still Poliziano said he envied a brook bathing the lady's foot (*Scelta* I, 180). Many other examples could be given. It is not surprising that as far as I know there is no parallel to Shakespeare's envying the virginal, seeing that this instrument came into wider use only well into the 16th century and chiefly in England and Germany. In any case it is clear that Shakespeare's CXXVIII belongs to the first-mentioned type of the envy-theme.

What we find in Constable's sonnet, on the contrary, is an

---

[5] Ben Jonson's editors, HERFORD & SIMPSON (IX, 1950, p. 461), point out that Marston satirized the conceit in *The Scourge of Villanie* (Sat. VIII). The passage in Ben Jonson to which MCNEAL called attention is also satirical. This, however, is hardly the case with any of the passages referred to above.

example of a different topic: 'lady's charm enhanced by her playing and singing'. This is perhaps less common than the envy-theme, but is well attested in Renaissance, particularly French, poetry. A typical instance is Marot's *D'Anne iouant de l'espinette* (vol. IV, no. CCXCIII):

> *Lors que ie voy en ordre la brunette,*
> *Ieune, en bon poinct, de la ligne des dieux,*
> *Etque sa voix, ses doigts & l'espinette*
> *Meinent vn bruyt doulx & melodieux,*
> *I'ay du plaisir, & d'aureilles & d'yeulx,*
> *Plus que les sainctz en leur gloire immortelle :*
> *Et aultant qu'eulx ie deuien glorieux,*
> *Des que ie pense estre vn peu aymé d'elle.*

Scève is similarly enraptured in no. CXCVI:

> *Tes doigtz tirantz non le doulx son des cordes,*
> *Mais des haultz cieulz l'Angelique harmonie, etc.,*

and Jamyn in XLIV is *ravi* by the sound of the lute played by his lady. Louise Labé (*Sonnets*, X) praises a friend who might induce trees and rocks to follow him while he is playing his lute, and Tyard in *Sonnets d'Amour* (p. 175) says that a lute, a spinet, or a lyre touched by his lady's hands would make the wildest creature tame and the saddest happy. One of the less common Italian instances occurs in a poem by Benedetto Guidi (Atanagi II, 154 r.):

> *Mentre Vittoria il plettro*
> *Moue, & accorda seco le parole*
> *Chiare, souaui, amorosette, & sole;*
> *I pargoletti Amori*
> *Ch'al suo bel uiso adorno*
> *Volan sempre dintorno;*
> *Prendon mill'alme, & ardon mille cori.*

One of the earliest examples of the theme is found in Propertius II, i, 9 ff.

Thus though of course Shakespeare's and Constable's sonnets both praise the lady's charms, they are examples of quite different conventional topics. What makes a connection possible is really no more than the word *kiss* and the details in ll. 12 and 9—10 respectively: *Making dead wood more blest then liuing lips* and *A lute of senselesse wood by nature dumbe | Toucht by thy hand doth speake devinelye well*. The latter contrast is of the same kind that we find in Campion, *A Booke of Ayres* VI, *When to her lute Corrina sings, | Her voice reuiues the leaden stringes*, and even in Heywood's *A Woman kilde with Kindnesse* (p. 148), where Anne's husband meditates on the lute she has left behind: *Oft hath she made this melancholly wood | (Now mute and dumbe for her disastrous chance) | Speake sweetly many a note*, etc. The 'dumb-speaking-instrument' contrast is also found in Spenser, Sidney, Drummond,[6] and others and, in fact, would seem to be conventional. — Thus Shakespeare's antithesis is wholly conditioned by the envy-theme, while the *senselesse wood ... doth speake* in Constable's sonnet occurs in a different context and is an antithesis of a different kind. The lines in both authors make the impression of being spontaneous work, and the 'dumb-dead-wood' idea may well have occurred to either independently.

Thus of the four parallel pairs discussed we may regard the influence from Constable on Shakespeare as certain in the first two cases, as highly probable in the third, but as incapable of proof in the fourth.

The 'Sonnets' and 'Parthenophil and Parthenophe'

After weighing various conceivable instances of a direct connection between Shakespeare's sonnets and Barnes's sequence of sonnets, madrigals, elegies, etc.,[7] I cannot find more than one parallel pair that may be seriously regarded as a case in point. One member of the pair is Shakespeare's no. CXIX:

> *What potions haue I drunke of Syren teares*
> *Distil'd from Lymbecks foule as hell within,*
> *Applying feares to hopes, and hopes to feares,*
> *Still loosing when I saw my selfe to win?*
> *What wretched errors hath my heart committed,*

[6] Spenser, *Verses upon the said Earles Lute* (*Fragments, Minor Poems* II, p. 269 and comm. p. 510); Sidney, *Arcadia*, lib. III (ed. FEUILLERAT II, p. 35); Drummond, II, son. VIII.
[7] Entered in the Stationer's Register in May, 1593.

Whilst it hath thought it selfe so blessed neuer?
How haue mine eies out of their Spheares bene fitted
In the distraction of this madding feuer?
O benefit of ill, now I find true
That better is by euil still made better.
And ruin'd loue when it is built anew
Growes fairer than at first, more strong, far greater.
　　So I returne rebukt to my content,
　　And gaine by ills thrice more then I haue spent.

This sonnet, as commentators point out, continues the theme of CXVIII, *potions* apparently harking back to the *drugs* of CXVIII, 14 (*Drugs poyson him that so fell sicke of you*).[8] TUCKER remarks: "The 'tears' were those of false women among his baser company. For their 'siren' influence ... cf. *A Lover's Complaint* 'What a hell of witchcraft lies / In the small orb of one particular tear'. He 'drank' them by allowing them to work upon him like a drug." Whether the tears were those of 'false women' or of the dark lady (BEECHING) we can only guess; the meaning of the vituperative phrase is clear and natural. The resemblance of this sonnet to Barnes's no. XLIX was early pointed out, as ROLLINS notes (I, p. 300), by LEE (*Life of Shakespeare*, 1st ed., 1898) in a note to the chapter on 'The Supposed Story of Intrigue in the Sonnets' (p. 152). This note was cancelled in the 14th edition of 1931 and possibly earlier. Barnes's sonnet reads:

---

[8] The whole of CXVIII reads as follows:

　　Like as to make our appetites more keene
　　With eager compounds we our pallat vrge,
　　As to preuent our malladies vnseene,
　　We sicken to shun sicknesse when we purge.
　　Euen so being full of your nere cloying sweetnesse,
　　To bitter sawces did I frame my feeding;
　　And sicke of wel-fare found a kind of meetnesse,
　　To be diseas'd ere that there was true needing.
　　Thus pollicie in loue t'anticipate
　　The ills that were not, grew to faults assured,
　　And brought to medicine a healthfull state
　　Which rancke of goodnesse would by ill be cured.
　　　　But thence I learne and find the lesson true,
　　　　Drugs poyson him that so fell sicke of you.

The last line, as POOLER points out, means: "The intercourse with 'unknown minds' left me in a worse state than when I was weary of the monotony of my happiness with you".

Coole coole in waues, thy beames intollerable
  O sunne, no sonne but most vnkinde stepfather,
  By law nor nature sier but rebell rather,
  Foole foole these labours are inextricable,
A burthen whose weight is importable,
  A Syren which within thy brest doth bath her
  A fiend which doth in graces garments grath her,
  A fortresse whose force is impregnable:
From my loues lymbeck still still'd teares, oh teares!
  Quench quench mine heate, or with your soueraintie
  Like Nyobe conuert mine hart to marble:
Or with fast-flowing pyne my body drye
  And ryd me from dispaires chyll'd feares, oh feares!
  Which on mine heben harpes hart strings do warble.

This is LEE's comment: "The fine exordium of Sonnet CXIX: 'What potions have I drunk of Siren tears, / Distill'd from limbecks foul as hell within', adopts expressions in Barnes's vituperative sonnet (No. XLIX), where, after denouncing his mistress as a 'siren', the poet incoherently ejaculates: 'From my love's limbeck [sc. have I] still [di]stilled tears'." SARRAZIN in 1906 repeated and modified LEE's suggestion: "Diese Sonettensammlung erschien 1593 im Druck. Vielleicht hat Shakespeare sie gekannt."[9] There are three dubious statements in LEE's brief note: That Shakespeare adopted Barnes's expressions, that the latter's sonnet is vituperative, and that *still still'd* means 'have I still distilled'. Barnes's poem is not of the vituperative kind à la Jodelle and others but deals with the lady's power and fascination, too great for the poet to endure. (The theme is thus similar to that of no. XXII in Drayton's *Idea* (cf. p. 75 above)). The first quatrain compares her intense radiance to that of a sun shining with unendurable heat, much as Sidney in no. LXXVI speaks of *her shining twins* burning too hot: *But loe, while I doe speake it groweth noone with me, / Her flamy glittering lights increase with time and place: / My heart cryes oh it burnes,*[1] etc. Each

---

[9] *Aus Shakespeares Meisterwerkstatt*, p. 108, n.
[1] The conceit of 'eyes=scorching suns' is found in many other passages: Barnes uses it in another sonnet in *Parthenophil* (XXII), Watson in *Hekatompathia* XLIV, Greville in *Caelica* VIII, Spenser in *The Faerie Qveene* II, ii, 7, 6, Alexander in *Aurora*, son. LXII and

line of the second quatrain in Barnes's sonnet is a variation on this theme: the insupportable burden, the (very unexpected) bathing siren, the fiend in "graces' garments", and the impregnable fortress are all powers which the poet is unable to resist. Only from his own tears can he expect relief.

Of the details in this sonnet, the combination 'siren — alembic' is particularly curious. Sirens are mentioned occasionally by the sonneteers, alembics are rare (although the theme of 'distilled tears' is not unusual in Petrarchan poetry; cf. *Phillis* xxxviii, *Fidessa* xxx, *Delia* xxi, 2, Pontoux cxxiii, etc.). There is an instance of alembics in Lodge's *Phillis* xxxvii: *The limbec is mine eye that doth distil the same;* an earlier one in Tyard (*Erreurs Amoureuses* I, xxiii): *L'eau sur ma face ... Vient à mes yeux ... Par l'alambic d'amoureuses chaleurs;* and Desportes at some length describes the process whereby tears are produced (*Diane* I, xlix):

> *Mon amour sert de feu, mon cœur sert de fourneau,*
> *Le vent de mes souspirs nourrît sa vehemence,*
> *Mon oeil sert d'alambic par où distile l'eau.*

But the combination of siren and alembic is to my knowledge unparalleled. Now the boldness and extravagance of Barnes's conceits are well known, and it has been shown (LEE ed. I, pp. lxxvi ff.) that many of them were inspired by other models: Ovid, Petrarch, Melin de St. Gelais, Desportes, Sidney. It is more than probable that 'siren+alembic' has a direct connection with Shakespeare's cxix. While the 'siren' conceit is unintegrated and highly eccentric in *Parthenophil*, it is natural and suits the context in the *Sonnets*, and — which is important — continues the *poyson* metaphor of no. cxviii. Again, the parallel in Shakespeare helps us to construe the obscure l. 9 of Barnes's poem, which can hardly be read as it was by LEE. Obviously *still'd* is a participle going with *teares* and qualified by *From my loues lymbeck* — just as in Shakespeare —, but not the main verb of an implied 'I have'. In short, there can be little doubt that Barnes used the expressions in Shakespeare's sonnet (conspicuously occurring in the first two lines) in order to enhance the effect of his own poem. In so doing he broke

Madr. 4; even Beaumont & Fletcher have recourse to it in *Philaster* (IV, iv, 74 ff). The prototype is Italian.

up what is in Shakespeare one coherent metaphor and produced two different conceits at two different points.

The 'Sonnets' and 'Fidessa'

When dealing with the relationship between Shakespeare's sonnets and those of Drayton, Constable, and Barnes, we have discussed theories that have been canvassed before. To my knowledge, however, the similarity that exists between a part of Griffin's sonnet-sequence *Fidessa* (published in 1596) and the *Sonnets*, and which is the subject of this section, has not been observed earlier. As in the case of Barnes's *Parthenophil and Parthenophe* I shall focus my discussion on one single pair of sonnets. The resemblance on this point may possibly be of some interest for the textual criticism of the Shakespearean sonnet, which is the well-known no. CXLVI:

> *Poore soule the center of my sinfull earth,*
> *[My sinfull earth] these rebbell powres that thee array,*
> *Why dost thou pine within and suffer dearth*
> *Painting thy outward walls so costlie gay?*
> *Why so large cost, hauing so short a lease,*
> *Dost thou vpon thy fading mansion spend?*
> *Shall wormes inheritors of this excesse*
> *Eate vp thy charge? Is this thy bodies end?*
> *Then soule liue thou vpon thy seruants losse,*
> *And let that pine to aggrauat thy store;*
> *Buy tearmes diuine in selling houres of drosse:*
> *Within be fed, without be rich no more,*
> > *So shalt thou feed on earth, that feeds on men,*
> > *And death once dead, ther's no more dying then.*

There is almost unanimous agreement that the first three words of l. 2 are a repetition of the last three of l. 1,[2] and conjectures have

---

[2] One of the very few attempts to defend the Q reading was made by TUCKER: "Meanwhile it must be admitted that the repetition of 'my sinful earth' may be deliberate, as emphasising 'the pity of it', and the error may be in the latter part of the line. If so, a possible reading is *My sinful earth these rebel powers array* (i.e. 'which these rebel powers array', the words *that thee* being an interpolation)." This explanation is rhetorically far-fetched, since *anadiplosis* of the type suggested does not occur in the *Sonnets*, as I have shown elsewhere (*op. cit.*, pp. 138 ff.). Moreover, TUCKER's proposal involves replacing one corruption by another.

been raining over the line ever since MALONE in 1780 proposed *Fool'd by those*.[3] The latest contributions are SISSON's *Fenced by* in 1956[4] and CLARKE's *Rob'd by* in 1958,[5] neither emendation any likelier than many others that have been suggested earlier.[6] However, before we briefly comment on this point we shall turn to the parallel sonnet in *Fidessa*, no. XXVIII:

> *Well may my soule immortall and diuine,*
>   *That is imprison'd in a lump of clay,*
> *Breath out laments, vntill this bodie pine:*
>   *That from her takes her pleasures all away.*
> *Pine then thou lothed prison of my life;*
>   *Vntoward subiect of the least aggrieuance,*
> *O let me dye: mortalitie is rife,*
>   *Death comes by wounds, by sicknes, care, & chance*
> *Oh earth, the time will come when i'le resume thee,*
>   *And in my bosome make thy resting place:*
> *Then doe not vnto hardest sentence doome me,*
>   *Yeeld, yeeld betimes, I must and will haue grace.*
> *Richly shalt thou be intomb'd, since for thy graue,*
>   *Fidessa, faire Fidessa thou shalt haue.*

It has often been pointed out that authors of love-sonnets occasionally use the phraseology characteristic of religious verse, but in such cases we have to do with a spiritualization of the theme of love: the lady is a divine being and the object of religious devotion. The *Fidessa* sonnet does not deal with such things at all. Its subject is the common one of the poet's desire to die because of hopeless love, but the way in which this theme is expressed is anything but common. The poem may be summarized as follows: The poet yearns for the fetters of the flesh to break so that his soul may be set free at last. He will return to the earth again, and invoking it to show mercy he gets the comforting reply that Fidessa will be his tomb. In the sestet we have two instances of the 'heart-tomb'

---

[3] Cf. the critical apparatus in ROLLINS I, p. 374.

[4] *New Readings in Shakespeare* I, p. 214.

[5] *The Shakespeare Newsletter* VIII:2, p. 11.

[6] The latest writer on the passage so far (A.S. GÉRARD, *Iconic Organization in Shakespeare's Sonnet CXLVI*, English Studies XLII, 1961, pp. 157 ff.) prefers SISSON's emendation.

motif (cf. p. 25). The sense of the first instance (l. 10) is: Earth shall fill my bosom, I shall be transformed to dust.[7] The sense of the second (ll. 13—14) is: The lady will cherish your memory. The latter example is thus a more normal one and reminiscent particularly of the Magno passage quoted on p. 25 above. The quatrains form an odd introduction to these conceits. While reading ll. 1—4 we expect the poem to deal with the immortality of the soul and the transience of the body; when we have read the whole of the poem, seeing that it deals with something else, we wonder why the poet began at all in the way he did. Now Griffin was a pilferer, which is not in itself surprising; what is remarkable is the fact that he practically always chose English poets for his victims.[8] Daniel he plagiarized even more boldly than Daniel plagiarized others; for Watson and Sidney he had also a special liking. As to *Fidessa* XXVIII, I know nothing similar to it except Shakespeare's CXLVI, and we may well ask if we cannot add some details in that poem to the list of property annexed by Griffin. The author of *Fidessa, more chaste than kind*, does not otherwise show the slightest interest in the immortality and divineness of the soul — except in no. XXIX, about which more anon. His whole attention, on the contrary, is focussed on erotic themes, unmasked or in disguise,[9] and no conceit is too strange for him, no theft too bold, in his dealing with this main subject. In no. V he pictures himself 'arraigned at the bar of beauty', closely imitating Gascoigne's *The Arraignement of a Lover* (*At Beautyes barre as I dyd stande*); in XXI he expands a line in Sidney's LXIV (*Nor doe aspire to Cæsars bleeding fame*), building nearly a whole sonnet on that motif as a fitting contrast to his last line, *I must Fidessa's be, or else not be*. In XLI, taking as his starting-point Daniel's no. XIV, which as we have seen deals with the common theme of 'lady's locks are nets, her eyes shoot darts', etc., he

---

[7] In LEE's edition, the pronouns in l. 10 have changed places: *And in thy bosom make my resting-place*. There is no indication at all in LEE's text that an alteration has been made here. LEE's reading involves a normalization, not to say a trivialization, of the text: the bold use of the 'heart-tomb' motif here is by no means impossible in a poet like Griffin.

[8] For Griffin's strange conceits, his plagiarism, and his form experiments cf. PEARSON, *op. cit.*, pp. 126 ff. PEARSON agrees with LEE's verdict (ed. I, p. ciii): *Fidessa* is "but a mosaic of borrowed conceits and diction". Cf. also SCOTT's Appendix, p. 321.

[9] Cf. SIEGEL's article *The Petrarchan Sonneteers and Neo-Platonic Love*, (SP XLII, 1945, p. 173) on the erotic nature of Griffin's sonnets.

transforms the lady's face into a prison, his own thoughts into bolts, his food into *the pleasing looks of thy faire eyes*,[1] etc.

It would seem that in XXVIII, an analogous instance, he saw an opportunity to tackle the old theme of 'death delivering lover from torments' in a new and baffling way by adding elements that are not normally found. It is natural to assume that he was influenced by Shakespeare's poem: both sonnets begin by speaking of the soul confined in the body — *sinfull earth, a lump of clay;* in both the word *pine* is used in the third line, in both there is the *-ay* rhyme in ll. 2 and 4, in both there is the word *diuine* and the use of sustained apostrophe. Again, there is l. 9 in *Fidessa: Oh earth, the time will come when i'le resume thee*, a reminiscence of *Gen.* 3,19, *Donec reuertaris in terram de qua sumptus es*, but a reminiscence possibly evoked by two details in Shakespeare's CXLVI: the *earth* of l. 1 and the 'worm' theme of ll. 7 f. All these details are unexpected in a sonnet of the type found in *Fidessa*. They are, moreover, instances of the vice of language known as *bomphiologia*, defined by Puttenham as the use of words "a great deale to high and loftie for the matter" (pp. 259—60).

There are also, of course, differences between Griffin's and Shakespeare's sonnets, and I am not suggesting that Griffin copied slavishly. But there are certain resemblances which indicate that he had Shakespeare's CXLVI in mind when writing his own poem: the point is that the details that resemble each other are traditional and organic parts of the religious theme treated in the *Sonnets* CXLVI, but practically unique expressions of the theme of *Fidessa* XXVIII. There is really no reason why the *Fidessa* poet should express himself as he does in XXVIII, particularly ll. 1—4, unless influenced by Shakespeare's sonnet. If we accept this reasoning, we must assume that Griffin had seen Shakespeare's sonnets — or rather this Shakespeare sonnet — in MS.

If I am right in connecting the *Sonnets* CXLVI with *Fidessa* XXVIII, the following reconstruction of the corrupt second line of the former poem may be somewhat hesitantly suggested: ⟨*Imprison'd by*⟩ *these rebbell powres that thee array*. We should thus get a metaphor that seems fitting enough: the soul imprisoned in the body by

---

[1] These and other borrowings of Griffin's are listed by Scott, *ibid.*

'rebel powers' preventing it from getting out. Similar metaphors occur in those very works by Shakespeare that probably date from the beginning and the middle of the 1590's (*KJ* III, iv, 21, *3 Hen. VI*, II, i, 74, *Luc.* 1726, *Tit. A.* I, i, 99, III, ii, 10). If we read *imprison'd*, *array* would get the double meaning of 'dress out' and 'afflict' demanded by the context. Metrically, we should get the initial sequence ⏑⏓⏑⏑⏑⏓, amphibrach+anapest, a fairly frequent one in the *Sonnets* (cf. LXIV, 6, LXXXIX, 9, CXLII, 11, etc.); or ⏑⏓⏑⏑⏓⏓, amphibrach+bacchius (cf. XII, 13, LII, 4, CXXIV, 3). In itself the emendation I propose is no more acceptable than dozens of others,[2] but it has to be considered owing to the parallel in *Fidessa* XXVIII.

Before we leave *Fidessa* another point might be noticed. No. XXVIII is immediately followed by a sonnet on a similar theme, the poet's desire to die because of hopeless love:

> *Earth, take this earth wherin my spirits languish,*
>   *Spirits, leaue this earth that doth in griefs retaine you:*
> *Griefs, chase this earth, that it may fade with anguish,*
>   *Spirits, auoide these furies which doe paine you;*
> *Oh leaue your lothsome prison, freedome gaine you,*
>   *Your essence is diuine, great is your power:*
> *And yet you mone your wrongs & sore complaine you,*
>   *Hoping for ioye which fadeth euery howre.*
> *Oh Spirits your prison loath, & freedome gaine you!*
>   *The destinies in deepe laments haue shut you*
> *Of mortall hate, because they doe disdaine you,*
>   *And yet of ioy that they in prison put you.*
> *Earth, take this earth with thee to be inclosed:*
> *Life is to me, and I to it opposed.*

The theme of this sonnet is thus as different from Griffin's usual motifs as that of no. XXVIII. However, Shakespeare's sonnet had no direct influence on XXIX. Yet since XXVIII is probably dependent on Shakespeare's CXLVI, there is an indirect dependence of XXIX

---

[2] The weakness of the conjecture is of course that the number of syllables is still greater than normal. Yet REIMER is wrong in saying (*Der Vers in Shakespeares nicht-dramatischen Werken*, Bonn, 1908, p. 44) that the six feet in CXLVI, 2 Q are unique in the *Sonnets*: XV, 4 and XXXIII, 14 are also hypermetrical. It is, moreover, a common prejudice that an emendation is always more likely to be correct the more perfect it is from the point of view of metre.

on the same sonnet, XXIX being in the nature of a variation on the theme of XXVIII. In any case, what is in Shakespeare's sonnet a religious contrast motif of a well-known type becomes, in *Fidessa*, a far-fetched conceit like many others in the same work, intended merely to arrest the attention of *blasé* readers.

The 'Sonnets' and 'Caelica'

The name of Fulke Greville has earlier been mentioned once or twice in the discussion of Shakespeare's sonnets, but so far as I know a direct connection between these and Greville's works has not been assumed. My starting-point in establishing such a connection is Shakespeare's no. CXXXII:

> *Thine eies I loue, and they as pittying me,*
> *Knowing thy heart torment me with disdaine,*
> *Haue put on black, and louing mourners bee,*
> *Looking with pretty ruth vpon my paine.*
> *And truly not the morning Sun of Heauen*
> *Better becomes the gray cheeks of th' East,*
> *Nor that full Starre that vshers in the Eauen*
> *Doth halfe that glory to the sober West*
> *As those two morning eyes become thy face:*
> *O let it then as well beseeme thy heart*
> *To mourne for me since mourning doth thee grace,*
> *And sute thy pitty like in euery part.*
> > *Then will I sweare beauty her selfe is blacke,*
> > *And all they foule that thy complexion lacke.*

This sonnet has often been compared with *Astrophel and Stella* VII. The first to make the comparison, KRAUSS in 1881,[3] also assumed that Shakespeare was indebted to Sidney, and this idea has been repeated several times, for example by LEE[4] and BROOKE.[5] Sidney, like Shakespeare, expresses the idea that the lady's eyes are black because they mourn for desperate lovers; in the *Astrophel and Stella*

---

[3] Cf. ROLLINS I, p. 338.
[4] *Life of Shakespeare*, 1931, p. 191, n.
[5] *Shakespeare's Sonnets*, 1936, p. 333.

sonnet this explanation is given as the last one in a series of alternatives:

> *When nature made her chiefe worke, Stellas eyes,*
> *In collour blacke, why wrapt she beames so bright?*
> *Would she in beamy blacke like Painter wise,*
> *Frame daintiest lustre mixte with shaddowes light?*
>   *Or did she els that sober hewe devise,*
> *In object best, to strength and knitt our sight:*
> *Least if no vaile these brave beames did disguise,*
> *They Sun-like would more dazell than delight.*
>   *Or would she her miraculous power shewe,*
> *That whereas blacke seemes Beauties contrarie,*
> *Shee even in blacke doth make all Beauties flowe:*
> *But so and thus, she minding Love should bee*
>   *Plaste ever there, gave him this mourning weede:*
>   *To honour all their deathes, who for her bleede.*

Praise of dark eyes, though a small minority in the 'praise of eyes' group, is not hard to find. WOLFF (p. 183 f.) and SCOTT (p. 304) refer to several instances. But in none of the Ronsard, Tasso, and Marullus passages indicated by them do we find the 'mourning' conceit used by Sidney and Shakespeare. What we find are such things as Ronsard's *Qui t'a noircy les arcs de tes soucis* (BLANCH. I, p. 198) and Marullus' *Dum nunc ocello dulce subrides nigro* (*Ad Neæram* LXI), or Tasso's more enthusiastic *Occhi leggiadri e belli,* | *Nel vostro dolce nero* | *Un fanciul diventò, scherzando, arciero* (272) and *Due nere stelle c'han virtù possente* | *Di far parere un uom di selce o finto*[6] (son. 233). Examples can be multiplied. There is for instance the beginning of an anonymous sonnet in *A Poetical Rhapsody*, p. 59: *The fairest Eies, (O Eies in blacknesse faire!)*; again the curious *strambotto* by Philoxeno which begins, *Qual donna ami tu ioue in caldo zelo*;[7] again a fine sonnet by Magno (*In quell'oscuro Amor*

---

[6] Cf. also the Tasso sonnet quoted on p. 116 below.

[7] Although the mourning conceit is not to be found in this poem, the second half of it bears a certain resemblance to ll. 7—8 of Sidney's no. VII and to Tasso's sonnet no. 572 (cf. p. 116):

> *... perche inuolta in tenebroso uelo*
> *per temprar il splendor che in lei si serra*
> *se obscuro al lume suo non fosse intorno*
> *faria uincendo il sol de nocte giorno.*

nascosto assale, l. 5, Atanagi II, 118), and Horace's *Lycum nigris oculis nigroque | crine decorum* (*Carm.* I, 32, 11 f.). Sylvester (son. XXII) says that his lady's eyes, though black, can illumine the darkness of night. It is sometimes implied that dark complexion is no ideal; yet it does not prevent the lady being beautiful, the poet infatuated. Thus we read in an Asclepiades epigram in the Greek Anthology v, 210, εἰ δὲ μέλαινα, τί τοῦτο; καὶ ἄνθρακες· ἀλλ' ὅτε κείνους / θάλψωμεν, λάμπους', ὡς ῥόδεαι κάλυκες,[8] and the same idea underlies Ovid's words in *Amores* II, iv, 40: *Est etiam in fusco grata colore Venus*. In Tofte's *Laura* (III, xxxi) someone who objects to the dark complexion of the poet's mistress receives the answer, *Yet loue I her although that brown she be*. But 'mourning' conceits, to my knowledge, cannot be gleaned from any Continental poet, classical or Renaissance. If we return to Shakespeare, however, there are some passages similar to that in no. CXXXII, though there are also differences. In comments on no. CXXXII we are referred to CXXVII, where dark eyes also mourn. Yet in this poem they mourn the fact that those who are not beautiful in themselves, but only possess artificial beauty, dishonour genuine and natural fairness:

> *In the ould age blacke was not counted faire,*
> *Or if it weare it bore not beauties name :*
> *But now is blacke beauties successiue heire,*
> *And Beautie slanderd with a bastard shame,*
> *For since each hand hath put on Natures power,*
> *Fairing the foule with Arts faulse borrow'd face,*
> *Sweet beauty hath no name, no holy boure,*
> *But is prophan'd, if not liues in disgrace.*
> *Therefore my Mistresse hairs[9] are Rauen blacke,*
> *Her eyes so suted, and they mourners seeme,*
> *At such who not borne faire no beauty lack,*
> *Slandring Creation with a false esteeme.*

---

[8] "If she is dark, what does it matter? So are the coals, but when we light them, they shine like roses". The same theme recurs in two epigrams by Philodemus (v, 121, 132). Asclepiades' lines were often adapted by French and Italian poets (cf. HUTTON, *The Greek Anthology in France*, p. 609, *The Greek Anthology in Italy*, p. 455).

[9] With various editors I adopt WALKER's conjecture, supported by *Rauen*. The Q reading *eyes* is obviously due to the printer's eye straying to *eyes* in l. 10.

Yet so they mourne becomming of their woe,
That euery toung saies beauty should looke so.

Commenting on this sonnet, TUCKER pointed out that the idea of
dark eyes mourning the triumph of artificial beauty also occurs in
Love's Labour's Lost IV, iii, 255 ff., where Berowne defends the
dark beauty of his lady:

O if in blacke my Ladies browes be deckt,
It mournes, that painting and vsurping haire
Should rauish doters with a false aspect :
And therfore is she borne to make blacke faire, etc.

Thus our four 'mourning' passages fall into two groups: one consists
of Sidney's VII and Shakespeare's CXXXII (mourning for unhappy
lovers), the other of Shakespeare's CXXVII and *LLL* IV, iii, 255 ff.
(mourning for dishonoured beauty). What is the genesis of this
non-continental conceit, and what is the relationship between these
groups?

This question makes it necessary for us to discuss certain differences in the working-out of the conceit which do not coincide with
the difference of grouping to which we have just referred. How
have the eyes become mourners? Nature, says Sidney, gave Love
'plaste ever there' a mourning weed. Shakespeare in CXXVII says the
eyes are suited to hair (if WALKER's conjecture is correct) or to
brows (according to a less probable conjecture by STAUNTON),
and then compares them to mourners (*they mourners seeme*). But
in *LLL* he says that his mistress's brows are *deckt in blacke*, and in
CXXXII that the lady's eyes have 'put on' black. A conceit which is
fanciful in itself becomes even more so in the last-mentioned form.
That Nature made Stella's eyes black is expressed in an artificial but
not unexpected way, tying up with the common 'Cupid-in-eyes'
conceit; that eyes are suited to something else that is black is neither
artificial nor surprising; that brows are decked in black is both to
some extent — but that eyes 'put on' black is a striking and, as far
as I know, almost unique idea. It is high time to turn to a *Caelica*
poem which constitutes another parallel to the four passages we
have discussed, in particular to two of them. This poem is no.
LVIII:

The tree in youth proud of his leaues, and springs,
His body shadowed in his glorie layes;
For none doe flie with Art, or others wings,
But they in whom all, saue Desire, decayes;
   Againe in age, when no leaues on them grow,
   Then borrow they their greene of Misseltoe.

Where Caelica, when she was young and sweet,
Adorn'd her head with golden borrowed haire,
To hide her owne for cold; she thinkes it meet
The head should mourne, that all the rest was faire;
   And now in Age when outward things decay,
   In spite of age, she throwes that haire away.

Those golden haires she then vs'd but to tye
Poore captiu'd soules which she in triumph led,
Who not content the Sunnes faire light to eye,
Within his glory their sense dazeled:
   And now againe, her owne blacke haire puts on,
   To mourne for thoughts by her worths ouerthrowne.[1]

This poem thus deals with 'Caelica's discarding her wig' (Bullough's note on p. 258): her golden wig dazzled the sense of spell-
bound souls, and Caelica, by 'putting on' her own dark hair,
mourns for these victims. This idea may have been the original
conceit developed by Shakespeare, with a substitution of eyes for
hair. Of the three 'mourning' conceits in Shakespeare, that in no.
cxxxii is most similar to *Caelica* lviii where, however, 'put on' is
used in a less extravagant way than it is in Shakespeare's sonnet: in
Caelica the lady does in a sense substitute dark hair for golden, in
no. cxxxii there is of course no change from fair to dark. It is not
unlikely that the conceits in *LLL* and in cxxvii represent further
developments of the idea, replacing 'mourning for captive souls'

---

[1] Greville uses the mourning conceit in yet another poem in *Caelica* (lxxv, 11 ff.):
   Her haire Nature dyed browne,
   To become the morning gowne,
   Of hopes death which to her eyes,
   Offers thoughts for sacrifice.
This instance of the conceit is not relevant in a discussion of Shakespeare's sonnet.

by 'mourning for dishonoured beauty,' and abandoning the original idea of 'putting on' black (in CXXVII there may still be a trace of it — fitted into a more natural context — in l. 5: *For since each hand hath put on Natures power*). However this may be, these Shakespearean 'mourning' passages, containing as they do an unconventional conceit, do not seem to be far apart chronologically whatever their relative order.[2]

But what about the conceit in Sidney's no. VII? WARD[3] and CROLL[4] take it for granted that Greville's poems were inspired by Sidney's; SCOTT (p. 58) and Greville's editor BULLOUGH appear to follow them.[5] None of these critics, however, mentions *Astrophel and Stella* VII and *Caelica* LVIII, but these pieces were perhaps thought to be included in the list "twice as long" (as the cases in which one entire poem is prompted by another) that "could be made of lines, quatrains and stanzas in *Caelica* which have been suggested by *Astrophel and Stella*" (CROLL, p. 9). This view as to the one-sided influence of Sidney's sonnets is perhaps a somewhat mechanical one. Yet in the case of *Astrophel and Stella* VII and *Caelica* LVIII it seems well-founded enough. We can analyse the relationship of these poems more easily by turning first to the source of Sidney's poem,

---

[2] It is well known that *Love's Labour's Lost* was revised, though opinion is divided as to the year when this happened. In any case the play was revised before 1598. Discussing the relationship of Shakespeare's 'dark lady' sonnets to *LLL*, BALDWIN (*Genetics*, p. 322) for quite insufficient reasons assumed that the play is earlier than the sonnets (cf. below, p. 160). He added: "Rosaline of *Love's Labor's Lost* was at least put into final form in 1598. It follows that the black beauty of this series of sonnets is not earlier than 1598" (p. 323). But this really does not follow, whatever view we take of the relative order of play and sonnets: as there is nothing to indicate that there was no dark beauty in the original version of *LLL*, the revision tells us nothing about the date of the sonnets. It is pretty generally agreed that the revisions in *LLL* affected Berowne's long speech in IV, iii (287—362), further the last scene of the play, and various details at the beginning of acts II, III, IV, and V. But there is no reason to doubt that Berowne's retort to the King at IV, iii, 255 ff., containing the 'mourning' conceit, formed part of the original version. (Cf. the latest Arden editor, DAVID, 1951 (5th ed. 1956), pp. xx ff.). As to the date of this original version, DAVID and others argue for 1593—94 (on the basis of stylistic affinities with the early poems), while SCHRICKX (*Shakespeare's Early Contemporaries*, Antwerp, 1956, pp. 246 ff.) holds that allusions to the Harvey-Nashe quarrel point to the autumn of 1592.

[3] *The English Poets* I, London, 1914, pp. 367 ff.

[4] *The Works of Fulke Greville*, Philadelphia, 1903, pp. 8 ff.

[5] The latter, however, with modifications: ... "The tone of his poems is rarely like that of Sidney's; when he takes over images, he usually remodels them entirely to achieve a different effect", etc. (p. 39). But BULLOUGH does not go so far as to assume a mutual influence.

which, as shown by SCOTT (pp. 41 f.), is a Tasso sonnet (SOLERTI III, no. 572) entitled *Loda gli occhi de la signora Lavinia de la Rovere*:

> Spettacolo a le genti offrir Natura
> Volle in angusto spazio il paradiso,
> E nel seren di pargoletto viso
> Formò due soli ardenti oltra misura:
> Ma vide che quel lume e quell' arsura
> Senso d'umane tempre avrian conquiso;
> Onde, perché ci sia chi miri e fiso
> Vagheggi di sua man l'alta fattura,
> Di dolce negro avvolse il lume loro
> E temprò il foco, e il bello e il dolce a i rai
> Accrebbe; e come il fece, essa l'intende.
> Oh novo de' duo soli almo lavoro!
> Tanto più bel del sol, quanto egli rende
> Cieco chi'l mira e tu cerviero il fai.

Sidney thus seizes on the general idea that Nature created the lady's eyes for a special reason, and reproduces Tasso's lines on Nature's veiling their too brilliant light out of concern for humanity. The 'mourning' conceit, however, is an addition of Sidney's. Greville moves further away from the original idea; the setting of his poem is a different one, hair is substituted for eyes, but the idea of the too strong light of the sun remains, and the couplet keeps close to Sidney by reproducing the 'mourning' conceit.

Thus it would seem that *Caelica* LVIII is an intermediary link between *A. & S.* VII and the *Sonnets* CXXXII: in spite of the difference between eyes and hair, lines 3—4 of CXXXII are more similar to Greville's couplet than to Sidney's. As to the question of date, CROLL (p. 16) assumed that most *Caelica* poems between nos. XL and LXXXIV were written in the post-Sidneyan period (between 1586 and 1600), but BULLOUGH (p. 41) gives strong reasons for a date before 1586 for the first seventy-six poems. If this is correct, and if my assumption of an influence from *Caelica* LVIII on Shakespeare's CXXXII is acceptable, it would mean that Shakespeare had seen *Caelica* LVIII in manuscript since the work was not printed until 1633.

Since the 'mourning eyes' conceit in our five passages is an isolated one in the 'dark-eyes' motif group and since there are certain verbal similarities, it can hardly be doubted that these passages are mutually interdependent. It is also fairly certain that Sidney was the first to use the 'mourning eyes' conceit. *If*, however, Shakespeare's no. CXXXII, 3—4 is not, as I believe it is, influenced by the poem in *Caelica*, we can be fairly sure that at least it owes something to Sidney's no. VII. In the former case the *terminus a quo* may be put as early as 1586, in the latter it is probably 1591, the year when *Astrophel and Stella* was published. That CXXXII is independent of both *A. & S.* VII and *Caelica* LVIII, on the other hand, is highly improbable.

I have earlier suggested a possible connection between a line in *Caelica* LXIV and Shakespeare's 'Will-sonnets' (CXXXV and CXXXVI),[6] but since I do not now regard the similarities as close enough the matter will not be discussed here.

The 'Sonnets' and 'Edward III'

Our last group of parallels is one that has in part been discussed for a long time. The best known similarities between the *Sonnets* and the anonymous play *The Raigne of King Edward the Third* (registered in 1595, printed in 1596) were first pointed out as early as the late seventeen-hundreds.[7] In his Shakespeare edition of 1780, STEEVENS observed that the last line of sonnet XCIV, *Lillies that fester, smell far worse then weeds*, is also found, word for word, in *Edw. III* II, i, 451. In the edition of 1790, MALONE made the same observation in the case of the phrase *their scarlet ornaments* in CXLII, 6, which occurs in *Edw. III* II, i, 10. A further resemblance between the *Sonnets* and the play was noted by LEE in his 1907 *Sonnets* edition: in no. XXXIII, 1 f. we find *Fvll many a glorious morning haue I seene, | Flatter the mountaine tops with soueraine eie*, and *Edw. III* I, ii, 141 f. reads *Let not thy presence, like the Aprill sunne, | Flatter our earth.*[8] Since *flatter* does not elsewhere seem to be used in a similar context, a connection may reasonably be assumed between these passages.

[6] *Op. cit.*, pp. 166 f.
[7] Cf. ROLLINS I, pp. 234, 364.
[8] Cf. ROLLINS I, p. 96.

In addition, ØSTERBERG in 1929 compared l. 12 of XCIV, *The basest weed out-braues his dignity*, with *Edw. III* II, i, 164 *Who smiles vpon the basest weed that growes*.[9] ØSTERBERG also called attention to certain general resemblances between the *Sonnets* LXXVIII ff. and *Edw. III* II, i, 65—183.[1] Moreover, beyond the cited parallels there are some that have so far escaped notice, and we shall discuss them all in due order and in their proper context. Taken together, these parallels seem to point in the same direction.

There is thus an accumulation of resemblances in the first scene of the second act of the play, and an isolated one in the second scene of the first. The passage in I, ii, 141 f. is to be found in a scene that describes the Countess's attempts to persuade King Edward to stay after he had delivered her and the Castle of Roxborough from the Scots. The Countess's plea is in twenty rather turgid lines:

> *Let not thy presence, like the Aprill sunne,*
> *Flatter our earth and sodenly be done.*
> *More happie do not make our outward wall*
> *Then thou wilt grace our inner house withall.*
> *Our house, my liege, is like a Country swaine,*
> *Whose habit rude and manners blunt and playne*
> *Presageth nought, yet inly beautified*
> *With bounties, riches and faire hidden pride.*
> *For where the golden Ore doth buried lie,*
> *The ground, vndect with natures tapestrie,*
> *Seemes barrayne, sere, vnfertill, fructles, dry;*
> *And where the vpper turfe of earth doth boast*
> *His pide perfumes and party colloured cost,*
> *Delue there, and find this issue and their pride*
> *To spring from ordure and corruptions side.*
> *But, to make vp my all to long compare,*
> *These ragged walles no testimonie are,*
> *What is within; but, like a cloake, doth hide*
> *From weathers Waste the vnder garnisht pride.*
> *More gratious then my tearmes can let thee be,*
> *Intreat thy selfe to stay a while with mee.*

---

[9] ROLLINS I, p. 235. *Edward III* is here quoted according to BROOKE's edition in *The Shakespeare Apocrypha*, Oxford, 1918, pp. 69 ff.

[1] *The 'Countess Scenes' of 'Edward III'*, SJ LXV, 1929, pp. 73 f. Cf. below, p. 131.

What is remarkable about this speech is that the whole imagery, except for that of the first two lines, turns on the contrast between a rugged and unpretentious exterior and a precious interior or between splendour without and corruption within. Ll. 141—42 fall wholly outside of this homogeneous series of metaphors. The Shakespearean sonnet with which LEE compared these lines is as follows:

> Fvll many a glorious morning haue I seene,
> Flatter the mountaine tops with soueraine eie,
> Kissing with golden face the meddowes greene;
> Guilding pale streames with heauenly alcumy:
> Anon permit the basest cloudes to ride,
> With ougly rack on his celestiall face,
> And from the for-lorne world his visage hide
> Stealing vnseene to west with this disgrace:
> Euen so my Sunne one early morne did shine,
> With all triumphant splendor on my brow,
> But out alack, he was but one houre mine,
> The region cloude hath mask'd him from me now.
>   Yet him for this, my loue no whit disdaineth,
>   Suns of the world may staine, when heauens sun staineth.

Thus the similarity extends further than appears from LEE's *Edw. III* quotation with a full stop after *earth*: the second half of the line, *and sodenly be done*, is paralleled in ll. 11—12 of the sonnet: *But out alack, he was but one houre mine,* | *The region cloude hath mask'd him from me now*, describing the friend withdrawing from the poet's sight or possibly "the first clouding of friendship" (POOLER). Thus in no. XXXIII the whole poem consists of one coherent sun metaphor and turns on the contrast between a fine morning and a cloudy afternoon, while that in *Edw. III* is much briefer and has no organic connection with the rest of the imagery.

This in itself is not sufficient to establish a direct relationship between the two passages, still less imitation on either part. But there is one more thing to be observed. LEE did not notice that there is another resemblance between *Edw. III* and XXXIII not farther away than 27 lines, in ll. 3—5 of Act II, scene i. These lines in their turn are near to 'the scarlet ornaments' compared by MALONE with the phrase in no. CXLII. Both these similarities are found in the speech by Lodowick in which he meditates on the signs of the king's passion for the Countess:

> I might perceiue his eye in her eye lost,
> His eare to drinke her sweet tongues vtterance,
> And changing passion, like inconstant clouds
> That racke vpon the carriage of the windes,
> Increase and die in his disturbed cheekes.
> Loe, when shee blusht, euen then did he looke pale,
> As if her cheekes by some inchaunted power
> Attracted had the cherie blood from his:
> Anone, with reuerent feare when she grew pale,
> His cheekes put on their scarlet ornaments;
> But no more like her oryentall red,
> Then Bricke to Corrall or liue things to dead.
> Why did he then thus counterfeit her lookes?
> If she did blush, twas tender modest shame,
> Being in the sacred presence of a King;
> If he did blush, twas red immodest shame,
> To vaile his eyes amisse, being a king:
> If she lookt pale, twas silly womans feare,
> To beare her selfe in presence of a king;
> If he lookt pale, it was with guiltie feare,
> To dote amisse, being a mighty king.

Let us first concentrate on the cloud image, which resembles ll. 5—7 of no. XXXIII: *Anon permit the basest cloudes to ride, | With ougly rack on his celestiall face, | And from the for-lorne world his visage hide.* If we ask which metaphor is the more suitable one in the context, the answer is not hard to find. The metaphor in the Shakespearean sonnet is of the same kind as many other sun-cloud images in the Shakespeare canon, all dealing with the transience of beauty or with the symbolic contrast between light and shadow in various contexts: *Two Gent.* I, iii, 84 ff. *O, how this spring of love resembleth | The uncertain glory of an April day, | Which now shows all the beauty of the sun, | And by and by a cloud takes all away!, Tam. of Sh.* IV, iii, 174 f. *And as the sun breaks through the darkest clouds, | So honour peereth in the meanest habit, Rich.* II I, i, 41 f. *Since the more fair and crystal is the sky, | The uglier seem the clouds that in it fly,* and *I Hen. IV*, I, ii, 196 ff., closely resembling no. XXXIII: *Yet herein will I imitate the sun, | Who doth permit the base contagious clouds | To smother up his beauty from the world*, etc.[2] In contexts like these the cloud metaphor is perfectly natural, as natural as it is in the sonnet describing the beauty of the friend hidden away for some reason from the poet. Equally natural are such uses of the cloud metaphor as are given by the NED under the heading "Anything that darkens or overshadows with gloom, trouble, affliction, suspicion; a state of gloom, etc.; also, a darkening of the countenance", illustrated by such examples as *These duskie cloudes of thy uniust dispaire* (1601), *Wrapped up in that melancholic Cloud* (1674).

But what are the clouds doing in King Edward's face? Here is the young monarch in the lady's presence, neither sad nor suspicious nor furious, just hopelessly infatuated, unable to turn away his eye, listening intently, now blushing, now pale. It is an extraordinary idea to describe such signs of passion as clouds 'increasing and dying in his disturbed cheeks', as if the king were alternately more or less dejected. I do not know any parallel to this use of the image.[3] The natural explanation is that the author of the play made use of the metaphor of XXXIII in two different places: at I, ii, 141 f., on 'the flattering sun', he condensed it into two lines and attached it loosely to his main image, that on the 'without — within' motif. It was then probably the detail of the *soueraine eie* that induced him

---

[2] Similar metaphors occur in *All's Well* V, iii, 34 f., *Rich. II*, III, iii, 65 ff., *2 Hen. VI*, II, iv, 1, *3 Hen. VI*, II, v, 2, V, iii, 4 f., *Tit. Andr.* III, i, 211 ff., *Macb.* III, iv, 111. Some of these passages are quoted by editors as parallels to no. XXXIII. BALDWIN tries to establish a chronological sequence of Shakespearean sun-cloud images (*Genetics*, pp. 233 ff.) in which also that in no. XXXIII has a part, but his statements are not convincing. Cf. further p. 158 f. below.

[3] Roses and fire are the images normally used for blushing; another common image is the red tinge of the morning or evening sky. More isolated are glowing coals (*VA*), apples, and ivory painted purple (Ovid, imitated by Davies in *Orchestra*). In *Endimion and Phoebe* Drayton describes colour coming and going as follows (536 ff.):

> So to and fro his colour came and went;
> Like to a Christall neere the fire set,
> Against the brightnes rightly opposet,
> Now doth reteyne the colour of the flame,
> And lightly moved againe, reflects the same.

Equally natural is such a use of the cloud metaphor as the following (*Peirs Gaveston*, 461 f.):

> So are his cheereful browes eclips'd with sorrowe,
> Which cloud the shine of his youths-smiling morrow.

to apply it to the king. At II, i, 3—5 he used the metaphor in a context in which it does not normally belong, but without condensing it as he did in the first passage.

And now for 'the scarlet ornaments'. This is Shakespeare's no. CXLII, where it occurs in a context different from that in *Edw. III*:

> *Loue is my sinne, and thy deare vertue hate,*
> *Hate of my sinne, grounded on sinfull louing:*
> *O but with mine, compare thou thine owne state,*
> *And thou shalt finde it merrits not reproouing,*
> *Or if it do, not from those lips of thine,*
> *That haue prophan'd their scarlet ornaments,*
> *And seald false bonds of loue as oft as mine,*
> *Robd others beds reuenues of their rents.*
> *Be it lawfull I loue thee as thou lou'st those,*
> *Whome thine eyes wooe as mine importune thee:*
> *Roote pittie in thy heart that when it growes,*
> *Thy pitty may deserue to pittied bee.*
>   *If thou doost seeke to haue what thou doost hide,*
>   *By selfe example mai'st thou be denide.*

Opinions are divided as to the appropriateness of *their scarlet ornaments* in *Edw. III* and in CXLII respectively, and even as to the meaning of the phrase. The earlier discussion is summed up in ROLLINS I, p. 364. LEE regarded it as unlikely that Shakespeare was the borrower, and PLATT said that the phrase, meaning 'scarlet wax with which the bond is sealed', is less fitting in the play ("King Edward's cheeks put on scarlet ornaments! Is comment needed?"). MACKAIL also thought that *scarlet ornaments*, used about the lady's lips in the sonnet, is compared to a wax seal, but thought that the expression in the play, "whether Shakespeare's own or another's, had clung in his mind and was here reproduced by him in a new application". ØSTERBERG believed that the metaphor, with other similarities, proved Shakespeare's authorship of *Edw. III*. ROBERTSON and BROOKE (sonnet edition 1936) regarded *scarlet ornaments* as used more naturally about blushing cheeks in *Edw. III* than of lips in CXLII. To these comments we may add that by FORT, who, like ROBERTSON and BROOKE, said that *scarlet ornaments* in *Edw. III* "denotes more appropriately blushing cheeks".[4] In his *Genetics* BALDWIN takes it for granted that Shakespeare was the borrower (p. 332). The latest writer on the passage, T. W. HERBERT in *Explicator*, 1955,[5] says that *scarlet ornaments* refers to the robe worn by various high officials in Elizabethan England, and rejects the sense of 'wax'. The second quatrain, according to HERBERT, means that the behaviour of the lips "is unbecoming to one who wears the bright tokens of authority".[6] All these three points had already been made by TUCKER in his notes to CXLII in 1924. TUCKER is not mentioned by HERBERT.

Before we continue, two things must be made clear. First, it is meaningless to argue the question whether *scarlet ornaments* is more appropriately used about lips than about cheeks or the reverse. Both uses were common; in *Diana* III, iii, 4, 9 Constable says *Youre lips in skarlet clad my iudges be*, and Sidney employs the same metaphor in *A & S* LXXIII, 11 *Those scarlet Judges, threatning blooddie paine*. (These passages thus confirm the sense suggested by TUCKER and HERBERT.) ROBERTSON, then, cannot convince us that "no man could have struck out [the lip conceit] as an original idea".[7] As for cheeks, we 'blush scarlet', and Shakespeare in *Romeo and Juliet* II, v, 70 f. says *Now comes the wanton blood up in your cheeks, | They'll be in scarlet straight at any news.* — Second, the obviously fundamental sense of *scarlet ornaments* in CXLII, 'official scarlet robe', does not exclude a second sense, 'wax', by association with the subsequent line *And seald false bonds of loue as oft as mine*. The expression is thus ambiguous, but the ambiguity is strengthened by the underlying conception of 'authority, compulsion, obligation'.

It now becomes easier to appraise *their scarlet ornaments* as used in CXLII and *Edw. III*, respectively. It is fairly obvious that the expression has its full force and meaning only in the sonnet. The red 'ornament' of the lady's lips represents "the proper recognition of a high ceremony of love" (TUCKER) as well as the sacred obligation of a bond, both desecrated and profaned by infidelity. In the play

---

[4] *A Time Scheme for Shakespeare's Sonnets*, notes to no. CXLII.

[5] *Shakespeare's Sonnet CXLII*, Expl. XIII, 38.

[6] HERBERT points out that Shakespeare elsewhere uses the "false wearing of scarlet as a profanation of the cloth", for example in *I Hen. VI*, I, iii, 56, and V, i, 54.

[7] *The Problems of the Shakespeare Sonnets*, London, 1926, p. 156.

there is no similar motivation for the metaphor, as appears clearly from the context. 'Scarlet ornaments' in *Edw. III* is a misnomer, since the ornaments are no more like *her oryentall red, | Then Bricke to Corrall or liue things to dead*. Again, and above all, what do the ornaments describe? Nothing fundamentally dignified, but simply Edward's blushing with *red immodest shame, | To vaile his eyes amisse, being a king*. Thus not only does the phrase lack a deeper significance in *Edw. III*, but is actually at variance with a pejorative context and is thus a case of *bomphiologia*. It can hardly be doubted that the phrase was borrowed from the sonnet and tacked on to the description in the play — as an ornament.

It may be added, which does not seem to have been observed before, that there seems to be yet another trace of no. CXLII, 5 ff. in the same scene. When the king has confessed his love for the Countess, she represents to him the enormousness of an act that involves breaking sacred oaths. The first two lines of her reproof read:

> But that your lippes were sacred, my Lord
> You would prophane the holie name of loue (249 f.),

and it is reasonable to believe that here the poet gleaned some of the details from the same lines that provided him with 'the scarlet ornaments':

> Or if it do, not from those lips of thine,
> That haue prophan'd their scarlet ornaments,
> And seald false bonds of loue as oft as mine.

I do not know of any third contemporary passage that could be adduced as a close parallel, and the other similarities between *Edw. III* and the *Sonnets* increase the probability that there is a direct connection on this point as well. If so, however, the poet was far more successful at II, i, 249 f. than he was at l. 10 of the same scene. This is thus a case where we can put a certain construction on a "neutral" parallel with the aid of parallels of the "original + imitation" type.

The same would seem to be the case with yet another 'neutral' resemblance between the *Sonnets* and the first scene of Act II in *Edw. III*. In ll. 143 ff. the king is displeased with Lodowick's poem on the Countess, in which the lady is compared to the moon:

> *Comparest thou her to the pale queene of night,*
> *Who, being set in darke, seemes therefore light?*
> *What is she, when the sunne lifts vp his head,*
> *But like a fading taper, dym and dead?*
> *My loue shall braue the ey of heauen at noon,*
> *And, being vnmaskt, outshine the golden sun.*

There is nothing particularly remarkable about this passage in itself. It becomes more interesting, however, if compared with Shakespeare's sonnet VII:

> *Loe in the Orient when the gracious light,*
> *Lifts vp his burning head, each vnder eye*
> *Doth homage to his new appearing sight,*
> *Seruing with lookes his sacred maiesty,*
> *And hauing climb'd the steepe vp heauenly hill,*
> *Resembling strong youth in his middle age,*
> *Yet mortall lookes adore his beauty still,*
> *Attending on his goulden pilgrimage:*
> *But when from high-most pich with wery car,*
> *Like feeble age he reeleth from the day,*
> *The eyes (fore dutious) now conuerted are*
> *From his low tract and looke an other way:*
> > *So thou, thy selfe out-going in thy noon:*
> > *Vnlok'd on diest vnlesse thou get a sonne.*

Various creatures lift their heads in Renaissance poetry, but the sun does so less often than one would expect. In *Poems* (xi, 9) Drummond of Hawthornden invokes the sun:

> *Ah, from those watrie Plaines thy golden Head*
> *Raise vp, and bring the so long lingring Morne,*

a passage for which there does not seem to be any direct source; and earlier Quirino used the same image about Aurora (*Rime di div.* I, 187). The image is also found in isolated passages elsewhere. As to the rhyme *noon* — *sun / sonne* it must be very uncommon; at least it does not occur anywhere else in Shakespeare, nor is it found in Spenser, Sidney, Barnfield, or any of the sonneteers.[8] Thus what

---

[8] Nor can I find it in Greville, Daniel, Breton, Deloney, Chapman or in Marlowe's poems; and only twice in Drayton (*Her. Ep.* II, 105f., *Shep. Sir.* 216f.).

we have in the passages in *Edw. III* and son. VII is a combination of a not very common image and a very rare rhyme. This combination, to my knowledge, is unique and can hardly be due to chance, the less so if taken in conjunction with the other parallels between these texts. Now it could be argued that the contrast between the *fading taper* and the sun lifting his head in *Edw. III* is not rhetorically impeccable and that personification is more consistent in the sonnet. But these are no serious flaws in the passage of the play and do not in themselves indicate imitation. It is the series of other similarities between the two texts, most of which clearly showing the direction of influence (cf. further below), that would seem to clinch the matter also in the case of no. VII and *Edw. III* II, i, 143 ff. It seems difficult to avoid concluding that the playwright caught up the image in VII, 2 as well as the couplet rhyme (which in *Edw. III* is similarly used at the end of the passage), and that *out-going* and *Vnlok'd* suggested to him *outshine* and the (somewhat unexpected) *vnmaskt*, respectively. Both these words, like those in Shakespeare's poem, occur towards the end of the passage.

If thus the parallel above may be called 'neutral', the same is hardly true of another parallel, hitherto unobserved, which remains to be discussed before we arrive at the 'lilies that fester'. After Lodowick's monologue in the same act and scene, the king approaches and begins to praise the Countess (ll. 25—48). This is part of his praise:

> *Wisedome is foolishnes but in her tongue,*
> *Beauty a slander but in her faire face,*
> *There is no summer but in her cheerefull lookes,*
> *Nor frosty winter but in her disdayne* (40 ff.).

L. 41 is remarkable: if only *her* tongue is wise and others', though said to be so too, are foolish on comparison, if there is no summer but in *her* looks and no winter but in *her* disdain, we should expect that there is no beauty but in *her* face. But the text yields something else. 'Beauty a slander but in her fair face' is something entirely out of the ordinary in this hyperbolical series of antitheses. 'Slander' here can only mean 'disgrace'.[9] But to say, even in very strong praise

---

[9] *Slander* in its modern sense is logically out of the question here: either we say, "so-and-so is so ugly that talk of ugliness in others is mere slander", or "so-and-so is

of someone's beauty, that beauty in others is a disgrace is odd in a
text of this period and, in fact, of any period. According to current
rhetorical rules, the context merely demands a contrast between
beauty in the eulogized person and plainness or ugliness in other
alleged beauties — a common simile compares the beloved to the
sun whose radiance obscures the light of stars and planets. The
hyperbolical contrast between beauty and disgrace is not only too
violent rhetorically but really beside the mark. Now a natural use of
slander='disgrace' in contrasts is found in such common phrases as
'to be a slander to honour, truth, chivalry, purity, courage, beauty,'
and the like. In a Shakespearean sonnet which we have already
discussed we find this very kind of contrast. I quote again the beginning of no. CXXVII:

> In the ould age blacke was not counted faire,
> Or if it weare it bore not beauties name:
> But now is blacke beauties successiue heire,
> And Beautie slanderd with a bastard shame,
> For since each hand hath put on Natures power,
> Fairing the foule with Arts faulse borrow'd face,
> Sweet beauty hath no name no holy boure,
> But is prophan'd, if not liues in disgrace.

This context bears a certain similarity to that in l. 41 of the play in
that both passages deal with the contrast between real and specious
beauty, and certain details resemble one another closely. But in
the sonnet passage beauty is really disgraced, 'slandered'; in *Edw. III*
the opposition *beauty — slander* is unnatural. The easiest way to
account for it is to assume that the author of the play culled the
word *slander* with other details from the first two quatrains of Shakespeare's sonnet to provide an antithesis corresponding with those of
ll. 40, 42, and 43. The idea of a contrast between 'foul' and 'fair'
in the sonnet seems to have appealed to him, but when he took over
slander he went too far and overdid his job. It is very unlikely that
beauty a slander would have occurred to him but for the lines in the
sonnet. The playwright may also possibly have had in mind another

so beautiful that praise of beauty in others is mere nonsense". To my knowledge, furthermore, *slander* in the sense 'somebody or something as an object of slander' is not
recorded.

passage in a Shakespeare sonnet combining 'beauty' and 'slander'
(in its modern sense) in a natural way, namely, no. LXX, ll. 1—6:

> *That thou art blam'd shall not be thy defect,*
> *For slanders marke was euer yet the faire,*
> *The ornament of beauty is suspect,*
> *A Crow that flies in heauens sweetest ayre.*
> *So thou be good, slander doth but approue,*
> *Their worth the greater beeing woo'd of time,* etc.

But if the author of *Edw. III* knew both sonnets, it is likely that he
was influenced more by CXXVII than by LXX. I do not know any
other relevant parallels to these 'beauty-slander' passages.

The most debated resemblance between *Edw. III* and a Shakespeare sonnet is doubtless that between II, i, 451 and no. XCIV —
the 'lilies that fester' parallel. The phrase in the play forms part of a
speech in which the Countess's father, Warwick, commends his
daughter's decision to withstand the king's temptations, stressing
the gravity of a sin committed where high rank demands a corresponding moral standard:

> *A spatious field of reasons could I vrge*
> *Betweene his glorie, daughter, and thy shame:*
> *That poyson shewes worst in a golden cup;*
> *Darke night seemes darker by the lightning flash;*
> *Lillies that fester smel far worse then weeds;*
> *And euery glory that inclynes to sin,*
> *The shame is treble by the opposite* (447 ff.).

Sonnet XCIV, of which the much-debated line forms the end, is one
of the most well-known in the sequence:

> *They that haue powre to hurt, and will doe none,*
> *That doe not do the thing, they most do showe,*
> *Who mouing others, are themselues as stone,*
> *Vnmooued, could, and to temptation slow:*
> *They rightly do inherrit heauens graces,*
> *And husband natures ritches from expence,*
> *They are the Lords and owners of their faces,*
> *Others, but stewards of their excellence:*

The sommers flowre is to the sommer sweet,
Though to it selfe, it onely liue and die,
But if that flowre with base infection meete,
The basest weed out-braues his dignity :
 For sweetest things turne sowrest by their deedes,
 Lillies that fester, smell far worse then weeds.

As appears from ALDEN's and ROLLINS's[1] summing-up of earlier critical opinion, DOWDEN, SMITH, ROBERTSON, and GRAY believed that Shakespeare borrowed from the play, while DELIUS, SARRAZIN, ISAAC, LEE (1898), and PLATT held the opposite view. BEECHING, ALDEN, and POOLER took a neutral attitude, and LEE by 1915 thought better of it and sided with them; while CHAMBERS, ØSTERBERG, and BROOKE (sonnet ed. 1936) regarded Shakespeare as the author of the scene in the play. The second act of *Edw. III* was assigned to Greene by ROBERTSON.[2] It may be added that, among the sonnet editors, ROLFE, TYLER, WALSH, REED, TUCKER, and RIDLEY left the matter open and that BROOKE, editing the *Shakespeare Apocrypha* in 1908 (2nd edition 1918), believed the author of *Edw. III* to have been the debtor. FORT[3] said that the passage in the play was the original of the sonnet passage. Finally, BALDWIN in his usual way took it for granted that Shakespeare quoted from *Edw. III* (*Genetics*, pp. 287, 332). — The question as to whether Shakespeare wrote the Countess scenes is a special problem discussed by several critics besides CHAMBERS, ØSTERBERG, and BROOKE. We shall return to it in a moment.

First of all it is clear that the problem of the relationship between XCIV, 14 and *Edw. III* II, i, 451 cannot be discussed separately from the other resemblances between the play and the *Sonnets*. The analysis of these that has been made on the preceding pages tends to put a certain construction on the double occurrence of the 'festering

---

[1] ALDEN pp. 220 f., ROLLINS I, pp. 234 f.

[2] *An Introduction to the Study of the Shakespeare Canon*, London, 1924, pp. 343 ff., 352 ff., repeated in *The Problems of the Shakespeare Sonnets*, pp. 156 f. ROBERTSON's attribution is no better substantiated than his attribution of various plays to Peele, which was rightly criticized by SAMPLEY ("*Verbal Tests*" *for Peele's Plays*, SP XXX, 1933, pp. 473 ff.). GOLDING (*The Authorship of 'Edward III'*, NQ CLIV, 1928, pp. 313 ff.) ascribed the play to Robert Wilson and CRUNDELL (*Drayton and 'Edward III'*, NQ CLXXVI, 1939, pp. 258 ff.) to Drayton, both on quite insufficient grounds.

[3] *A Time Scheme*, note to no. XCIV.

lilies'. Nevertheless, let us for the moment leave these other similarities out of account. As earlier critics have pointed out, it cannot
be denied that the metaphor in l. 14 of the sonnet winds up and
summarizes, in an epigrammatic way, the more extended flower
imagery of ll. 9—13. In other words, the last line does not depart
from the main idea of the poem: the best and purest, if sullied, become more wretched than the basest thing. In the play there is a
difference of technique, just as there is in the case of 'the flattering
sun': the festering lilies in *Edw. III* is a metaphor inserted into a
succession of other metaphors and has no connection with them.
The idea is also different. What Warwick gives is a *field of reasons ...
Betweene his glorie, daughter, and thy shame*: the Countess's sin would
appear the more loathsome if committed with a person of so high a
rank as the king. *Lillies that fester smel far worse then weeds* is no
adequate expression of this idea. This point was made very clearly
by PLATT fifty years ago: "Here" (in *Edw. III*) "the lily and the
weeds are not led up to as they are in the sonnet. Not only that,
but the simile is irrelevant. If the Countess of Salisbury stoops to
sin with a king, the high position of the king will but make the sin
the fouler. Poison is worse in a gold cup than in earthenware, the
lightning but makes the night look blacker. If lilies are to be
dragged in after this they should be so to the effect that a lily in
the hand of ugliness only shews up the ugliness more plainly. But
what is the festering of the lily or the contrast of lily and weed
doing in this context? Set the two passages before any unprejudiced
person and ask him which is the original."[4] With this I entirely
agree. I also agree with BROOKE's early note on the passage in
Edw. III: "The only safe inference from the coincidence seems to
be that the author of our play had seen the sonnets in MS."[5] For
my part, in the course of my study of the parallel passages in *Edward III* and the *Sonnets*, I have come to visualize the playwright as
having at his elbow a MS. copy of Shakespeare's sonnets, or of
some of them, dipping occasionally into the slender volume to
appropriate an image or a phrase. If so, he had access to the poems
only while composing the last part of I, ii and the first scene of

---

[4] *'Edward III' and Shakespeare's Sonnets*, MLR VI, 1911, pp. 511 ff.
[5] *The Shakespeare Apocrypha*, p. 423.

Act II. As appears from our analysis, he was in most cases rather unsuccessful as a borrower.

Our discussion thus tends to show that the parallels between *Edw. III* and the *Sonnets* are due to the dramatist's imitating Shakespeare. But several critics have assigned the play to Shakespeare or at least suggested that he had a hand in it. Particularly the scenes in which most parallels with the *Sonnets* occur, the Countess scenes, have interested these critics. What justification is there for this opinion? If acceptable, can it be reconciled with the view that the author of *Edw. III* imitated Shakespeare's sonnets?

In the discussion as to whether Shakespeare had a hand in the play or not, most participants, pro and contra, have contented themselves with brief and general statements or with insufficient analysis. Thus ØSTERBERG, to whom we have referred several times, dismissed the matter in two pages, satisfied that phrases and ideas in *Edw. III* could also be found in the *Sonnets* and other Shakespearean works, but without analysing technique and context and without asking himself how common similar details are in other contemporary plays and poems. Entirely subjective judgment was the basis for SWINBURNE's opinion that "Shakespeare had not a finger in the concoction of *King Edward III*. He was the author of *King Henry V*."[6] FLEAY presented the result of vocabulary and metrical tests to support a contrary opinion,[7] but these were shown to be unsatisfactory by SMITH[8] who, however, based his denial of Shakespeare's authorship on equally inadequate grounds (the play "is by no means up to Shakspere's level"; there is the lack of external evidence and the fact that the play was not considered Shakespeare's until the eighteenth century; in his authentic plays, Shakespeare did not use Froissart as a source, therefore he had no hand at all in the play, etc.).

If these and other similar arguments call for little attention there are others, presented later, which do: those of HART[9] and MUIR.[1] The former made various vocabulary tests intended to show the relative frequency of words in some of Shakespeare's plays, in

---

[6] *A Study of Shakespeare*, 5th impr., London, 1909, p. 274.
[7] *A Shakspere Manual*, London, 1876, pp. 303 ff.
[8] *Edward III*, JEGP x, 1911, pp. 90 ff.
[9] *Shakespeare and the Homilies*, Melbourne, 1934, pp. 219 ff.
[1] *A Reconsideration of Edward III*, SS vi, 1953, pp. 39 ff.

Marlowe, in various other non-Shakespearean plays, and in *Edw. III*. He also examined the use of certain prefixes and suffixes, of compound words, and of compound participial adjectives in plays by Shakespeare, Marlowe, Greene, Peele, and in *Edw. III*. On the basis of these tests he concluded that Shakespeare was the author of *Edw. III*: "The other possibility is to accept the facts, confess our ignorance, and permit the play to remain authorless" (p. 241). As MUIR remarks, the word tests do not seem to prove much since the figures arrived at do not show a marked enough difference between the Shakespearean plays and *Edw. III* on the one hand and Marlowe's plays on the other. More significant differences appear from the examination of prefixes and suffixes — details, incidentally, that easily escape attention and therefore do not lend themselves to imitation. Also HART's analysis of the use of compound participial adjectives is of importance: his figures, modified by MUIR so as to show the use per 1000 lines of different kinds of adjectival compounds, show a correspondence between Shakespeare's usage and that in *Edw. III*, and marked differences between this use and that found in Marlowe, Greene, and Peele. To HART's tests MUIR adds that of the occurrence of words not before used in the Shakespearean plays, and the result shows differences between the scenes that have been suspected as Shakespeare's and the remainder of the play. The figures for the former scenes "are not incompatible with Shakespeare's authorship, assuming the play was written 1594—96".

The main part of MUIR's article deals with the imagery in *Edw. III* and in comparable Shakespearean plays. It is pointed out that iterative images in the *Edw. III* scenes assigned to Shakespeare are strongly suggestive of Shakespeare's authentic work, that the same to some extent holds for clusters of images of the type analysed by ARMSTRONG in Shakespeare's plays and poems,[2] and that certain images are linked together by puns — a favourite device with Shakespeare. MUIR finally calls attention to a series of parallels between *Edw. III* and *Measure for Measure*: the passages in the latter play are throughout more poetical and more dramatically effective than those in *Edw. III*. MUIR comments on this: "Certainly Shakespeare, having written the *Measure for Measure* passage,

---

[2] *Shakespeare's Imagination*, London, 1946.

would not later produce the inferior version of *Edward III*; but if, as is generally agreed, the passage in *Edward III* was written first, it would be in accordance with Shakespeare's usual custom for him to refine on a passage he had written earlier. Hundreds of examples could be given of similar recurrences in plays whose authenticity no one disputes; and in nearly every case the second version is more pregnant and impressive than the first" (pp. 46 f.). MUIR's conclusion is that Shakespeare "was hastily revising a play by another dramatist, certain scenes being entirely rewritten and the remainder being left with comparatively few alterations" (p. 47). This conclusion has been accepted by RIBNER in his work on the Elizabethan history play.[3]

The use of the tests described above is open to some criticism, the most conspicuous weakness being the fairly limited comparative material.[4] Yet it is not so easy to explain away the cumulative force of the evidence: it is in fact quite possible that if Shakespeare had a finger in the main part of *Edw. III*, he had at least a hand in the Countess scenes. But how does this fit in with our assumption that the author of *Edw. III* imitated some of Shakespeare's sonnets? If HART and MUIR are right, there seems to be one possible conclusion: *Edw. III* was originally written by some playwright imitating these poems and possibly some of the early Shakespeare plays,[5] and Shakespeare later revised it more or less thoroughly, retaining the imitations and probably other matter as well. The parallels with the *Sonnets* and those with *Measure for Measure*, respectively, would thus be traces of different stages or layers of composition, the former originating from the imitator, the latter from Shakespeare himself. In fact MUIR suggests that this was what happened, for in a note indicating various parallels between *Edw. III* and *King John*, *King Lear*, and *Hamlet*, he remarks: "Parallels with the *Sonnets* and early plays have been omitted as they might be imitations by the author of *Edward III*." It is instructive to compare the parallels

---

[3] *The English History Play in the Age of Shakespeare*, Princeton, 1957, p. 147.

[4] Furthermore, the development of Shakespeare's images and figures is a far more complicated problem than would appear from MUIR's statement (cf. pp. 173 ff. below). Yet as MUIR says there is no question of chronology here: *Measure for Measure* was probably composed in 1604 and at any rate several years later than *Edw. III*.

[5] MUIR (p. 45) refers to resemblances between the Lady Grey scene in *3 Hen. VI* and the Countess scenes.

between *Edw. III* and the *Sonnets* with those between *Edw. III* and *Measure for Measure*: in the latter set of parallels the passages in *Edw. III* may be less "pregnant and impressive" than those in *M. f. M.*,[6] but they are not logically and rhetorically objectionable like most passages in *Edw. III* that resemble those in the *Sonnets*. There is thus something to be said for the idea that the group of parallels in *Edw. III* and *M. f. M* is wholly Shakespeare's own work, while that in *Edw. III* and the *Sonnets* is only partly so. This explanation is in no way incompatible with what we know about literary imitation in the Renaissance[7] and about the habits of Elizabethan dramatists.

When was the earlier version of *Edw. III* composed? The play, as we have said, was registered in 1595 and published in 1596, but as pointed out by several critics it is announced on the title-page as having "bin sundrie times plaied about the Citie of London". There was thus a first version possibly several years earlier than 1595. BALDWIN refers to a play of Edward III performed by English comedians in Danzig as early as 1591,[8] but it is doubtful whether this is identical with the play we are discussing. At any rate, our evidence

---

[6] Among the parallels adduced by MUIR are the following:

> An euill deed, done by authoritie,
> Is sin and subbornation: Decke an Ape
> In tissue, and the beautie of the robe
> Adds but the greater scorne vnto the beast (*Edw. III*, II, i, 443 ff.),

>   Proud man,
> Drest in a little brief authority,
> Most ignorant of what he's most assured,
> His glassy essence, like an angry ape,
> Plays such fantastic tricks before high heaven
> As make the angels weep (*MfM* II, ii, 117 ff.);

> The freshest summers day doth soonest taint
> The lothed carrion that it seemes to kisse (*Edw. III*, II, i, 438 f.),

>   But it is I,
> That, lying by the violet in the sun,
> Do as the carrion does, not as the flower,
> Corrupt with virtuous season (*MfM* II, ii, 165 ff.).

The latter pair of course reminds us of the *god kissing carrion* in *Hamlet*, II, ii, 182.

[7] REESE (*op. cit.*, p. 397) describes the attitude to imitation in Shakespeare's age as follows: "Plagiarism gave no offence; indeed, the borrower was apt to plume himself on the range and quality of his appropriations and the creditor to feel himself complimented." On the whole, this description is adequate; the cited epigram on Daniel is therefore all the more interesting (cf. p. 70 above).

[8] *On the Literary Genetics of Shakspere's Plays*, Urbana, 1959, p. 233.

points to the existence of certain Shakespearean sonnets a good deal earlier than 1595. If with RIBNER we assume that *Edw. III* was written in 1592 or 1593,[9] it would follow that nos. VII, XXXIII, XCIV, CXXVII, and CXLII were then available to the playwright.

[9] *Op. cit.*, p. 146.

II. PARALLELS BETWEEN THE 'SONNETS' AND OTHER SHAKESPEAREAN WORKS

If we accept the suggestions made in the preceding chapter, the next step in our analysis is to consider more closely the datings that have emerged from the comparison of parallel passages. As we have seen, there are three questions that must be answered: a) Are there any valid objections to the datings that follow from this comparison? b) Are there sonnets so intimately connected with those already discussed that they must share the datings proposed for these? c) Is it possible to narrow down the suggested limits of dating? We shall attempt an answer to these questions, closely interwoven, by studying the relationship between the analysed sonnets and other Shakespearean works. A few extra-Shakespearean parallels will also be considered in this connection. As said before, it is not certain that all the suggested borrowings can be accepted as such, but as a working hypothesis we shall assume that they can. They will thus form the basis of the following discussion. Our starting-point, then, is the following series of sonnets: XVII, LXVI, LXVII, LXVIII, LXXXI, XCII, CXLII (suggested date before 1592), CXVIII and CXIX (suggested date before 1593), XXXVIII, LXXV, XCVI, CIV (suggested date before 1594), VII, XXXIII, XCIV, CXXVII, CXLVI (suggested date before 1595—6, possibly, in the case of the first four, before 1592—93), CXXXII (suggested date after 1586, or, in any case, 1591), XXXI, CVI (suggested date after 1591), XCVIII, XCIX (suggested date after 1592), V, XII, XIII, XVIII, XIX, LIV, CV, CXXXIX (suggested date before 1601; CXLIV: before 1599).[1] Since the most comprehensive and systematic

---

[1] I thus assume that LXVI is closely connected with LXVII and LXVIII, XCVIII with XCIX, and CXVIII with CXIX. I further choose the earliest possible dates: before 1592 (instead of 1599) for LXXXI, before 1595, possibly 1592—93 (instead of 1601), for XCIV, and before 1592 (instead of 1594) for CXLII. If RIBNER is right in dating the first version of *Edw. III* as early as 1592—93, this would fit in well with a date before 1592 for CXLII as suggested also by *Delia* XXVI A.

treatment so far of the chronology of these and other sonnets is found in BALDWIN's *On the Literary Genetics of Shakspere's Poems & Sonnets*, we shall often have reason to discuss the views set forth in this work.

Before 1592

No. XVII is the last of the procreation sonnets. As I have pointed out before, the procreation theme does not form part of the sonnet convention or, indeed, of any poetic convention, though it has a traditional background as a didactic motif. Does this then mean that the procreation sonnets deal with contemporary realities? It is only possible, not certain, that the procreation sonnets should be regarded in this way. Hence it is of little use to try and identify the 'fair youth' for dating purposes when we do not even know if these sonnets were intended for a real person. We cannot disregard the possibility that the procreation group should be looked upon as a mere literary innovation, the poet utilizing, in a sonnet cycle, a motif otherwise found in dramatic and narrative literature. Yet from whatever point of view we regard them, it is more than probable that they all hang together, are intended as a coherent series of variations on the same theme, and were therefore written at about the same time. In other words, it would seem that the remaining sixteen sonnets of the group (except for no. xv) were probably also, like no. XVII, written before 1592 or else, at least, not long after. Are there any objections to this assumption? This depends in the first place on the nature of the relationship between these sonnets and some datable works of the 1590's, in the first place Shakespeare's *Venus and Adonis* (registered in 1593).

As early as 1821, BOADEN in BOSWELL's third *Variorum* edition stated his opinion that Shakespeare's procreation sonnets — with nos. XVIII and XIX — were based on a passage in *Venus and Adonis*: the sonnets "will be found only to expand the argument" of *VA* 169—174.[2] The idea of the dependence of the sonnets on *VA* has been vindicated in great detail by BALDWIN. The gist of his argu-

---

[2] Cf. ROLLINS I, p. 6. In the following account nos. XVIII and XIX will not be included in the procreation group, their theme being immortality and praise of beauty, not the necessity of bringing forth children.

ment is to be found in his discussion of Shakespeare's no. 1 (*Genetics*, pp. 181 ff.). The relevant stanza (ll. 169 ff.) in *VA* is as follows (Venus is trying to seduce the reluctant Adonis):

> *Vpon the earths increase why shouldst thou feed,*
> *Vnlesse the earth with thy increase be fed?*
> *By law of nature thou art bound to breed,*
> *That thine may liue, when thou thy selfe art dead:*
> *And so in spite of death thou doest suruiue,*
> *In that thy likenesse still is left aliue.*

BALDWIN comments: "As we have seen, these arguments in *Venus and Adonis* are an interpretation of the source story in Ovid. It is likely, therefore, that they are the original. Besides, as Boaden indicates, the sonnets are an expansion of the argument in *Venus and Adonis*" (p. 181). The last statement remains to be proved; as for the first, on turning to BALDWIN's discussion of the sources of *VA*, we find a much more problematical state of affairs than appears from his remarks on p. 181. Before we continue, however, it is necessary to quote a line and a stanza preceding ll. 169 ff. in *VA*. In l. 96 Venus exclaims, *Tis but a kisse I begge; why art thou coy?*, an entreaty repeated and varied in ll. 115 ff.; in 157 ff. she adds:

> *Is thine owne heart to thine owne face affected?*
> *Can thy right hand ceaze loue vpon thy left?*
> *Then woo thy selfe, be of thy selfe reiected:*
> *Steale thine own freedome, and complaine on theft.*
> *Narcissus so him selfe him selfe forsooke,*
> *And died to kisse his shadow in the brooke* (157—162).

Now, discussing the sources of *VA*, BALDWIN observes: "The idea of an Adonis unwilling to kiss and procreate is from the story of Salmacis and Hermaphroditus, and of the possible reason being self-love is from the Narcissus story; but the details of the arguments used are Shakspere's own 'invention', though not in the least original. The law of Nature is probably always the primary argument on such occasions, as it is here, and 'gather ye rosebuds' had long been coupled with it" (p. 18). In other words: the arguments (i.e. the procreation theme ll. 169 ff.) which on p. 181 are "an interpretation of the source story in Ovid" are found on p. 18 to lack any support in that author.[3] Again, though it is probable enough that Salmacis-Hermaphroditus and Narcissus are the basis of details in *VA*, it is far from certain that ll. 96 and 157 ff. were derived from Ovid, not least because the drowning of Narcissus does not occur in the *Metamorphoses*.[4] Therefore, when BALDWIN quotes Shakespeare's no. 1 —

> *From fairest creatures we desire increase,*
> *That thereby beauties Rose might neuer die,*
> *But as the riper should by time decease,*
> *His tender heire might beare his memory:*
> *But thou contracted to thine owne bright eyes,*
> *Feed'st thy lights flame with selfe substantiall fewell,*
> *Making a famine where aboundance lies,*
> *Thy selfe thy foe, to thy sweet selfe too cruell:*
> *Thou that art now the worlds fresh ornament,*
> *And only herauld to the gaudy spring,*
> *Within thine owne bud buriest thy content,*
> *And tender chorle makst wast in niggarding:*
> > *Pitty the world, or else this glutton be,*
> > *To eate the worlds due, by the graue and thee —*

with the following comment: "The first quatrain of Sonnet I is thus based principally on the stanza numbered three in our quotations from *Venus and Adonis* [ll. 169—174]. The second quatrain, the Narcissus theme, is based on the first stanza [ll. 157—162]. In *Venus and Adonis* the reference is explicit and grows out of the source background, whereas in the sonnet it is implicit and derivative, even though Shakspere does echo the words of Ovid" (p. 186), it may be said that the first statement is groundless, the second highly dubious, the third and fourth consequently dubious too, and the fifth at variance with BALDWIN's own reasoning. For if anywhere in these texts, it is in the sonnet that a direct influence from

---

[3] Cf. also PRINCE, the latest editor of Shakespeare's *Poems* (London, 1960), p. xxxii.

[4] Cf. BALDWIN, *op. cit.*, pp. 19 ff. The discussion of Shakespeare's indebtedness to Ovid in *VA*, which is a complicated problem, is summed up by ROLLINS in his edition of Shakespeare's *Poems*, pp. 391 ff. The drowning of Narcissus, not in Ovid, can be found in various English authors: Lydgate, Warner, Marlowe (cf. ROLLINS, pp. 23 f.), Lodge, and Edwards (cf. BALDWIN, p. 20). Cf. also BULLOUGH, *Narrative and Dramatic Sources of Shakespeare* I, London-New York, 1957, p. 163, n. 1.

Ovid is ascertainable: BALDWIN himself notes that v. MAUNTZ in 1894 pointed out the striking correspondence between *Met.* III, 464 and 466 (*uror amore mei : flammas moveoque feroque; ... quod cupio mecum est: inopem me copia fecit*) and 1, 6 and 7 (*Feed'st thy lights flame with selfe substantiall fewell, | Making a famine where aboundance lies*), whether Shakespeare's rendering derives directly from Ovid or indirectly through Golding.[5]

In short: the assumption of a relationship 'Ovid > *VA* > sonnet 1' is a baseless construction. The only thing that can be said for certain is that *VA* 157—162 and 169—174 contain the same themes as does no. 1, but the suggested evidence is insufficient as a basis for chronological conclusions.[6]

As regards the remaining procreation sonnets, many of BALDWIN's conclusions are equally doubtful, based as they are on his views of the genesis of no. 1. It is doubtful, for reasons already given, whether the *VA* line *Narcissus so him selfe him selfe forsooke* (161) "rings through" sonnets such as IV, X, XIII, and XIV; it is doubtful whether ll. 163 ff. in *VA* —

> *Torches are made to light, iewels to weare,*
> *Dainties to tast, fresh beautie for the vse,*
> *Herbes for their smell, and sappie plants to beare.*
> *Things growing to them selues, are growths abuse,*
>   *Seeds spring from seeds, & beauty breedeth beauty,*
>   *Thou wast begot, to get it is thy duty* —

along with two later *VA* lines (*Foule cankring rust, the hidden treasure frets, | But gold that's put to vse more gold begets,* 767—68) "have been developed" into no. II, dealing with the theme of 'miser versus money-lender' (p. 192 f.). It is doubtful whether no. XI ('beauty dies unless perpetuated') was "suggested" in *VA* 173 f. (*And so in spite of death thou doest suruiue, | In that thy likenesse still is left aliue*) (p. 205). There is no sufficient evidence for these statements, any more than there is for the conclusion that the 'decayed

---

[5] The text in Golding reads (ll. 584, 587):
> *I am inamored of my selfe, I doe both set on fire ...*
> *The thing I seeke is in my selfe, my plentie makes me poore.*

[6] BULLOUGH (*op. cit.*, pp. 161 ff.) gives no hint that it is a problem to what extent Ovid influenced *VA* directly. As regards his views on the order of *VA* and the sonnets, he observes that the two works were probably written at about the same time (p. 164).

house' images of nos. x and xiii "assume" a more developed figure in *Two G. V*, iv, 7 ff. and are thus later than that play (p. 204). It is equally doubtful whether no. xii "reworks a passage" from *VA* and that "both reflect a parent passage in Ovid" (p. 206). On these two last-mentioned points the weaknesses of BALDWIN's reasoning are as apparent as they are in the case of no. 1. The lines in *VA* read:

> *Make vse of time, let not aduantage slip,*
> *Beautie within it selfe should not be wasted,*
>   *Faire flowers that are not gathred in their prime,*
>   *Rot, and consume them selues in litle time* (129—132).

BALDWIN observes: "Wyndham compares the last two lines with two from Ovid, *Ars Amatoria* II, 115—116. But the first two lines also find their parallel in the two preceding lines of Ovid. This same passage in Ovid lies behind the very beautiful lines three and four of Sonnet xii (*When I behold the violet past prime, | And sable curls all siluer'd ore with white*). Ovid had warned his young lover against Time, as Venus warns Adonis and as Shakspere warns his lovely boy.

> *Forma bonum fragile est, quantumque accedit ad annos*
>   *Fit minor, et spatio carpitur ipsa suo.*
> *Nec violae semper nec hiantia lilia florent,*
>   *Et riget amissa spina relicta rosa.*
> *Et tibi iam venient cani, formose, capilli;*
>   *Iam venient rugae, quae tibi corpus arent.*
> *Iam molire animum, qui duret, et adstrue formae:*
>   *Solus ad extremos permanet ille rogos* (II, 113—120).

... In the two lines from Sonnet xii above, beautiful though they be, one does not directly see any connection between violets and silvered hair, nor does he see any particular appropriateness in the violet at all. But on the background of Ovid's passage, the thought becomes clear. We need Ovid's thought concerning the violet and his connection of it with gray hair in order to get Shakspere's application of the thought, in which he associates the violet and gray hair. It was Ovid who established that association in his mind. And Shakspere knew the passage in Ovid before he wrote this corresponding passage in *Venus and Adonis*" (pp. 206 f.).

Extensive as is this passage from BALDWIN, it has been necessary to quote it in its entirety. First of all, it is well known that the theme of "transitoriness — withering flowers" is a commonplace. Yet it is probably true that the connection between violets and gray hair links up Ovid's passage with Shakespeare's sonnet passage. What conclusions can we draw from this? We can infer that Shakespeare probably draws on Ovid in no. XII but not necessarily in *VA* 129 ff. since this passage is a commonplace which does not connect flowers with hair and does not mention violets. Nor is there anything to indicate that Shakespeare has "reworked" the passage from *VA*. Thus BALDWIN's suggested chronology is again found to lack foundation in facts. In other words, there seems to be nothing that compels us to assume that *VA* precedes the procreation sonnets.

Comparison with Ovid, then, does not help us to determine the relationship between *VA* and the *Sonnets*. ROBERTSON made a different attempt to solve the problem,[7] suggesting that the procreation theme in *VA* is out of key with the context: "What primary plausibility, it may be asked, even on the most liberal conception of poetic license, is there in representing the enamoured Venus as wooing Adonis with an argument to the effect that he ought to have a child? Is it the kind of appeal that would seem likely to suggest itself in any episode of *seduction*, on either side?" ROBERTSON's own suggestion is that the sonnets, previously written and urging marriage on the young Southampton, might have supplied Shakespeare with "some items of poetic conversation in a discursive poem, written for the market in a time of closed theatres, on the subject of the realistic amour of a Renaissance Venus for a new Adonis ... Anything that served for some not too irrelevant stanzas was grist for the mill"[8] (p. 127). Quite apart from the uncertainty as to the identity of the 'fair friend' — if he has an identity — ROBERTSON's objections to the appropriateness of the procreation theme in *VA* are anachronistic. It is true, as said before, that the theme is mostly found in didactic contexts in Renaissance literature:

---

[7] *The Problems of the Shakespeare Sonnets*, p. 126.

[8] In his note on l. 168 in *VA* (*Thou wast begot, to get it is thy duty*), PRINCE also seems to think that *VA* is later than the sonnets: "This and the following lines repeat the theme of the first seventeen Sonnets." However, no motivation is given.

some mentor, fictitious or not, advises a young man or a young woman to obey the laws of nature by marrying and bringing forth children (Barnfield, Chapman, Sidney, Vaenius, Tasso, Guarini).[9] But does not Leander use 'procreation' arguments when wooing Hero (*H & L*, I, 234 ff., 262 ff.),[1] does not Disteo try to persuade Dardanea in the same way in Perez's *Diana* (Bk. VIII),[2] and does not King John in Drayton's *Legend of Matilda* resort to similar arguments when trying to seduce the girl:

> *Hoord not thy Beautie, when thou hast such store :*
> *Wer't not great pittie it should thus lye dead,*
> *Which by thy lending might be made much more?* (232 ff).

It is thus impossible to argue that the theme is used in a natural way in the *Sonnets* but employed a second time in a less suitable context in *VA*. If we are to get some idea of the probable chronological relationship between *VA* and the procreation sonnets, we must proceed along different lines. It is necessary to examine the relation of the two works to their literary background.

As is well known, there are various interesting parallels between the procreation sonnets and some *Venus and Adonis* stanzas on the

---

[9] We also find the advice given in more general terms, forming part of didactic disquisitions (Plato, Erasmus, Palingenius). A Capello love-sonnet indicated by WOLFF (*op. cit.*, p. 172) as an instance of the procreation theme hardly belongs here, dealing merely as it does with the *carpe diem* motif.

[1]
> *Then treasure is abus'd,*
> *When misers keep it : being put to loan,*
> *In time it will return us two for one* (234 ff.);

> *Base bullion for the stamp's sake we allow :*
> *Even so for men's impression do we you* (265 f.).

In Musaeus' poem, Leander tries to persuade Hero in a similar way; his arguments are less blunt than those in Marlowe's 265 f.:

> Παρθένον οὐκ ἐπέοικεν ὑποδρήσσειν Κυθερείῃ,
> παρθενικαῖς οὐ Κύπρις ἰαίνεται. ἢν δ'ἐθελήσῃς
> θεσμὰ θεῆς ἐρόεντα καὶ ὄργια κεδνὰ δαῆναι,
> ἔστι γάμος καὶ λέκτρα (143 ff.)

('It is not fit for a maiden to serve the goddess of love: Kypris does not rejoice in maidenhood. If you want to know the sweet laws and the cherished rites of your goddess, they are wedding and marriage-bed.' Λέκτρον is also used metonymically for 'child'). — The editor of Edwards's *Cephalus and Procris*, W. E. BUCKLEY (Roxburghe Club, 1882), adduced Marlowe's *treasure is abus'd* etc. as a parallel to the lovesick Aurora's words to Cephalus: ... *Is it not heartie gaine, | Vpon aduantage to take double fee? | Thou shalt haue double, treble, pleaseth thee* (p. 16). But this only means: "Love me, and you shall be amply rewarded." Procreation ideas are hardly in Aurora's mind.

[2] Burgos edition, 1564, fol. 219 v.

one hand and Palingenius' *Zodiake*, Sidney's *Arcadia*, Wilson's *Arte of Rhetorique*, and Marlowe's *Hero and Leander* on the other. HANKINS has demonstrated that in *VA* and sonnets I—XVII Shakespeare draws fairly amply on the *Zodiake* as translated by Googe.[3] In *VA* 168, *to get it is thy duty* seems to echo 289 a of the older work, which speaks of *duty ... Encrease to get*; again in the next stanza of *VA* (ll. 169—174), *By law of nature thou art bound to breed* is reminiscent of the *Zodiake* 288 a: *Natures hest, | Which would the bred should breede agayne*. *VA* 171—173, 'offspring challenging death', deals with the same theme as a subsequent passage in the *Zodiake*, 289 g. In the same way the *fruitlesse chastitie, the Loue-lacking vestals, and selfe-louing Nuns*, and the *barraine dearth of daughters* of *VA* 751 ff. are no doubt derived from the *Zodiake* 288 f., *Let them more chaste than Sibyls be, or Nunnes of Vestal weede*, and from the continuation in 288 g, *the barreine bows that fruteless fade*. *VA* 211 *Fie, liuelesse picture, cold and senceless stone* resembles 294 k *More deafe, than pictures which be made of Parus Marble stone*. Thus coherent paragraphs and groups of passages in the *Zodiake* have apparently coloured various stanzas in *VA*.[4]

HANKINS points out similar parallels between the *Zodiake* and the procreation sonnets.[5] No. I, l. I, *From fairest creatures we desire increase* seems to echo the *fayre encrease* of 288 d, while the continuation, on the father's survival in children, is reminiscent of the *Zodiake* 289, including the *Boy of small and tender yeares* (289 d) corresponding to the *tender heire* of I, 4. In no. III several *Zodiake* images coalesce. *Looke in thy glasse* seems to echo 297 f, *Thou shalt thy glasse perceiue*, the context being identical: the looking in the glass is a signal for the unloving youth not to die childless. Again in the same sonnet the wrinkles, the face passed on to children, and the surviving image recall various passages in the *Zodiake* 288 and 289. No. IV echoes other phrases in Palingenius' work, l. 11, *when nature calls thee to be gone*, combining 289 f, *the day wherein thou must be gone*, and Nature's speech in 264 h, *when the houre last shal come wherin I byd you go*. The 'decaying house' image in Shakespeare's nos. X and XIII has a background in the *Zodiake* 243 a, *The highest houses often fall and*

---

[3] *Shakespeare's Derived Imagery*, Lawrence, 1953, ch. 18.
[4] *Op. cit.*, pp. 234 ff., 239 f.
[5] *Op. cit.*, pp. 246 ff.

come to meere decay; and *When I perceiue that men as plants increase* (XV, 5) recalls *And all the body doth increase, as plants,* etc. Many more parallels of the same type are adduced by HANKINS.

Before this, MASSEY had demonstrated that in *Arcadia* III, V, containing Cecropia's advice to Philoclea, there is a string of passages, closely following one another, to which there are striking correspondences in some successive procreation sonnets.[6] Thus in the relevant paragraphs in *Arcadia* we find parallels to the 'liquid prisoner pent in walls of glass' in no. V,[7] to the happy bestower of no. VI, to the harmony of strings of no. VIII, to 'you must live, drawn by your own sweet skill' of no XVI, and to yet other details. The *unkindnes* in rebelling against Nature's laws in the same paragraph in *Arcadia*, as HANKINS points out, may colour *VA* 203—204, on the mother dying 'unkind' unless bringing forth a child. Similarly the words on *your children ... in whom you are (as it were) eternized* resemble *VA* 172 f. *That thine may liue, when thou thy selfe art dead: | And so in spite of death thou doest suruiue.* In the first book of *Arcadia* (ch. 19) there is another passage resembling both a *VA* stanza and, to a lesser extent, one of the procreation sonnets. Geron says to Histor:

> *Thy common-wealth may rightly grieved be,*
> *Which must by this immortall be preserved,*
> *If thus thou murther thy posteritie.*
> *His very being he hath not deserved,*
> *Who for a selfe-conceipt will that forbeare,*
> *Whereby that being aye must be conserved.*[8]

In ll. 757 ff. of *VA* Venus says:

> *What is thy bodie but a swallowing graue,*
> *Seeming to burie that posteritie.*
> *Which by the rights of time thou needs must haue,*
> *If thou destroy them not in darke obscuritie?*

[6] *Shakspeare's Sonnets Never Before Interpreted,* London, 1866, pp. 36 ff.; summarized by ROLLINS II, pp. 119 f., and by BALDWIN, *Genetics,* pp. 194 ff. The section in *Arcadia* is found in FEUILLERAT's edition, 1912, pp. 379 ff.

[7] This metaphor is extremely rare outside *Arcadia* and no. V (cf. SCHAAR, *op. cit.*, p. 166). Shakespeare uses it again in *Mids. N. D.* I, i, 76.

[8] This passage is cited as a parallel to *VA* 168 ff. and *Son.* XIII, 14 by POOLER in his edition of *VA*, but the similarities referred to above are closer. Geron's speech is quoted from FEUILLERAT's edition, p. 139.

> *If so the world will hold thee in disdaine,*
> *Sith in thy pride, so faire a hope is slaine.*

Ll. 7—8 of sonnet III ask:

> *Or who is he so fond will be the tombe,*
> *Of his selfe loue to stop posterity?*

It is noteworthy that this burial motif also occurs in Disteo's letter to Dardanea in Perez's *Diana* (*ibid.*): "Is not Nature rightly annoyed when you hide away her treasure?"

> *No es justo que se enoje, si entendiesse*
> *qu'entierras su thesoro, pretendiendo*
> *ella, que su riqueza paresciesse? ...*
> *sepultas lo primero y esto entierras,* etc.[9]

To these resemblances may be added those between the *Sonnets-VA* and Erasmus' *Epistle* as translated by Wilson in his *Arte of Rhetorique*.[1] Here again we find the law of Nature, the blessing of getting children and of living in them for ever, the observation that anyone who refuses to 'encrease his posterity' is a *Parricide, or a murtherer,* etc. We also find a parallel to the 'tillage-of-husbandry' image in no. III:[2] *What punishment is he worthie to suffer, that refuseth to Plowe that land which being Tilled, yeeldeth children.* — As to the similarities between the procreation sonnets and certain lines in Leander's speech in *Hero and Leander*,[3] there are such things as the 'miser' theme *H & L* 234 f. — *Son.* IV, the 'stamp-and-impression' theme *H & L* 265 f. — *Son.* XI, and the 'ruined house' image *H & L* 239 f. — *Son.* X and XIII. It is conceivable that Marlowe derived the latter detail from the *Zodiake*, but it is hardly possible to unravel the relationship on this point in detail.

To a great extent the themes and images are thus the same in these texts on the procreation motif, and seem to be traditional

---

[9] HARRISON (*Shakespeare and Montemayor's Diana,* Texas Studies in English 6, 1926, pp. 115 f.) refers to these and other details of Disteo's letter in the English version of *Diana* and is inclined to connect them directly with the procreation sonnets by Shakespeare. But the letter in *Diana* only represents one out of many instances of the procreation theme.

[1] BALDWIN (*Genetics,* pp. 183 ff.) quotes the epistle, which was first mentioned in connection with the *Sonnets* by FRIPP in 1924 (BALDWIN, p. 183, n. 8).

[2] Pointed out by HANKINS, p. 251.

[3] These similarities have been stressed by many scholars ever since they were pointed out by ISAAC in 1884. The discussion of the point is summarized by ROLLINS in II, p. 124.

ingredients. The point is, however, that sonnets I—XVII and certain stanzas in *Venus and Adonis* are saturated with the phraseology of the procreation motif as handled above all by Palingenius-Googe and Sidney, and that traces of this phraseology are much fainter in later (and rarer) procreation passages in Shakespeare's works, such as *Romeo and Juliet* I, i, 214 ff., or *All's Well* I, i, 139 ff.[4] It seems impossible to determine in detail the mutual order of the *VA* stanzas and the sonnets on the procreation theme, and it is indeed doubtful whether there is any "order". The simplest and most natural way of explaining the striking accumulation of procreation phraseology in these poems appears to be that the author was occupied simultaneously with both works at a time when he had at his disposal the Palingenius and Sidney texts and probably also others. It is possible that these texts were included in some anthology or commonplace book in part devoted to the procreation theme. The strong dependence of sonnets I—XVII on traditional phraseology and *Topik* to some extent supports the idea that these poems are literary exercises rather than exhortations directed to a real contemporary person.

As to the date of composition, *Venus and Adonis* was registered early in 1593, and it is thus natural to assume that it was composed in 1592, the rough date we have proposed for sonnets I—XVII. Earlier discussions of the date of composition do not invalidate this suggestion.[5]

Sonnets LXVI, LXVII, and LXVIII, as we have seen, belong closely together, while the links between these sonnets and LXIII—LXV, not to speak of those between them and XIX, XXI, and CV, as suggested by

---

[4] In *RJ* the phraseology only comes out in three lines: *When she dies, with beauty dies her store … For beauty, starved with her severity, | Cuts beauty off from all posterity.* In *All's Well*, the relevant passage is more extended but the phraseology has changed as compared with that in *VA* and the *Sonnets: There's little can be said in't; 'tis against the rule of nature. To speak on the part of virginity is to accuse your mothers, which is most infallible disobedience. He that hangs himself is a virgin: virginity murders itself, and should be buried in highways out of all sanctified limit, as a desperate offendress against nature,* etc. Thus the old formulas have disintegrated and combined with other ideas and images.

[5] This earlier discussion is summed up by ROLLINS in his edition of the Shakespeare poems, pp. 384 ff. The suggested dates range from the middle 1580's down to 1593 and are largely founded on guesswork. A date around 1592 is in any case perfectly possible. It is unlikely, as REARDON and others thought (cf. ROLLINS, p. 385), that Lodge's *Scillaes Metamorphosis* (1589) was inspired by *VA*; the reverse is more probably the case. Marlowe's

STIRLING (*op. cit.*), seem pretty weak. In discussing the date of LXVI—LXVIII, we shall have to consider a parallel between LXVIII and *The Merchant of Venice*.[6] Bassanio, 'commenting on the caskets to himself', is absorbed in broodings on the deceitfulness of outward beauty:

> Looke on beautie,
> And you shall see 'tis purchast by the weight,
> Which therein workes a miracle in nature,
> Making them lightest that weare most of it:
> So are those crisped snakie golden locks
> Which makes such wanton gambols with the winde
> Vpon supposed fairenesse, often knowne
> To be the dowrie of a second head,
> The scull that bred them in the Sepulcher (III, ii, 94 ff.).

MALONE called attention to this passage in his notes to no. LXVIII, which as we remember is concerned with artificial beauty as a symptom of the depravity of the age. Ll. 5—8 of that poem read:

> (*Thus is his cheeke the map of daies out-worne ...*)
> Before the goulden tresses of the dead,
> The right of sepulchers, were shorne away,
> To liue a second life on second head,
> Ere beauties dead fleece made another gay.

It should be added that earlier on in *The Merchant of Venice* (I, i, 179 f.) Bassanio, telling Antonio about Portia, speaks of her *sunny locks* that *Hang on her temples like a golden fleece*. BALDWIN traces the relationship between *Mer. V.* and no. LXVIII as follows: "It is clear that Shakspere developed this idea in the corresponding five lines of blank verse in *Merchant of Venice* and then compressed it into a Procrustean three in Sonnet LXVIII, with a repetitive fourth line to

Hero and Leander, which has also played a part in the discussion, cannot be dated with certainty, so little can be built on the relationship of *VA* to that work alone. — In the dedication of *VA*, Shakespeare speaks of the poem as 'the first heire of my inuention', but it is quite wrong to conclude from this, as RIDLEY (*Son.* ed., p. xiv) and before him many others did, that the sonnets are later than 1593. Sonnet-writing — more or less every cultured gentleman's occupation in the late 1500's — did not count for much as compared with a mythological narrative poem.

[6] LEVER (*op cit.*, p. 210) points out a parallel between no. LXVII, 9 ff. and *Mer. V.* III, i, 48 f. There is no doubt a similarity, but one of little use in a discussion of date.

tie it in, though this line also echoes the 'golden fleece' of Portia. It will be noticed also that these three lines are compressed allusion, not direct statement. It follows that Sonnet LXVIII is later than the corresponding passage in *Merchant of Venice*" (p. 283). LEVER (pp. 210 ff.) also stresses the parallel without drawing the same conclusions as BALDWIN. But if we cannot accept the latter's premisses we cannot accept his conclusion. Shakespeare did not develop the idea in *Mer. V.* and compress it in no. LXVIII: what makes the former passage more extended is the fact that two lines describe the 'snakie golden locks'. The essential point, the origin of the wig, is rather dealt with in somewhat greater detail in LXVIII, which describes the process of obtaining false hair from dead bodies. As compared with this description ('the golden tresses of the dead, the right of sepulchres, were shorn away to live a second life on second head') the passage in *Mer. V.* is less explicit ('golden locks are often known to be the dowry of a second head, the skull that bred them in the sepulchre'). Thus it is the three lines in LXVIII that may be called direct statement, while the two in *Mer. V.* are more metaphorical and allusive. Why, finally, should *fleece* in LXVIII be an echo of Portia's *golden fleece?* The latter expression occurs in a passage totally different from that on the false hair in *Mer. V.*, and *fleece* began to come into general use towards the end of the 16th century in the sense 'mass of hair'.[7] There is thus nothing that forces us to conclude that LXVIII is later than *Mer. V.*; the reverse is equally probable, if not even more so.[8]

In the case of nos. LXXXI, XCII, and CXLII there are no parallels to be discussed in connection with the dating, except for the 'scarlet ornaments' in CXLII and *Edw. III* which we have already examined. What is relevant here is instead the subject-matter of these poems and its relation to that of other sonnets. No. LXXXI, on the poet's verse immortalizing the recipient though the poet himself may be dead and forgotten, does not seem to be intimately connected with any other particular poem or poems, and the theme is conventional.

---

[7] Shakespeare uses it again in *Titus Andronicus* (II, iii, 34).

[8] It could be added that the 'false hair from dead bodies' theme is also found elsewhere: HALLIWELL (cf. ALDEN's ed., p. 171) refers to Drayton's *Moon-Calfe* (492 ff.); and Guarini uses the theme in *Il Pastor Fido* II, vi (*malvagia | Incantatrice, che i sepolchri spoglia, | E da i fracidi teschi il crin furando | A'l suo l'intesse*, etc.).

BALDWIN suggests that LXXXI combines LV and LXXIV: "In LV the friend was to be eternized in the poet's verse. In Sonnet LXXIV, though the poet's body be the prey of worms, yet the better part of him will live in his verse, which is to remain with his friend. Then Sonnet LXXXI reverses the situation for the poet, contrasting it with that of the friend" (p. 292). But this is not enough to show that LXXXI has any connection with either LV or LXXIV, let alone that it is later than both.

As to XCII, it no doubt continues the theme of XCI and is in its turn continued by XCIII. In XCI the poet says that whatever the delight of others, it is surpassed by his own love, and he is "wretched in this alone", that the friend may take it all away. No. XCII ties up with this in the first few lines (*But doe thy worst to steale thy selfe away, | For tearme of life thou art assured mine*) and goes on to say that the poet's life depends entirely on the friend's love; however:

> But whats so blessed faire that feares no blot,
> Thou maist be falce, and yet I know it not (ll. 13—14).

This couplet is obviously alluded to at the beginning of no. XCIII:[9]

> So shall I liue, supposing thou art true,
> Like a deceiued husband, so loues face,
> May still seem loue to me, etc.

The subsequent three sonnets are not in the same way formally linked up with XCI—XCIII, but their theme is closely connected with that of these poems. The 'lilies that fester' theme of XCIV for example, as BALDWIN notes (p. 296), is reminiscent of the end of XCIII:

> How like Eaues apple doth thy beauty grow,
> If thy sweet vertue answere not thy show,

and XCV and XCVI elaborate the theme of the friend's suspected fault, the *canker in the fragrant rose*:

> How sweet and louely dost thou make the shame,
> Which like a canker in the fragrant Rose,
> Doth spot the beautie of thy budding name?
> Oh in what sweets doest thou thy sinnes inclose!

---

[9] Cf. POOLER and several other editors.

That tongue that tells the story of thy daies,
(Making lasciuious comments on thy sport)
Cannot dispraise, but in a kind of praise,
Naming thy name, blesses an ill report.
Oh what a mansion haue those vices got,
Which for their habitation chose out thee,
Where beauties vaile doth couer euery blot,
And all things turnes to faire, that eies can see!
    Take heed (deare heart) of this large priuiledge,
    The hardest knife ill vs'd doth loose his edge (xcv).

Some say thy fault is youth, some wantonesse,
Some say thy grace is youth and gentle sport,
Both grace and faults are lou'd of more and lesse :
Thou makst faults graces, that to thee resort :
As on the finger of a throned Queene,
The basest Iewell wil be well esteem'd :
So are those errors that in thee are seene,
To truths translated, and for true things deem'd.
How many Lambs might the sterne Wolfe betray,
If like a Lambe he could his lookes translate.
How many gazers mighst thou lead away,
If thou wouldst vse the strength of all thy state?
    But doe not so, I loue thee in such sort,
    As thou being mine, mine is thy good report. (xcvi).

These poems are thus connected in that they describe an identical situation, and are limited by xc ('If you must leave me, do so at once without delay') and xcvii ('How like a winter has my absence been from thee'); thus by sonnets on motifs which do not fit in with the series xci—xcvi. The couplet of xcvi is the same as that in xxxvi, but this does not link these poems together: the themes are different and it is possible, as some editors suggest, that xcvi was imperfect in the manuscript and that the couplet was filled up from an earlier sonnet. However this may be, it is not far-fetched to regard such poems as xcv and xcvi, dealing with the same situation, as composed within the same short period even if the situation described has no autobiographical background.

No. CXLII, finally, treats the same main motif as nos. CXXXV—CXLI:[1] the lady's faithlessness and depravity, the poet's desperation and hatred. Thematically these poems form such a homogeneous group that it is natural to regard them all as written within a short time even though, formally, CXLII is connected only with no. CXLI: *That she that makes me sinne, awards me paine* (CXLI, 14) — *Loue is my sinne, and thy deare vertue hate* (CXLII, 1; cf. BALDWIN, p. 331). Various rearrangements have been suggested, but to determine the exact order in which these and possibly other sonnets were composed is an impossibility. That CXLII immediately follows CXLI may in any case be considered fairly certain, and is conceded even by several rearrangers. Although the exact chronological relationship of these two sonnets to the rest of the series is not clear, it is not going too far to group them all together and assume that they were written at about the same time.

To sum up: there seems to be no valid objection so far to the assumption that the procreation sonnets I—XVII (except for no. XV), LXVI—LXVIII, LXXXI, XCI—XCVI, and CXXXV—CXLII were composed before or around 1592. But it does not seem possible to arrive at a more precise dating.

Before 1593

No. CXIX is connected with CIX, CX, CXVII, CXVIII, and CXX in much the same way as CXLII with CXXXV—CXLI: an identical situation ties these poems very closely together, and as mentioned

---

[1] As a representative of this group I quote no. CXXXVII:

> Thou blinde foole loue, what doost thou to mine eyes,
> That they behold and see not what they see:
> They know what beautie is, see where it lyes,
> Yet what the best is, take the worst to be:
> If eyes corrupt by ouer-partiall lookes,
> Be anchord in the baye where all men ride,
> Why of eyes falsehood hast thou forged hookes,
> Whereto the iudgement of my heart is tide?
> Why should my heart thinke that a seuerall plot,
> Which my heart knowes the wide worlds common place?
> Or mine eyes seeing this, say this is not
> To put faire truth vpon so foule a face,
>   In things right true my heart and eyes haue erred,
>   And to this false plague are they now transferred.

Cf. also no. CXXXIX as quoted on p. 60.

earlier the *poyson* of CXVIII, 14 and the *potions* of CXIX, I connect
these two sonnets formally. The close interrelationship of most of
these sonnets is also pointed out by LEVER, who, however, includes
nos. CXI and CXII (*op. cit.*, p. 236). But the subject of these two sonnets
is different (cf. below). The situation described in CIX, CX and
CXVII—CXX is of a particular kind in that the poet gives vent to
regret, self-blame, and relief when 'ruin'd love is built anew' after a
period of estrangement in his relations with the friend.[2] It is natural
to assume that these sonnets are not far apart chronologically. It
is possible that no. LVI should also be included (*Sweet loue renew thy
force*), but of this I feel less certain. BALDWIN regards all the sonnets
between C and CXX as a close sequence, but only those I have referred
to are clearly homogeneous thematically. The other poems from
C to CXX deal with various other themes: the poet blames his Muse
for negligence in praising the friend (C—CI), 'My love is strengthen'd
though more weak in seeming' (CII), the friend's beauty surpasses
all description (CIII), though he does not seem to grow older, he is
subject to change like everything else (CIV), the poet's verse, always
praising the same things, braves time (CV, CVIII), beauty described
in bygone days prophesied the friend's beauty (CVI), the poet's
love 'looks fresh', no longer threatened by dangers, and is immortalized by his verse (CVII), his love consoles him when his name
'receives a brand' (CXI—CXII), his eyes see nothing but the friend
(CXIII—CXIV), his love is ever growing (CXV), true love never
changes (CXVI). — There is nothing in the more uniform group

---

[2] No. CXX may be quoted as typical of this group:

> That you were once vnkind be-friends mee now,
> And for that sorrow, which I then didde feele,
> Needes must I vnder my transgression bow,
> Vnlesse my Nerues were brasse or hammered steele.
> For if you were by my vnkindnesse shaken
> As I by yours, y' haue past a hell of Time,
> And I a tyrant haue no leasure taken
> To waigh how once I suffered in your crime.
> O that our night of wo might haue remembred
> My deepest sence, how hard true sorrow hits,
> And soone to you, as you to me then tendred
> The humble salue, which wounded bosomes fits!
>   But that your trespasse now becomes a fee,
>   Mine ransoms yours, and yours must ransome mee.

Cf. also no. CXIX (p. 101 f).

CIX, CX, and CXVII—CXX that makes it possible to narrow down the dating.

Before 1594

Of the four sonnets XXXVIII, LXXV, XCVI, and CIV which we have proposed to date before 1594, XCVI has already been dealt with and placed within more narrow limits. BALDWIN finds a place for no. XXXVIII in a sequence comprising sonnets XXXIII—XLII, which he says "is probably later than May, 1594. Its first sonnets, at least, are probably earlier than the summer of 1595" (p. 244). This conclusion is based on the following premisses: "Most of them [i.e. sonnets XXXIII—XLII] center upon sonnets XXXIII—XXXV, which are later than passages in *Two Gentlemen*, *Titus Andronicus*, and *Lucrece*; but are earlier than *Richard II*, and *I Henry IV*, and show affinities with *Richard III* and *King John*. We can thus date them as probably not earlier than May, 1594, but probably earlier than the summer of 1595" (*ibid.*). Whether we can accept this or not depends above all, then, on our answer to this question: Do sonnets XXXIII—XLII constitute a homogeneous sequence? If so: Is it certain or at least probable that XXXIII—XXXV are later than passages in *Two G.*, *Tit. Andr.*, and *Lucrece*, but earlier than *Rich. II* and *I Hen. IV*, and show affinities with *Rich. III* and *K. John?*

BALDWIN reads a continuous story into the sequence, dealing with the poet's love for his friend and the complications it involves. This is right as far as nos. XXXIII—XXXV are concerned, dealing as they do with the clouding of friendship. Nos. XXXIII—XXXV are also grouped together by LEVER (pp. 221, 224). The connection between nos. XXXIII and XXXIV is particularly close, both poems being based on the 'overcast day' image (cf. p. 157 below). However, the link between XXXV and XXXVI (*Let me confesse that we two must be twaine*) is not strong, though we may possibly agree with BALDWIN that "in Sonnet XXXVI the poet assumes all guilt for the separable spite to save his friend, since he had decided in Sonnet XXXV to corrupt himself to excuse his friend's guilt" (p. 239). The same idea had earlier been expressed by DOWDEN. But it is hard to agree with BALDWIN that "the sequence continues in Sonnet XXXVII" (*ibid.*). In this poem there is no question of dissension; the poet merely

assures us that, 'made lame by fortune's dearest spite' he takes 'all
his comfort' from the friend's 'worth and truth' and is no more
unhappy. No. XXXVIII, again — the starting-point of our discussion
— deals with a related theme: the friend inspires the poet's Muse.[3]
With this theme that of XXXIX may or may not be connected: no.
XXXIX suggests that poet and friend should 'live divided', so that
the former may sing the latter's praise properly although the friend
is 'all the better part' of the poet. But if there is at least a possible link
between XXXVIII and XXXIX, it is far more difficult to see one between XXXIX and XL, in which Shakespeare blames his friend for
playing a rival's part (*Take all my loues, my loue, yea take them all,* /
What hast thou then more then thou hadst before?) BROOKE separates
XXXVIII—XXXIX from XL—XLII, CELLINI, XXXVIII from XXXIX. It is
not enough to connect XXXIX with XL by saying that the 'twain-
self in unity' of the former sonnet "carries over into Sonnet XL"
(BALDWIN, p. 240). It is much easier, in fact it is inevitable, to
connect XL with XLI and XLII, for these sonnets go on speaking, in
unequivocal terms, of the friend as a rival, and of the 'loving
offenders' (cf. p. 166 below).

Thus there is nothing that compels us to regard XXXIII—XLII
as a continuous sequence. It is easier, on the contrary, to regard
XXXIII—XXXVI as one group, XXXVII—XXXIX as another — though
much more loosely interrelated —, and XL—XLII as a third and very
homogeneous group. The break between XXXVI and XXXVII is
particularly hard to ignore. It follows that it cannot reasonably be
necessary for us to regard nos. XXXVI—XLII as in any way 'centred
upon' XXXIII—XXXV, and we need not therefore now discuss the
datings of these sonnets that have been proposed by BALDWIN. We
shall have reason to do so below in a different context (pp. 157 ff.).

Thus we may conclude that there is no clue to the dating of no.
XXXVIII beyond that suggested on p. 37. As regards the connection
of this poem with others, there is, as we have found, a similarity

---

[3] POOLER thinks that this poem "continues" XXXVII, 5—8 (*For whether beauty, birth, or
wealth, or wit,* / *Or any of these all, or all, or more* / *Intitled in their parts, do crowned sit,* / *I
make my loue ingrafted to this store*). But this means, as TUCKER says, that the poet grafts his
love "upon all this richness, and so [draws] life and strength from it". That the friend is his
only real source of inspiration of course need not be a "continuation" of this theme. But
we may agree that there is a strong similarity of motif.

of motif in nos. XXXVII—XXXIX. However, this similarity is not in my opinion strong enough to make it probable that these sonnets belong together chronologically. In particular, they do not seem to deal with an identical — real or fictitious — situation.

No. LXXV begins by assuring the friend of the poet's unreserved love: *So are you to my thoughts as food to life, | Or as sweet season'd shewers are to the ground.* The continuation expresses a conflict, 'such strife as 'twixt a miser and his wealth is found': now the lover wants the world to 'see his pleasure', now he prefers to be alone with him; now he is feasting on his sight, now starved for a look. This poem, as POOLER says, bears a certain similarity to the subject of those sonnets which hint at the friend's possible inconstancy. In LXXV such a hint would be found in l. 6, which gives the motivation for the poet's desire 'to be with you alone': *Doubting the filching age will steale his treasure.* But this does not necessarily express more than any lover's natural mistrust of others, mixed with pride and a desire to show his treasure to the world. It is therefore not certain that no. LXXV should be connected, as POOLER thinks, with XLVIII, which is entirely concerned with the danger that the recipient may be 'stolen away'. Even less is there a clear connection with no. XLIX, which speaks openly of the possibility of the friend's indifference:

> *Against that time when thou shalt strangely passe,*
> *And scarcely greete me with that sunne thine eye.*

In fact no. LXXV is a fairly isolated poem in the *Sonnets*, though details of it may be paralleled in other pieces. Above all it does not form part of a sequence, its theme being different from that of LXXIV ('poet is mortal, his verse makes beloved immortal') as well as from that of no. LXXVI ('poet's verse monotonous because always dealing with beloved'). Apart from the parallel we have discussed on p. 61, there is nothing to indicate a date for no. LXXV.

As to no. CIV, this sonnet played a considerable part in earlier criticism as a "dated" poem. According to FORT it was composed in March or April, 1596, since it was found to allude to a certain stage of Shakespeare's friendship with Southampton.[4] FORT's theory gave rise to a discussion pro and contra. Several years earlier, how-

---

[4] *The Two Dated Sonnets*, pp. 21 f., 29. Cf. ROLLINS II, pp. 59 ff.

ever, LEE had pointed out that the three-year period referred to by
FORT (*Three Winters colde, | Haue from the forrests shooke three sum-
mers pride*) was conventional in sonneteering;[5] the Southampton
theory, moreover, is no very reliable support for a dating. In a
discussion of FORT's hypothesis, BALDWIN rightly observes that "we
simply do not know" (*Genetics*, p. 319). On the other hand BALD-
WIN's own statement that no. CIV was preceded by no LXXVII, where
the poet also speaks of a dial, is an unwarranted conclusion (*ibid.*,
p. 308). Beyond the somewhat questionable parallel in *Delia* (cf.
p. 61) there seems to be no clue at all to the dating of no. CIV.

Before 1595 and -96

For nos. VII and XCIV we have already suggested a dating around
1592. As to the other sonnets of the group, nos. XXXIII—XXXVI, or
at least XXXIII—XXXV, have been found to form a continuous
sequence. It is now necessary to examine the relationship between
these sonnets and *Two Gent,, Tit. Andr., Lucrece, Rich. II, I Hen. IV,
Rich. III* and *K. John* as suggested by BALDWIN (cf. p. 154).

BALDWIN's argument is based on what he takes to be the development of the figure of 'the sun-bedimming clouds'. The first sonnet
of the sequence reads:

> *Fvll many a glorious morning haue I seene,*
> *Flatter the mountaine tops with soueraine eie,*
> *Kissing with golden face the meddowes greene;*
> *Guilding pale streames with heauenly alcumy:*
> *Anon permit the basest cloudes to ride,*
> *With ougly rack on his celestiall face,*
> *And from the for-lorne world his visage hide*
> *Stealing vnseene to west with this disgrace:*
> *Euen so my Sunne one early morne did shine,*
> *With all triumphant splendor on my brow,*
> *But out alack, he was but one houre mine,*
> *The region cloude hath mask'd him from me now.*
> > *Yet him for this, my loue no whit disdaineth,*
> > *Suns of the world may staine, when heauens sun staineth.*

[5] Sonnet ed. 1907. Cf. ROLLINS I, p. 255.

According to BALDWIN this figure of the sun has 'grown out' of another figure in Sonnet XXVIII, 9—10:

> *I tell the Day to please him thou art bright,*
> *And do'st him grace when clouds doe blot the heauen.*

But as BALDWIN says himself, "Here the real sun is behind the clouds, and the friend takes the sun's place in distributing brightness" (p. 233). Thus here the context is quite different from that in XXXIII, and there is nothing to show why XXVIII must be the basis of the sun figure. The same objection can be raised to BALDWIN's next attempt to fix the chronology of XXXIII, which he does with the aid of some lines in *Two Gentlemen* (I, iii, 84—87):

> *O, how this spring of love resembleth*
> *The uncertain glory of an April day,*
> *Which now shows all the beauty of the sun,*
> *And by and by a cloud takes all away!*

BALDWIN declares categorically: "Here is the germ of Sonnet XXXIII" (*ibid.*); but he gives no reason for this statement. Here we have a sonnet describing the clouding of friendship after 'a glorious morning', and a passage in a play comparing the delicate spring of love to the 'uncertain glory' of an April day, now sunny, now overcast. Why must the latter be 'the germ' of the former? Because the passage in the play is shorter? But quite apart from the fact that there are differences between the images, why could not the *Two Gent.* lines be an allusion to or a summary of a more extended image used earlier? On p. 235, speaking of the figure of 'clouds poisoning the sun', BALDWIN observes that it is "developed in *Lucrece*, and assumed or alluded to in *I Henry IV*, a very frequent trick of Shakspere's with figures". How do we know that Shakespeare uses this trick in *Lucrece* and *I Hen. IV*, but not in *Two Gent.* and XXXIII?

But to continue. The chronology of nos. XXXIV and XXXV BALDWIN tries to determine by referring to various details in other Shakespearean works. He first quotes two stanzas in *Lucrece* (771—84), where the ravished maiden beseeches the night to extinguish the light of the sun: *Knit poysonous clouds about his golden head ... With rotten damps rauish the morning aire* (777 f.), an idea that is varied throughout the stanza. A "companion piece" to these details he finds in some lines in *Tit. Andr.* III, i, 210 ff.:

> *Heaven shall hear our prayers;*
> *Or with our sighs we'll breathe the welkin dim,*
> *And stain the sun with fog,* etc.

A similar idea is found in no. xxxv, l. 3 of which reads, *Cloudes and eclipses staine both Moone and Sunne,* a metaphor excusing the friend. It is concluded that xxxv is later than *Tit. A.* 210 ff. — and also later than xxviii, for in that poem day and night are mentioned ... Nor is this all. BALDWIN also tells us that nos. xxxiii and xxxiv come between *Lucrece* and *I Hen. IV.* In the latter play, as mentioned above, he finds an allusion to the 'clouds poisoning sun' image in *Lucrece.* The relevant lines in *I Hen. IV* read:

> *Who doth permit the base contagious clouds*
> *To smother up his beauty from the world* (I, ii, 197 f.).

These lines, according to BALDWIN, are at the same time "rephrased from" two of the sonnets. One is xxxiii, 5 ff.:

> *Anon permit the basest cloudes to ride,*
> *With ougly rack on his celestiall face,*
> *And from the for-lorne world his visage hide,*
> *Stealing vnseene to west with this disgrace.*

"The first lines of these quoted sections are almost identical, and the second line of one says the same thing as the second and third lines of the other. The condensed form is almost certain to be the later" (p. 235). This is quite possible, but how are we to know that it is not the 'germ' of the sonnet lines instead? Yet not only the image of xxxiii but also that of xxxiv (*To let bace cloudes ore-take me in my way, | Hiding thy brau'ry in their rotten smoke*) is regarded as a forerunner of the passage in *I Hen. IV:* "'The basest clouds' of Sonnet xxxiii, under the influence of 'base clouds ... in their rotten smoke' of Sonnet xxxiv (from the 'rotten damps' of *Lucrece*) have become 'base contagious clouds' in *I Henry IV.* Clearly the line in *I Henry IV* is later than the corresponding lines in Sonnets xxxiii and xxxiv" (*ibid.*). Very likely, but not on this evidence alone. Surely the only thing that is quite clear is that we can here merely deal with probabilities, and it is probable that those passages that resemble each other most are not too far removed in point of time from one another. On the other hand we cannot take it for granted that this is so, for reasons that will be discussed later (cf. pp. 175 f.). It should also be observed that the texts containing the 'sun-bedimming cloud' image range from *Tit. A.*, probably written in 1592, to *I Hen. IV*, probably written in 1596 or —97. At any rate, except for the cases where we are aided by external dates, attempts to trace in detail the genetics of the image are bound to be arbitrary: now the poet is said to condense something detailed, now to develop something embryonic, but we lack criteria that might help us to determine when one process takes place and not the other. BALDWIN uses the same kind of arguments as those cited here in order to show that a passage in *Rich. II* (III, iii, 62 ff.) is an "allusory capitulation" of the figure in nos. XXXIII and XXXIV, and again we do not feel convinced. On the other hand I agree with him when, observing (p. 237) that the 'cloud-cloak' figure in *Rich. III* and *KJ* is shared by no. XXXIV, he adds: "I see nothing to show relative order, but we now know that the three passages were not far apart chronologically." Provided that we do not regard the chronological limits as too narrow this goes, I think, for all the passages discussed above. In short, whether sonnets XXXIII—XXXV are later than *Lucrece* (printed in 1594) it is impossible to tell. They probably belong to the same main period, but I think it is plausible, for reasons I have given already, to assume that they are earlier than *Edw. III*.[6] We shall return to the matter later.

Also in the case of no. CXXVII I have given reasons for a date earlier than *Edw. III*, and have made some suggestions regarding its relationship to *Love's Labour's Lost* (pp. 114 ff.). These views do not coincide with those of BALDWIN who, following STEEVENS, regards no. CXXVII as "foreshadowed" in *LLL*. I have tried to show that the question of the genesis of the 'mourning eyes' conceit must be seen in a wider perspective, and I cannot agree with BALDWIN that "for Sonnet CXXVII Shakspere has simply and solely put Biron's paradoxical black beauty into sonnet form" (p. 323), and that this

---

[6] DARBY's interpretation of these sonnets (cf. p. 7 above), as ROLLINS points out (II, p. 62) is probably too literal.

poem, with others, is therefore not earlier than 1598. However, I need not repeat my discussion of these points, but pass on to no. CXLVI, for which poem I have proposed 1596 as the probable *ante quem* limit. BALDWIN remarks that this address to the poet's soul is not necessarily in sequence any more than CXLV (*Those lips that Loues owne hand did make*). With this I entirely agree, and there can be no objection to BALDWIN's summing-up: "These two sonnets ... have little, if any, connection, with each other or with any series" (p. 335).

After 1591

No. CXXXII, as we have seen, like CXXVII, is a variation on the theme of 'mourning eyes' for which BALDWIN proposes *Love's Labour's Lost* as the ultimate origin. As in the case of no. CXXVII, I refer to my discussion of the 'mourning eyes' conceit on p. 114. It seems *a priori* highly probable that CXXVII and CXXXII were written at about the same time since the conceit used in them is a rare one, and it is possible that CXXVII is later than CXXXII (cf. *ibid.* above). If this is right, both poems were written after 1586 or 1591, possibly before 1592—93, and in any case before 1595. For the rest, I shall here only observe that BALDWIN seems to be wrong in connecting nos. CXXVII and CXXXII with CXXX. No. CXXXII says that the lady's two mourning eyes become her face better than the sun becomes the east or the evening star the west. "This connects with Sonnet CXXX, where we are told, 'My mistress' eyes are nothing like the sun'. Now as mourners for him the poet defends them as more becoming than the sun. So this sonnet connects with both CXXVII and CXXX" (p. 326). But the 'more-than' figure in no. CXXXII is a hyperbolical praise of the lady's eyes, whereas no. CXXX is a satire on Petrarchan eulogy: though her eyes are not like the sun, though coral is redder than her lips and snow whiter than her breast etc., yet *by heauen I thinke my loue as rare, / As any she beli'd with false compare.*[7] Nor, for the same reason, has this theme anything to do with no. CXXVII.

---

[7] This poem has often been misunderstood and taken for a piece disparaging the lady's alleged beauty. But as TUCKER and others point out it is conventional hyperbole that is

Sonnet XXXI is one of several poems praising the friend, such as nos. XXIX and XXX, where the thought of him is enough to make the poet forget frustration and sorrow. The theme of XXXI — the poet's love for the friend sums up his love for dead friends — ties up closely with that of XXX, of which the main part describes the poet's sorrow for 'precious friends hid in death's dateless night'. This idea of 'love for dead friends — love for Friend' actually links these two sonnets so closely together that it is reasonable to regard them as written in sequence. The conceit of no. XXXI, as we have seen, seems derived from Constable and modified so as to fit the 'mourning-for-friends' theme. Though XXX and XXXI belong very closely together, it is not so certain that the same is true of no. XXIX, for here the poet's melancholy is not caused by the thought of dead friends but by his being *in disgrace with Fortune and mens eyes*. As regards the theme of 'love for dead friends summed up in love for Friend', BALDWIN finds an important parallel in no. XX, where the friend is referred to as "A man in hue, all 'hues' controlling". He also connects no. XXXI with LIII, where 'millions of strange shadows on you tend', and with no. VIII, where the friend is warned that "unless he emulates the music in being all in one and one in all he will prove none" (p. 174). Thus BALDWIN finds a continuous development of the theme of 'all in all, and all in every part', which as we have seen he traces back to the Plotinian doctrine of the soul. At the same time, however, he asks himself why Shakespeare harped "so everlastingly and so pointedly on this theme when addressing his friend", and finds the answer in a suggestion made by the signature W. C. J. in 1859 and later repeated by STOPES (1904), to the effect that Shakespeare was playing on Southampton's motto — or rather on that of the Wriothesley family —: *Ung par tout, tout par ung* (p. 175).

It may be true that the Plotinian doctrine of the soul forms the background of the 'all in one, one in all' theme, at least as regards nos. XX and LIII (cf. p. 95 above). It is far more doubtful, as we have seen, whether it colours no. XXXI, and there seems to be no reason to resort to it in order to explain the commonplace idea of musical

criticized, not the lady. Similar 'anti-Petrarchan' satires were common in the late fifteen-hundreds.

harmony resulting from the interplay of singing voices in no. VIII — imitated, incidentally, from Sidney's *Arcadia*.[8] So Shakespeare does not exactly 'harp' on the Plotinian theme, and do we need Southampton's motto to explain Shakespeare's use of it in two poems? Is it not fully motivated by the subject of the sonnets where it occurs? The theme — fixed in the 'all-in-all' formula — was used "widely" and belonged to the "current phraseology of the day" (BALDWIN, pp. 158, 161). It is therefore equally probable that the use of it by Shakespeare *and* by the Wriothesley family reflects this common contemporary use.

There seems to be no valid objection to our dating no. XXXI after 1591, but there is as yet nothing to indicate a date *ante quem*.

No. CVI does not seem to be connected with any other sonnet in the sequence besides possibly no. LIX, where in the same way a relationship is established between beauty in bygone ages and the beauty of the living friend. However, in that poem the author applies a different perspective, moving backwards from the present, desirous to see what 'the old world could say to this composed wonder of your frame'. In no. CVI he moves forwards from the past, whose descriptions of beauty are said to prophesy the beauty of the friend. Thus there is a similarity of motif along with certain differences, but the similarity is not of such a kind that we need group these sonnets together chronologically. Therefore CVI, but not necessarily LIX, should be dated after 1591.

After 1592

There is an obvious and very close connection between the 'flower' sonnets, XCVIII and XCIX, and it is reasonable to regard them as written more or less in sequence, not least since both, though chiefly XCIX, show traces of influence from *Diana* I, iii, 1. Besides, both speak of absence from the friend. It is true that this is also the case with no. XCVII. But 'absence from friend' was a conventional motif. Since no. XCVII is not formally connected either with XCVIII

---

[8] In his *Mortimeriados* (1170 ff.) Drayton illustrates the harmony of feelings by describing *Musicks language sweetly speaking playne, | When every string it selfe with sound doth fill,* and a similar image occurs in Lyly's *Loues Metamorphoses* (115 ff.). No one is likely to adduce these passages as instances of the 'all-in-all' formula.

or XCIX in the same way as these two poems are connected with each other, it is therefore not certain that XCVII was written at the same time as XCVIII and XCIX. It is equally possible that XCVII was grouped with the other two in the Quarto because of the similarity of theme. — Can we fix the date for XCVIII and XCIX with greater precision? A passage in *Lucrece* also makes use of the flower conceit as found in Constable (p. 89 above), so it is probable that no. XCIX was composed at about the same time as the *Lucrece* passage. The same would thus hold for no. XCVIII. It is fairly generally believed that *Lucrece* was written in 1593 -94. Therefore we are probably not far from the truth when assigning nos. XCVIII and XCIX to roughly the same date.

Before 1601

It remains for us to discuss the dating of nos. XVIII, XIX, LIV, CV, and CXLIV (before 1599). 'Before 1601' leaves us within fairly generous limits. Can we arrive at more precise dates for these sonnets?

Nos. XVIII and XIX immediately succeed the procreation sonnets and are concerned with the immortality theme. In XVIII Shakespeare declares that everything changes, but the friend's beauty will live for ever in the poet's verse. In XIX he says he will tolerate any act of violent change on the part of Time except one: 'Carve not with thy hours my love's brow' — yet whatever Time may do, the poet's love shall 'ever live young' in his verse. Though the theme is common to both sonnets it is not expressed in such a way as to impose continuity, and they do not describe or represent an identical situation in the way we have seen other poems do. Furthermore, sonnets on immortality are scattered throughout the sequence. Instances are nos. XV, LIV, LV, LX, LXIII, LXXIV, LXXXI, C, CI, and CVII, sonnets which all contrast transitoriness with immortality and which there is no reason to assign to the same short period or occasion (except for C and CI, both addressed to the poet's Muse). Many other sonneteers wrote sonnets on the immortality theme as long as they wrote at all. As to the mutual order of the two sonnets under discussion, BALDWIN assumes that XVIII is earlier than XIX,[9] as shown by their respective relation to the basis of the 'transitori-

---

[9] A similar view seems to be held by LEVER (p. 201) and by several editors.

ness — immortality' theme which he finds in Ovidian passages on the defeat of Time through verse. The "idea of defeating Time through the poet's verse" is introduced in no. xv, but "the thought is more or less of an accident, becomes clearer in xviii, and is fully conscious of itself only in Sonnet xix. Shakspere does not first consciously borrow a passage from Ovid and then shade off from it. Instead, he gropes through vague memories to full consciousness on one particular point" (p. 211). How do we know that this is what happened? Psychologically, one would imagine the reverse process to be the more natural one: the poet writes one sonnet under the direct influence of a passage in another author and then moves away from it, becoming gradually more independent as his memory of it grows indistinct. When trying to prove, in another connection, that sonnet I is earlier than a passage in *Lucrece*, BALD-WIN finds use for this latter reasoning: the second quatrain of no. I is built on a figure in Ovid. "Then four lines in *Lucrece* restate the idea of the four lines in the sonnet, being thus further away from the source"[1] (pp. 186 f.). So "the passage in sonnet I precedes that in *Lucrece*". Similarly on p. 314, "while it is not wholly certain, yet" it is found to be "highly probable" that a phrase in no. CXIV is later than a similar one in *King John*, "since the latter is more fully based" on a passage in Ovid. Why not assume that the same thing happened in the case of xviii and xix — *if* we are to connect them —, so that xix is built directly on Ovid, and xviii moves further away from the source? BALDWIN's discussion of nos. xviii and xix is a striking example of *petitio principii*.

However, BALDWIN makes it very probable (pp. 212 ff.) that there is some connection between no. xix and a *Lucrece* passage (925—59), even if I cannot agree with him that the latter must precede the sonnet. The stanzas in *Lucrece* contain a series of accusations and execrations hurled against Time ('Eater of youth', 'false slave to false delight', 'Base watch of woes', etc.) and a list of his destructive activities: his glory, among many other things, is to 'feed oblivion with decay of things', ... 'To pluck the quills from ancient ravens' wings', ... 'To dry the old oak's sap and cherish

---

[1] My emphasis.

springs,' ... 'To slay the tiger that doth live by slaughter', etc. It cannot be denied that such lines are in part strongly suggestive of the first five lines of no. XIX:

> *Deuouring time blunt thou the Lyons pawes,*
> *And make the earth deuoure her owne sweet brood,*
> *Plucke the keene teeth from the fierce Tygers yawes,*
> *And burne the long liu'd Phœnix in her blood,*
> *Make glad and sorry seasons as thou fleet'st;*

and it is very likely that, as many commentators have suggested, this is inspired by Ovid's *tempus edax rerum* etc. in *Met.* XV, 234. But the only permissible inference would seem to be that Shakespeare elaborated the Ovidian passage in a certain way in both XIX and *Lucrece* at about the same time, when these particular phrases and images were in his mind. So I would date XIX not far from the *Lucrece* passage, whether before or after I find it impossible to say. As to the exact date of no. XVIII I have no suggestions.

No. XLI, as we have found earlier, makes up a group with nos. XL and XLII: all three are addressed to the friend who has turned rival, all three describe the same situation. BALDWIN notes some parallels to a detail in XLI in order to fix it chronologically. In ll. 5 ff., Shakespeare makes an attempt to excuse the friend:

> *Gentle thou art, and therefore to be wonne,*
> *Beautious thou art, therefore to be assailed.*
> *And when a woman woes, what womans sonne,*
> *Will sourely leaue her till she haue preuailed.*

BALDWIN, with most commentators, points out the similarity of the last two lines to *Venus and Adonis* 201 f., where the disappointed goddess asks her unwilling companion:

> *Art thou a womans sonne and canst not feele*
> *What tis to loue, how want of loue tormenteth?*

According to BALDWIN, the *VA* passage is the earlier, and the idea of the sonnet derives from it (p. 241). But again it is hard to see how we can go beyond concluding — at most — that the passages may be fairly close to each other chronologically, similar ideas being expressed in much the same way.[2] BALDWIN is more convincing in his analysis of the relationship of XLI, 5—8 to passages in *Tit. Andr., Rich. III,* and *I Hen. VI.* In the former two the combination *woo — won* is used in a kind of formula: *She is a woman, therefore may be woo'd; | She is a woman, therefore may be won (Tit.* II, i, 82 f.); *Was euer woman in this humour woo'd? | Was euer woman in this humour won? (Rich. III,* I, ii, 228 f.). In *I Hen. VI,* V, iii, 78 f., BALDWIN observes, "the pattern of the figure is varied slightly from the strictly parallel form" (*ibid.*): *She's beautiful and therefore to be woo'd; | She is a woman, therefore to be won.* BALDWIN says that in no. XLI Shakespeare "adapts the figure as given in *I Henry VI …* He has reversed the conventional phrase into won and wooed, and has then substituted assailed for wooed," etc. (*ibid.*) Though BALDWIN seems to forget that *I Hen. VI* is probably earlier than *Rich. III* and *Tit. Andr.,* the similarity between XLI and *I Hen. VI* may be strong enough to link these particular passages together to the exclusion of those in *Rich. III* and *Tit. Andr.* It is, however, not necessarily true that *I Hen. VI* presents "the form from which Sonnet XLI was adapted" (p. 242). Here as in many other cases we cannot go beyond assuming that the passages referred to are not likely to be very far apart chronologically, representing as they do an accumulation of identical phrasing.

But if XL—XLII belong closely together in that they describe an identical situation, the same is true of CXXXIII, CXXXIV, and CXLIV, which by BROOKE are printed in the order CXLIV, CXXXIII, CXXXIV. TYLER also briefly refers to CXLIV in his note on CXXXIII. These three poems also explicitly deal with a triangle, a liaison between the friend and the dark lady, both of whom are within the poet's sphere of interest. However, the tone of these three poems is quite different from that in XL—XLII.[3] The latter sonnets, addressed to

---

[2] Incidentally, BALDWIN refuses to accept the old emendation *she* for Q *he* in XLI, 8: "Certainly, Malone's bachelor emendation from 'he' to 'she' is wrong, and the meaning of 'prevail' ought also to be sufficiently evident" (*ibid.*). The emendation — accepted by a vast majority of editors — is not MALONE's but TYRWHITT's, and what BALDWIN says in no way invalidates MALONE's simple motivation for the conjecture: "The lady, and not the man, being in this case supposed the wooer, the poet without doubt wrote … *she.*" And what becomes of the poet's excuse if we retain the Q reading?

[3] TYLER refers to XL in his notes on CXXXIII, TUCKER to the same sonnet in his notes on CXXXIV.

the friend, are sad and melancholy, mildly reproachful, trying even
to find excuses for the friend's fault:

> Then if for my loue, thou my loue receiuest,
> I cannot blame thee, for my loue thou vsest,
> But yet be blam'd, if thou this selfe deceauest
> By wilfull taste of what thy selfe refusest.
> I doe forgiue thy robb'rie gentle theefe
> Although thou steale thee all my pouerty:
> And yet loue knowes it is a greater griefe
> To beare loues wrong, then hates knowne iniury, etc. (XL, 5 ff.)

No. XLII even finds an excuse for both 'offenders':

> Louing offendors thus I will excuse yee,
> Thou doost loue her, because thou knowst I loue her,
> And for my sake euen so doth she abuse me,
> Suffring my friend for my sake to approoue her.

Nos. CXXXIII and CXXXIV, on the other hand, addressed to the lady,
are bitter and caustic:

> Beshrew that heart that makes my heart to groane
> For that deepe wound it giues my friend and me;
> I'st not ynough to torture me alone,
> But slaue to slauery my sweet'st friend must be?
> Me from my selfe thy cruell eye hath taken, etc.
>
> (CXXXIII, 1 ff.)

The poet also begs that he may 'bail his friend's heart':

> Thou canst not then vse rigor in my Iaile.
>   And yet thou wilt, for I being pent in thee,
>   Perforce am thine, and all that is in me.

To this last line no. CXXXIV alludes directly: *So now I haue confest
that he is thine,* and Shakespeare varies the 'heart-bail' image of
CXXXIII by using the image of forfeit in CXXXIV:

> My selfe Ile forfeit, so that other mine,
> Thou wilt restore to be my comfort still.

However, that hope is in vain, just as it was in vain in CXXXIII
to hope that the lady would not 'use rigor in my jail': the lady

refuses to restore the friend, the friend does not want to be free. At the same time it is the lady who is blamed, and the friend is exonerated: *For thou art couetous, and he is kinde* (l. 6). The lady in CXXXIV is a 'usurer that puts forth all to use', and 'sues a friend, came debtor for my sake'. Thus the ideas and structures of both poems have a great deal in common, and the sonnets would therefore seem to be fairly intimately connected. No. CXLIV, though also expressly dealing with the triangle, is differently conceived and uses the angel-devil imagery (cf. p. 76). BALDWIN believes (p. 333) that CXLIV was developed on the background of *2 Hen. IV*, II, iv, 362 ff., where we have a similar contrast of boy-angel and woman-devil. But it would be just as easy to hold the opposite view since the contrast in CXLIV is elaborate and that in *2 Hen. IV* more allusory. In any case, the three sonnets CXXXIII, CXXXIV, and CXLIV seem to be centred on the same situation, and CXLIV retains and strongly heightens the aversion vis-à-vis the lady and the tolerance vis-à-vis the friend: *The better angell is a man right faire: | The worser spirit a woman collour'd il*, etc. So what we have is this: three sad and tolerant poems addressed to the friend; two bitter and upbraiding poems addressed to the woman; one poem dealing with both and retaining and sharpening the contrast. Thus all these six sonnets seem to make up a group and fit one another exactly, and the difference in attitude towards friend and woman is clearly stated in the first quatrain of XLII:

> *That thou hast her it is not all my griefe,*
> *And yet it may be said I lou'd her deerely,*
> *That she hath thee is of my wayling cheefe,*
> *A losse in loue that touches me more neerely.*

The symmetry and deliberate structure of the group *may* be an indication that the conception is literary rather than autobiographical.

Among the sonnets surrounding CXXXIII, CXXXIV, and CXLIV there is not one that seems connectible with them in the same way as nos. XL—XLII. According to POOLER CXXXIII is a continuation of the 'mourning eyes' sonnet no. CXXXII (cf. p. 110); according to BALDWIN there is an unbroken sequence of thought "from CXXX through CXXXVIII, and CXXX continues CXXVII" (p. 330). But the 'mourning eyes' theme has nothing to do with CXXXIII, and the themes of CXXX—CXXXVIII are too diversified to form a sequence of thought. CXXXV and subsequent sonnets deal with the lady's wantonness, but nothing is really said to indicate whether the friend is involved or not. Therefore it is not certain that CXXXIII—CXXXIV were written in sequence with CXXXV ff., and we must confine ourselves to regarding CXXXIII, CXXXIV, and CXLIV as a homogeneous group intimately connected, from thematic and structural points of view, with XL—XLII. Since we found reason to date these latter before or around 1593, it is natural to assume that CXXXIII, CXXXIV, and CXLIV were also composed at about the same time: the very nature of the interrelationship of these six sonnets is such that it is reasonable to imagine them as written within a quite short period. But if this is acceptable, we need not avail ourselves of the well-known *ante quem* date for no. CXLIV, which was published in *The Passionate Pilgrim* in 1599 and probably pillaged in the same year by Drayton.

No. LIV is the next sonnet for which we have suggested a date not later than 1601. This sonnet is not closely linked up with any other poem in the Quarto. BALDWIN suggests a relationship which fails to carry conviction. This time we are invited to follow the development of the 'canker-and-the-rose' images. Since Shakespeare in LIV contrasts canker blooms 'whose virtue only is their show' with a fair rose made even fairer by its sweet odour, symbolizing truth, it is assumed that he must adapt this image from a passage in *I Hen. VI* (II, iv, 68 ff.) where he had symbolized truth as the thorn of a rose, and from no. V, which deals with the theme of 'distilled beauty'. But it is also assumed that LIV must in its turn be earlier than *I Hen. IV*, I, iii, 175 ff., where Richard, 'that sweet lovely rose', is contrasted with 'this thorn, this canker, Bolingbroke', and BALDWIN traces in detail the process by which these images are supposed to grow out of one another (pp. 198 f.). What BALDWIN thinks happened may indeed have happened, and the chronology seems in itself acceptable, but the evidence is too scanty to be convincing. Even less convincing is the statement that 'you canker-blossom' in *Mids. N.D.* III, ii, 282, by which Hermia accuses Helena of falsity, is earlier than LIV.[4] We must again content ourselves with assuming that those images which resemble one another closely may have been written at about the same time, though we must not regard this as a certainty. On the other hand, as to the canker-rose passages referred to here it is reasonable to believe that LIV and *I Hen. VI*, II, iv, 68 ff. are not too far apart in point of time since both establish the unusual connection between rose and truth instead of the conventional one between rose and beauty.

No. CV was connected with *The Merchant of Venice* by ROLFE, and BALDWIN tries to construct a chronology on the basis of this parallel. In the play, as BALDWIN had briefly indicated before (*Small Latine* II, p. 96, n. 61), there is an instance of a well-known figure, consisting of a triple division of concepts followed by a summary. We find it in Lorenzo's words to Jessica (II, vi, 52 ff.):

> *Beshrew me but I loue her heartily.*
> *For she is wise, if I can iudge of her,*
> *And faire she is, if that mine eyes be true,*
> *And true she is, as she hath prou'd her selfe:*
> *And therefore like her selfe, wise, faire, and true,*
> *Shall she be placed in my constant soule.*

Other examples of this correlative figure, indicated by BALDWIN in *Small Latine* (*ibid.*) are found in *LLL* III, i, 36 ff., IV, iii, 291 ff. and *KJ* II, i, 504 ff. The figure was extremely common in Renaissance poetry — not least in sonneteering — as shown by FUCILLA, who has examined the use of it in the Romance-speaking countries and in England.[5] In no. CV we do not have it in its regular form as in *Mer. V.*, but much more freely handled:

> *Let not my loue be cal'd Idolatrie,*
> *Nor my beloued as an Idoll show,*
> *Since all alike my songs and praises be*
> *To one, of one, still such, and euer so.*
> *Kinde is my loue to day, to morrow kinde,*
> *Still constant in a wondrous excellence,*

---

[4] BEECHING points out yet another parallel to the poem: *Hamlet* (I, iii, 40), but this is less close than the other parallels mentioned here.

[5] *A Rhetorical Pattern in Renaissance and Baroque Poetry* (Studies in the Renaissance III, New York, 1956, pp. 23 ff.).

Therefore my verse to constancie confin'de,
One thing expressing, leaues out difference.
Faire, kinde, and true, is all my argument,
Faire, kinde, and true, varrying to other words,
And in this change is my inuention spent,
Three theams in one, which wondrous scope affords.
Faire, kinde, and true, haue often liu'd alone,
Which three till now, neuer kept seate in one.

BALDWIN suggests, or rather states, that Shakespeare has "assumed and adapted" the theme of the *Mer. V.* figure in no. cv. This does not prevent him from adding: "He had in fact been praising the truth and beauty of his love throughout the sonnets. He can, therefore, take over fair and true, but wise does not fit the sonnet conditions. So Shakspere adds 'kind' as a more fitting word to complete his triplicity here, even though he has not much emphasized this characteristic elsewhere", etc. (p. 173). What does this amount to? First, to the fact that the poet did not need any instance of 'fair and true' in *Mer. V.* for adaptation in cv since he had used that theme throughout the sonnets; secondly, to the fact that 'kind' does not derive from *Mer. V.* Consequently, we are hardly prepared for the following conclusion: "So Shakspere in Sonnet cv assumes the figure which he had developed in *Merchant of Venice*, merely substituting kind for wise as his third theme, and the word itself had got suggested as an alliterative yoke-mate to constant. Sonnet cv is thus later than the passage in the *Merchant of Venice*" (*ibid.*). This inference is all the less necessary as the theme of 'fair, kind, and true', as WYNDHAM and HARRISON have pointed out,[6] is nothing but a restatement — in a natural order — of the old trinity of 'the Good, the Beautiful, and the True'. BALDWIN's dismissal of this idea does not alter the fact that the 'fair-kind-true' theme of cv is based on a Platonic commonplace and that 'kind', far from being a substitution for 'wise', forms part of this basic combination. If we *have* to connect the *Mer. V.* figure with cv, it is therefore just as likely — if not likelier — that the former was adapted from the latter as the reverse. However this may be, we cannot on the evidence adduced feel bound to date cv later than *Mer. V.*

---

[6] Cf. ROLLINS I, p. 259.

As regards the relationship of CV to other sonnets, it is not formally connected with the preceding or the subsequent poems, and as BEECHING observed in his note on the poem, there is "no connection with the subject of the previous five sonnets". STIRLING places CV as the last of his group, preceded by XIX and XXI.[7] His arguments I do not find convincing. The theme of CV, however, is paralleled in nos. LXXVI and CVIII. In LXXVI the poet asks himself why his verse is 'so barren of new pride, so far from variation or quick change', and he answers:

> O know sweet loue I alwaies write of you,
> And you and loue are still my argument.

In CVIII, a parallel stressed by DOWDEN and ROLFE,[8] he asks himself 'what's new to speak, what new to register', and the answer is similar to that in LXXVI:

> Nothing sweet boy, but yet like prayers diuine,
> I must each day say ore the very same,
> Counting no old thing old, thou mine, I thine,
> Euen as when first I hallowed thy faire name.

Thus LXXVI and CVIII are similar in theme and structure, whereas the resemblance is less marked between these two and CV. It is possible that LXXVI and CVIII were written on the same occasion as variations on the same theme, while this assumption is less natural in the case of no. CV. In any case I can see nothing to determine the date of any of these poems more closely.

As far as the 'before 1601' sonnets are concerned, then, it seems possible in most cases to suggest a narrowing of the limits of dating.

*

It will thus appear from our analysis that the assumed development of Shakespeare's images and figures is not a reliable criterion in determining the chronology of the sonnets. It should be emphasized in all fairness that BALDWIN makes reservations at the end of his book: "The base may be found to be inadequate, the direction of development as indeterminate; that is, some of our instances may be found to be only parallels and so useless in this analytical frame-

[7] Op. cit., passim.
[8] Cf. ROLLINS I, p. 258.

work" (p. 340). Naturally we can study the growth and change of images in plays which are datable by other means, and SPURGEON's, ARMSTRONG's and CLEMEN's researches show how images on certain themes expand or contract, grow or dwindle, absorb new elements and cast off old ones.[9] In other words, it is hardly possible, in the case of 'myriad-minded' Shakespeare, to lay down rules as to how images or ideas develop, so that a study of such developments could help us towards a dating where other criteria are lacking.[1] This method too often involves reasoning in a circle, and what should be proved turns out to be the starting-point of the argument. Shakespeare's mind was no machine combining and arranging material in a way that can be calculated and foreseen.[2] BALDWIN himself observes, in his discussion of the procreation sonnets, that "through Sonnet XIII we can follow Shakspere's mind as it meanders from one nucleus of thought to another. It reminds one a great deal of the antics of an amoeba" (p. 208). But how can we hope to predict such antics, and how can we be sure, when studying Shakespeare's thoughts in a number of undated short poems and in some dated works, that the order we suggest for the amoeba's movements is in fact the right one? On p. 340 BALDWIN gives a quite different picture of the mechanisms he has studied, a picture suggesting law and order instead of whimsical antics: his conclusion (namely, that probably all the sonnets were written from about 1593 to about 1599) "rests fundamentally on long accepted literary relationships, controlled by external facts. The fundamental principle of these literary relationships has been to discover the basic source of origin and thence to determine direction of evolution, just as in manuscript relations". But the external

---

[9] Cf. particularly SPURGEON, pp. 152 f., ARMSTRONG, p. 102, CLEMEN, p. 102 (completeness followed by scattering and allusion), SPURGEON, pp. 218 ff., ARMSTRONG, pp. 29, 30, CLEMEN, p. 61 (reverse process).

[1] Cf. similar objections to BALDWIN's method by STIRLING, op. cit., p. 348.

[2] ARMSTRONG makes some suggestive comparisons: "Shakespeare's images are seen to be like molecules in chemical reactions, making new combinations which constitute new substances with novel properties" (p. 30). He also speaks of "the strange frolics of his images as they changed partners like children in a game or dance, some dropping out to come in again later, or, perhaps, joining up with another group" (pp. 30—31). ARMSTRONG also justly observes: "The attempt to classify psychological processes into static logical categories is foredoomed to failure. It is seeking the living amongst the dead. Psychological modes of association cannot be accurately correlated with apparent literary affinities save when in the context or otherwise we are provided with additional clues" (p. 105).

facts often fail to come up to expectations, and it is odd indeed that nothing should be said about the obvious difference between literary relationships of the kind BALDWIN has examined and manuscript relations as conceived by the 'genetic' school. In the former case there is the uncertainty as to 'direction of evolution' due to the practically inexhaustible possibilities of the poet's mind to transform, arrange, separate, and fuse together ideas and images. There is, to be sure, a 'logic of poetry', but this is not of a kind to be codified and regularized. In the latter case we have to do with relationships of an entirely different kind, groupings being based on errors and peculiarities common to certain MSS. and not to others, and the relationship of MSS. is ultimately dependent on the mechanical habits of copyists — a machinery highly different from the working of a creative poetic mind.

It may be more fruitful to ask, however — as we have done often enough in this chapter —, if at least very close resemblances between details in different works do not suggest identical dating which can be fixed if one of the works compared is datable with some amount of certainty. Thus we have seen that the image of 'morning air polluted by mists' is found in *Titus Andronicus* and *Lucrece* (p. 159), both registered in 1594, and several critics have pointed out far-reaching correspondences between the imagery in *Hamlet*, registered in 1602, and *Troilus and Cressida*, registered in 1603. Does not this mean that no. XIX and some *Lucrece* stanzas, closely similar in the use of the 'devouring Time' image (p. 165), were written at the same time, and that this also, for identical reasons, is true of nos. XXXIII—IV and *I Hen. IV*, of no. XLI and *VA* 201 f., and of no. LIV and *I Hen. VI* (pp. 157 ff.)? In these cases, however, I have not gone beyond assuming that the texts may have been written 'at about the same time' or are probably 'not too far apart chronologically', since modern Shakespeare research has shown how a phrase, an image, or an image cluster can linger for a surprisingly long time in the poet's mind. This is for example true, as ARMSTRONG has pointed out, of Shakespeare's kite-images, and the same critic calls attention to the fact that certain images in *Midsummer Night's Dream* reappear, twelve (?) years later, in *King Lear*, and "in closer contiguity than when they first made their appearance together" (p. 21). Similar observations had earlier been made by SPURGEON. If we work through a tolerably full commentary on, say, *Macbeth*, we find numerous instances of phrases and images closely paralleled in plays sometimes many years earlier.[3] We must accordingly be careful when concluding simultaneous date from such resemblances. Yet in the case of the similarity between LIV and *I Hen. VI* I feel inclined to believe that the chronological difference, if any, is inconsiderable since the details discussed deviate from convention and would thus seem to have occurred to the poet at the same time ('rose — truth'). As to the other parallels, there are at least no specific objections to a simultaneous date for the 'Art thou a woman's son' formulas in XLI, *VA*, and *I Hen. VI*. Nor does there seem to be anything that definitely precludes the hypothesis that the 'devouring Time' images in XIX and *Lucrece* belong chronologically together. On the other hand we have seen from ch. I that strong objections can be raised to a simultaneous date (about 1597) for XXXIII, XXXIV, and *I Hen. IV* (cf. further p. 184 below). All things considered, the recommendable procedure would seem to be to regard very close resemblances as possible indications of a simultaneous date, unless other and weightier circumstances point in a different direction, but in any case to avoid mechanical conclusions. *If* we are to use data of group c), we need extensive overall comparisons and cumulative evidence — approximate though the conclusions must be — rather than studies of isolated intra-Shakespearean details and their assumed development. Some comparisons of this statistical type will be dealt with below (p. 190 f.).

Naturally I do not maintain that the method I have adopted in ch. I differs from the analysis of intra-Shakespearean parallels in having no disadvantages at all. I have pointed out several sources of error in the introduction, and there may be others. But it is at least less difficult to trace the direction of development of phrases, figures, and images when we leave the field of the same poet's imagination and pass from one poet's mind to another's. It is then possible to draw lines of demarcation and, as observed before, to

---

[3] I briefly refer to the following select instances (from MUIR's Arden *Macbeth*, 1951): *Macb.* I, iv, 28 f. — *All's W.* II, iii, 163, *Macb.* I, vi, 4 ff. — *Mer. V.* II, ix, 28 ff., *Macb.* I, vii, 35 ff. — *K.J.* IV, ii, 116 f., *Macb.* I, vii, 80 f. — *Hen. V* III, i, 16 f., *Macb.* II, iii, 140 f. — *Rich. III* II, i, 92, *Macb.* V, ii, 15 f. — *TC* II, ii, 30 ff.

suspect dependence when one of two otherwise closely similar details shows significant deviations from norms of style, convention, and logic. It is unlikely that such deviations were imitated in a "rhetorical" age. In every case we are also aided by the safely established date of one of the passages compared. In short, comparison of one poet with another provides a system of reference necessary in studies of literary chronology. The processes we have examined in ch. I may be compared to the transformations of a ray of light refracted in a succession of different media.

It will be seen that in chapter II I have connected different sonnets into chronologically coherent groups when three conditions can be regarded as fulfilled, separately or in combination. The first condition is that of the identical situation.[4] When we find such sonnets as CXXXV—CXLII, all dealing with the lady's faithlessness and with the poet's suffering, or CIX, CX, and CXVII—CXX, expressing certain feelings on the part of the poet after a period of estrangement, or XL—XLII, accusing and excusing the rival friend — then it seems natural to suppose that the members of these groups were composed, respectively, within the same short period, if not actually on the same occasion. For if these poems are mere literary productions, describing psychological processes, it is reasonable to assume that the various details of such matters were worked out without interruption and not at long intervals. A short story writer is not likely to work out the details of a brief story of jealousy and passion at intervals of months and years. If on the other hand these sonnets are autobiographical, they must be responses to certain definite situations, and the idea of composition at intervals is even more unnatural. — Of course *some* amount of personal experience must have played a part even in a 'literary' undertaking.

---

[4] LEVER has already stressed the importance of identical situations for classifying and ordering the *Sonnets*: "On the analogy of scenes in a drama, it is possible to consider the *Sonnets* as a number of groups, like that formed by the first nineteen sonnets of the Quarto, each based upon some well-defined theme or situation, expressed through all the technical resources of this medium. Such groups would in turn form part of a composite sequence — using 'sequence' in a more flexible sense than has been considered hitherto — developing not in steady progression from beginning to end, but through the juxtaposition of themes and situations parted by intervals of time and modifications of outlook" (*op. cit.*, p. 172; my emphasis).

The second condition is that of formal coherence. One type is of a simple kind and has been systematically applied by BRAY in rearranging the sonnets: endlinking, taken in a broad sense of the term. The linkings I have used do not involve rearrangements and have been known for a long time. Thus there can be very little doubt that, for example, the last line of no. XCI or of CXVIII is alluded to in the first of nos. XCII and CXIX, respectively (cf. pp. 150 ff.). This trick was a well-known commonplace in sonnet poetry. The case of nos. XL—XLII, CXXXIII, CXXXIV, and CXLIV is of a different type. What we have here is a group in which a symmetrical planning is perceptible, the several poems being corresponding parts within the whole. Also in this case is it reasonable to imagine that the various pieces that make up the symmetrical whole were composed at the same time, when the poet conceived and carried out his plan. Nos. LXXVI and CVIII are a simpler instance of a similar kind and strike the reader as structurally similar variations on the same theme. The idea of a long interval of composition seems far-fetched here, too. The group XL—XLII, CXXXIII, CXXXIV, CXLIV and the group LXXVI—CVIII fulfil both the condition of the identical situation and that of the formal coherence.

The third condition is that of common external influence. Even if the author's own phrases and images may recur after longer and shorter intervals, it is probable that those of his works that betray foreign influence issuing in similar phraseology were written at about the same time. The likelihood that this is so is of course particularly great if this phraseology does not later recur in Shakespeare's works or else recurs sporadically or in a different shape. Instances of this are the procreation sonnets and *Venus and Adonis* influenced above all by the *Zodiake* and *Arcadia*, no. XIX and *Lucrece* 925 ff. influenced by Ovid, and the 'flower' sonnets XCVIII and XCIX — with a *Lucrece* stanza — influenced by Constable's *Diana*. I have already pointed out the scarceness of parallels to the first group; as to the second, we find various other references to Time's destructive activity in later Shakespeare works, but no close parallels to the phraseology in no. XIX and *Lucrece*. The same goes for the 'flower' conceits: we find flowers used in many instances of praise of beauty, but we do not find any further cases of the 'charms-lent-to-flowers' formula — except in such an early text as *VA* (935 ff.). Venus here exclaims against Death who has robbed her of Adonis,

> *Who when he liu'd, his breath and beautie set*
> *Glosse on the rose, smell to the violet.*[5]

I have tentatively suggested that the second and third conditions, if fulfilled, may seem indicative of a purely literary, and not auto-biographical, origin of the sonnets. However, this is only a possibility: a strict attention to form and a marked literary influence are not necessarily incompatible with an autobiographical background, as shown for example by Tasso's and Tansillo's sonneteering.

It is not capable of absolute proof that these three conditions, if fulfilled, indicate a simultaneous date of composition. Nor do we have at our disposal a body of poems demonstrably written at about the same time by one particular author of the age. We must content ourselves with probabilities, and it is just as probable that the groups of Shakespeare sonnets indicated above belong together chronologically as it is probable that a scene in a Shakespeare play was written without long intervals in the composition. Thus if we apply the principles discussed here we are not in danger of reasoning in a circle since our arguments are based on what is psychologically natural and *a priori* probable.

*

Before we go on to consider what conclusions we may draw from the discussion in chapters I and II, it is in place to examine certain characteristic arguments based on data belonging to group e). EMERSON assigned the *Sonnets*, with the *Poems*, to Shakespeare's early work on the evidence of feminine rhymes and run-on lines,[6] and though his verdict that the *Sonnets* were probably "written about the time of *Lucrece*, or soon after" (p. 130) is not far removed from my own conclusions as regards a fair number of the *Sonnets*, I am not sure that *Venus and Adonis* and *Lucrece* are comparable to

---

[5] As LEE pointed out in his 1907 edition, the whole of Venus' speech against Death is closely paralleled in Metello Giovanni Tarchagnota's *Adone*, stanzas 54—59 (Venice ed. 1550). LEE's comment is recorded in ROLLINS's *Poems* edition.

[6] *Shakespeare's Sonneteering*, SP xx, 1923, pp. 111 ff. Results summarized by ROLLINS, II, p. 67.

the *Sonnets* in the respects discussed by EMERSON. It is evident that there is much truth in EMERSON's own remark on the danger of comparing proportions of run-on lines: "Perhaps the somewhat larger percentage in the *Sonnets* is partly accounted for by the longer stanza, or thought-unit of the sonnet with its fourteen lines, compared with the six-line stanza of the *Poems*" (*ibid.*). Other similar verse-tests seem equally unreliable in dating the *Sonnets*. FEUILLERAT[7] uses metrical data in his discussion of the chronology of the sonnets, but he regards the versification of the *Sonnets* merely as an illustration of a development which he has ascertained in advance.

SCHMIDT[8] also discusses differences between Shakespeare's early and his later style, but his arguments are vaguer than EMERSON's. Thus we learn that "die Sprache des jungen Shakespeare ist durch die Festigkeit seiner Prägungen bestimmt. Es fehlen die weichen Übergänge. Die Grenzen der Verse, der Sätze, der Sinn- und Themenabschnitte sind klar und hart" (p. 289). But "in den späteren Sonetten löst sich die starre Form. Die innere Bewegung, der Rhythmus strömt über die Versgrenzen, in einzelnen Fällen sogar über die Grenzen des Quartetts" (p. 304). These descriptions, however, are not founded on a detailed examination and do not agree with others that are (for example BROOKE's, whose investigation tends to show that on the contrary the number of run-on lines is somewhat higher in the earlier Q sonnets than in the later).[9] We must also, of course, allow for the different content of different sonnets. Another critic using stylistic criteria as an argument is BATESON, who in his criticism of HOTSON's early date for the *Sonnets* resorts to impressions such as, "The style of this sonnet [CVII] is more mature, not less mature, than that of either *Venus and Adonis* or *Lucrece*".[1] But these styles are not comparable for reasons we have referred to before. Again, there is "the absence from the sonnet of the rash of verbal antitheses that characterizes Shakespeare's early manner" (*ibid.*). However, HOTSON does not only discuss no. CVII but, by implication, the majority of Shake-

---

[7] *The Composition of Shakespeare's Plays.* New Haven, 1953, pp. 70 ff.

[8] *Sinnesänderung und Bildvertiefung in Shakespeares Sonetten*, Anglia LXII, 1938, pp. 286 ff.

[9] Edition 1936, p. 5. BROOKE also summarily characterizes the later Q sonnets as "rather less fluently written".

[1] *Op. cit.*, p. 87.

speare's sonnets, and I have shown elsewhere[2] that antithesis is a very common feature of the *Sonnets*. Particularly striking is the frequency of series of antitheses, which are commoner in the later Q sonnets than in the earlier. Does this, then, mean that the dark lady and the 'triangle' sonnets are earlier than the rest? If they are, it hardly appears from the frequency of antithesis: the subject-matter of these sonnets would seem to be of some importance.

J. M. NOSWORTHY, as we have seen another critic of HOTSON's early dating, compares a select number of the words used by Shake-speare in nos. CVII, CXIX, CXXI, CXXIII, and CXXIV with his use in the plays.[3] The sonnets examined "yield about twenty-five examples of what appear to be undeniably post-1600 or even Jacobean usages, and several of these are impressive" (p. 321). As a check, Nos-WORTHY applies this vocabulary test also to the two sonnets included in *The Passionate Pilgrim* and thus not later than 1599. No. CXXXVIII shows links with the *Henry VI* cycle and suggests a composition date in the early 1590's, while 1598—99 is the date proposed for no. CXLIV. These suggestions are not uninteresting, but the material is of course much too limited, and such a statement as "two rare and significant words [*limbecks* and *rebuked*] link it [CXIX] with *Macbeth*" (p. 319) is not reassuring,[4] any more than "there is nothing to suggest that the sonnet (CXLIV) is a particularly early one, and some weight, I think, attaches to the *Julius Caesar* links" (p. 323). These links consist in the use of *directly*, found in Shakespeare "at all periods, but eight examples out of a total of twenty-nine appear in *Julius Caesar*", and of *fire* (verb), found in *3 Henry VI*, *Richard II*, *Julius Caesar* (2), *Hamlet*, and *King Lear* (p. 322). Who can feel convinced on such evidence? Yet NOSWORTHY is "inclined to claim propinquity." He also ignores the fact that words are sometimes used at an early stage, are discarded, and crop up again later.[5] The distribution, for instance, of such words chosen at random and denoting common concepts as *brainsick* (*I Hen. VI*,

---

[2] *Op. cit.*, pp. 133 ff.

[3] *Op. cit.*, pp. 317 ff.

[4] The less so as the verb *rebuke* is also found in *Hen. V*.

[5] This is thus a different process from that pointed out long ago by BEECHING (ed., pp. xxiv ff.) and BECKWITH (*On the Chronology of Shakespeare's Sonnets*, JEGP xxv, 1926, pp. 227 ff.), namely, that Shakespeare sometimes repeats words just after he has first used them, and then never resorts to them again (cf. ROLLINS II, pp. 66 f.).

2 Hen. VI, Tit. A., Luc., TC), bruit (sb.) (*3 Hen. VI, TC., Tim. A*), bruit (vb) (*I Hen. VI, 2 Hen. IV, Ham., Macb.*), *countless* (*VA, Tit. A., Per.*), *livelihood* (*VA, All's W.*), *love-sick* (*VA, Tit. A., Ant. C.*), *pith* (*VA, Tam. Shr., Hen. V, Ham., M.f.M., Oth.*), *satiety* (*VA, Tam. Shr., Oth., Tim. A.*), *timorous* (*I Hen. VI, 3 Hen. VI, VA., Rich. III, All's W., Oth.*), *waned, waning* (*2 Hen. VI, 3 Hen. VI, Luc., Son. 126, Tam. Shr., Rich. III, Ant. C.*), *I wis* (*Rich. III, Tam. Shr., Mer. V., Per.*), and *workmanship* (*VA* (2), *Cy.*) should make us careful. Too much, in short, must not be made of Shakespeare's use of isolated words. On the contrary, conclusions drawn from resemblances on such points are of course even more hazardous than those based on similarities of imagery and figures. It is quite possible that some sonnets are late, but their being so must be proved in a different way. Thus as expected, such data as those adduced by EMERSON, SCHMIDT, BATESON, and NOSWORTHY — other examples could easily be given — do not seem more reliable in a discussion of chronology than the c) data as handled by BALDWIN.

CONCLUSIONS

'Before 1592' was the date suggested for no. XVII. But there is reason to believe that all the procreation sonnets were written within a short period. Therefore nos. I—XIV and no. XVI were probably also composed before 1592 or at least not much later. This is supported by parallels in *Venus and Adonis* (1592), which indicate a simultaneous date since there is a strong dependence of both texts on Palingenius' *Zodiake* and Sidney's *Arcadia*. So the procreation sonnets would date shortly before or about 1592. — Nos. LXVI—LXVIII are variations on the same theme and read like a continuous sequence. There is no objection to our dating them before 1592, but a more precise date does not seem possible. Nor is it possible to suggest one, beyond 1592 as an *ante quem* limit, in the case of no. LXXXI. No. XCII continues no. XCI and is in its turn continued in no. XCIII, and XCIV—XCVI vary the same theme: the poet's dependence on the friend's love and his suspicions that the friend may not be faithful. Since all these poems reflect the same situation it seems possible for all of them to share the date suggested for XCII: before 1592. A thematic resemblance of a similarly special kind ties up no. CXLII with CXXXV—CXLI: the lady's wantonness, the poet's suffering. But CXLII may be dated before 1592; therefore it is reasonable to regard CXXXV—CXLI as written at the same time or not much later.

Another psychological situation is described by nos. CIX, CX, CXVII—CXX, some of which are also formally connected: the poet's feelings vis-à-vis his friend after a period of estrangement. Since CXIX may be dated before 1593, it would follow that the other sonnets share a similar date. But there is nothing to indicate an *a quo* limit.

No. XXXVIII describes the friend as a perpetual source of inspiration for the poet. This poem does not seem clearly connectible, least of all chronologically, with any other. There is nothing to indicate a more precise dating than 'before 1594.' The situation is analogous in the case of nos. LXXV and CIV: there is no obvious link with any other sonnets, and it does not seem possible to narrow down the dating.

Nos. XXXIII—XXXV or possibly XXXVI form a homogeneous group dealing with the 'clouding of friendship', a theme that indicates a chronological connection. Parallels in *Edw. III* indicate some date possibly two or three years earlier than 1595 for these poems (cf. p. 135), while another parallel in *I Hen. IV* points to 1597 for at least XXXIII. But since the parallels between *Edw. III* and XXXIII seem to be more important than the similarities of phrasing between XXXIII, XXXIV, and *I Hen. IV*, the earlier date appears more probable than the later (cf. p. 119 f.).

Nos. CXXVII and CXXXII are closely connected and seem written some time between 1591 and 1595, possibly before 1592—93. No. CXLVI, on the other hand, is an isolated poem probably written before 1596.

Nos. XXX and XXXI form one group, and while we have an *a quo* date in 1591, there is no indication of an *ante quem* limit. The two 'flower' sonnets XCVIII and XCIX were assigned to a period later than 1592 with the aid of a parallel in Constable's *Diana*. This fits in with the fact that a parallel in *Lucrece* points to a date around 1593. The same date applies to no. XIX, dealing with the immortality theme. There is no *a quo* limit for no. XVIII, and no *ante quem* limit for no. CVI.

Nos. XL, XLI, and XLII all describe a triangle and obviously deal with an identical situation. The same holds for CXXXIII, CXXXIV, and CXLIV. But it is probable that XLI is not far removed in point of time from *I Hen. VI*, and nothing contradicts this assumption. Therefore the other poems seem written in the same period, and a parallel in *VA* may suggest that the time of composition falls some time between 1591 and 1593. LIV is another poem closely paralleled in *I Hen. VI*, and there is nothing to contradict 1591 -92 as a likely date. — As to CV, there is no clear indication of date except the *ante quem* year 1601.

It is necessary here to repeat the reservation made in ch. I, that although the bulk of the passages there analysed are in all probability originals and imitations, it is not certain that this is true of all of them. The problems discussed are delicate, and we must reckon with the possibility that some parallels have been misinterpreted and are merely accidental. In any case most of the dates I have suggested seem to me at least worthy of serious consideration. I should like particularly to stress the possibility that forty-six sonnets date before or around 1592. If this is correct, these sonnets would be earlier than commonly recognized.

We may then give the following answers to the questions asked on p. 136:

a) There seem to be no decisive objections to the datings suggested in ch. I; b) These datings, if correct, seem to be valid also for other sonnets than those examined in that chapter; c) In a number of cases it has been possible to narrow down the limits of dating.

Certain reservations made, the vast majority of the sonnets we have examined seem thus to have been written between 1591—92 and 1594—95. Before we continue our reasoning, we must take a look at the subject-matter of those we have dealt with, arranged in the approximate order of dating. Before 1592: I—XIV, XVI, XVII, procreation theme; LXVI—LXVIII, depravity of time, beauty and purity of friend; LXXXI, transitoriness-immortality; XCI—XCVI, poet entirely dependent on friend's love, suspected faithlessness; CXXXV—CXLII, lady's wantonness, poet's suffering. 1591—92: LIV, immortality in verse. After 1591: CVI, beauty of bygone days prophesies friend's beauty; XXX—XXXI, love for friend poet's only consolation. 1591—93: XL—XLII, CXXXIII—CXXXIV, CXLIV, rivalry, triangle. About 1593: CIX, CX, CXVII—CXX, poet and friend reunited after estrangement. Before 1592—93 and 1594—95: XXXIII—XXXV clouding of friendship, XXXVIII, friend poet's source of inspiration; LXXV, lover's mixed jealousy and pride, CIV, time and beauty, CXXVII, CXXXII, beauty of black eyes. 1593—4: XIX, immortality. Around 1593: XCVIII—XCIX, praise of beauty in 'flower' conceit. 1594—95: CXLVI, religious theme; flesh and spirit. Before 1601: XVIII, immortality, CV, monotony of poet's verse praising friend.

As will be seen, there is nothing to prevent us from reading a 'story' into this if we want to do so. We find the poet at an early stage praising the beauty and purity of the friend, promising to

make him immortal, assuring him that he is the poet's only consolation and source of inspiration, and that his life is 'dependent
on that love of thine', and at the same time hinting that the friend's
heart is 'in other place'. The sonnets on the lady fit in with this, as
well as the series on the triangle and on the clouding of friendship.
All these sonnets, if our datings are accepted, would be composed
some time between 1591 and 1593. About 1593 we find the sonnets
on reunion after an estrangement apparently due to the poet's
breaking with the friend and 'hoisting sail to all the winds that
should transport me farthest from your sight'. Thus a coherent
pattern, whether literary or autobiographical, would emerge from
our dating. After (?) these poems falls the sonnet on the flesh-
and-spirit theme, and at any time before 1601 that on the monotony
of the poet's verse. Some time around 1593 we find such sonnets
as the 'mourning eyes' and 'flower' ones, and the immortality
sonnet no. XIX. The procreation sonnets make up a group of their
own. It is reasonable to suppose that the poems on the 'triangle',
on the dark lady, and on the friend's inconstancy belong closely
together and that poems on beauty, immortality, etc. are more or
less scattered chronologically. This leads us to another question: We
have so far only discussed the dating of 64 sonnets, less than half
the number contained in the Quarto. What about the others?

As said in the introduction, I have not undertaken to suggest a
dating for all Shakespeare's sonnets, and what more I have to say is
entirely tentative. But just as we found it possible to perceive
certain units by starting from isolated poems, so it might perhaps
be worth while to see if we can continue this inductive process,
starting from the units we have arrived at. However, we must first
give a survey of the remaining sonnets and refer to some results of
previous research.

*

The poems we have not yet dealt with can be roughly divided
into three groups. The first group includes sonnets which deal
with love and beauty without calling either in question. In this
group, then, belong XV, LV, LXIII, LXV (beauty immortalized by
poet's verse), LX (friend's worth immortal in a transitory world),
XX ('a man in hue, all hues in his controlling'), XXII (exchange of
hearts), XXIII (eloquent looks), XXIV ('thy beauty's form in table

of my heart'), xxv (poet's love not subjected to change), xxvi ('written ambassage' sent to patron), xxvii (thought of friend keeps poet awake), xxviii ('day by night, and night by day', poet oppressed in friend's absence), xxix (thought of friend poet's sole happiness), xxxvi (though love is 'undivided', poet suggests separation lest friend should suffer harm), xxxvii ('made lame by fortune', poet finds consolation in love for friend), xliii (friend in dream illuminates poet's night), xliv—xlv (thought reduces distance from friend), xlvi—xlvii (conventional conceit of war between eye and heart), xxxix, l—lii (friend absent from poet), liii ('you in every blessed shape we know'), lix (beloved's image in ancient times), lxii (poet's self-love is love for friend), lxxi—lxxiv (transitoriness and strong love), xcvii ('How like a winter hath my absence been from thee'), cvii (love no longer threatened by dangers), cxi, cxii (friend's pity poet's consolation), cxiii, cxiv (poet's eye sees only friend), cxv (love still growing), cxvi, cxxiii—cxxv (constancy of love), cxxx (lady's beauty requires no artificial praise). Thus all these sonnets deal with worship of beauty and with intense and constant love. Some of the poems fall naturally into groups: xx and liii (friend's beauty reflected in all fair shapes; cf. p. 95), xxvii, xxviii, xliii (friend is in poet's thought at night), xxix, xxxvii, cxi, cxii (love for friend makes poet happy in distress), xliv, xlv, l, li (absence of beloved). In this group we might also include poems dealing more exclusively with the poet's verse but presupposing unlimited love and admiration: xxi, lxxvi, cviii (poet's verse unadorned and monotonous but expressing genuine sentiments), lxxviii—lxxx, xxxii, lxxxii—lxxxvi (others, though praising recipient more eloquently than poet, lack his feeling), c—ci (Muse must break her silence), cii (love stronger though not professed in verse), ciii (friend's beauty 'oergoes my blunt invention'). It is possible that a) nos. xxvii, xxviii, xliii, b) xxix, xxxvii, cxi, cxii, and c) xliv, xlv, l, li belong chronologically together since they seem to depict certain definite situations. On the other hand the themes of these groups are more conventional than those dealt with on the next page, so it cannot be excluded that the sonnets indicated were written at intervals.

The second group of sonnets differs from the first in that love and beauty are described as problematic: moods and feelings range from uneasiness to desperation, jealousy, and hatred. Friend and lady are unfaithful, passion resembles a disease. These sonnets are nos. XLVIII (friend is left the prey of 'every vulgar thief'), XLIX (self-humiliation and anticipation of friend's estrangement), LVI (reunion after 'sad interim'), LVII, LVIII (poet like slave waiting for friend to return), LXI (jealousy keeps poet awake), LXIX, LXX (suspicion of vice in friend), LXXXVII (poet renounces all demands on friend), LXXXVIII—XC, CXLIX (bitter self-humiliation, recipient's indifference), CXXXI, CXLIII, CXLV, CXLVII, CXLVIII, CL—CLII (passion, plea for mercy, jealousy, hatred), CXXIX ('the expense of spirit in a waste of shame is lust in action'). The grouping made here is a thematic one, and beyond the inference that poems hinting at or predicting estrangement might precede those dealing with relationships more obviously complicated,[6] there is nothing to suggest the chronological order.

A third group consists of some stray poems which fall outside the two categories indicated above. Nos. LXIV and CXXVI deal with the theme of transitoriness, which in these poems is not, as in many other sonnets, contrasted with that of eternizing verse. No. LXXVII is a gift sonnet possibly accompanying several different presents; CXXVIII, whose dependence on *Diana* is very doubtful, is addressed to a lady playing the virginal. Other sonnets in this group are CXXI ('Tis better to be vile than vile esteemed'), CXXII ('Thy gift, thy tables are within my brain'), and CLIII—CLIV (conventional 'Cupid's brand' conceit). No. CXXI may have some connection with other poems apparently dealing with the poet's personal situation (XXIX, XXXVII, CXI, CXII), and no. CXXII, as LEE suggests, with the gift sonnet no. LXXVII, but this is far from certain.

Various suggestions have been made as regards the dating of some of the sonnets in these three groups. We have already referred to some attempts to do so with the aid of stylistic criteria. Better known than these, however, are the efforts, mentioned in the introduction, to find topical allusions in nos. CVII, CXXIII, and CXXIV. Though it seems probable that these poems do contain such allusions, it has not been possible to identify them with any amount of

---

[6] This is obviously the case if the sonnets are autobiographical, if not, the inverse order is also possible.

certainty. The same, as we have seen, goes for other poems which are supposed to allude to contemporary events and persons. — BALDWIN is one of the very few critics who sees no topical allusions at all in no. CVII. Instead he suggests that the meaning of the sonnet may be brought out by comparing it with the first quatrain of no. LXV, which asks,

> *Since brasse, nor stone, nor earth, nor boundlesse sea,*
> *But sad mortallity ore-swaies their power,*
> *How with this rage shall beautie hold a plea,*
> *Whose action is no stronger than a flower?*

According to BALDWIN, this question is answered in the first quatrain of CVII, giving "the basic reply" elaborated and concluded in the remainder of the poem:

> *Not mine owne feares, nor the prophetick soule,*
> *Of the wide world, dreaming on things to come,*
> *Can yet the lease of my true loue controule,*
> *Supposde as forfeit to a confin'd doome.*

BALDWIN points out that both passages are in the same legal phraseology and that CVII, 4 refers to the theme of *tempus edax rerum*. "So the first quatrain of Sonnet LXV poses the Ovidian question in legal figure, and the first quatrain of Sonnet CVII answers that same question in legal figure. Failure to grasp the Ovidian reference has resulted in many needless conjectures as to possible specific allusions in this first quatrain. There are none here certainly" (p. 310). But CVII, 1—4 does not answer the question of no. LXV, which is: *How* shall fragile beauty 'hold a plea' with the rage of time and death; it merely expresses moods opposite to those expressed in LXV. The supposed Ovidian reference is carefully veiled, and legal figures are scattered through many other sonnets. BALDWIN's is hardly a valid argument against the topicality of CVII, and the assumed connection between CVII and LXV seems frail indeed.

BALDWIN suggests dates for several other sonnets of the three categories we have referred to above.[7] However, since his arguments are of the same kind as those we have already discussed at

---

[7] Nos. XX, XXII, XXVI, XXVIII, XLIII, XLVIII, L, LI, LII, LXXX, LXXXIII; pp. 166 ff., 224, 231, 249, 254 ff., 291, and 293.

some length, and are mostly no more acceptable than these, it may be permissible to pass them by.[8] It may be said, in short, that no attempts so far to give exact dates for any of the sonnets surveyed above seem to me to have been successful. We shall instead consider some facts of a more general and statistical character, from which certain approximate dates emerge.

Much work has been devoted to a large-scale mapping out of the resemblances of detail between the *Sonnets* and Shakespeare's other works at different periods. Thus ISAAC[9] and DAVIS[1] made estimates of this kind. The numbers of resemblances found by them were tabulated by ALDEN so as to facilitate a survey of the accumulation of parallels.[2] After the publication of ALDEN's *Variorum* edition including these tables (1916), DAVIS made a second estimate, arriving at higher values than in the first. This latter table, with the other two, is given by ROLLINS.[3] In order to make the survey still easier, I have drawn a diagram based on ISAAC's and DAVIS's figures and showing CHAMBERS's dates for poems and plays as supplied by ROLLINS.[4] The plain columns represent ISAAC's figures, the hatched ones DAVIS's before ALDEN's edition, the black ones DAVIS's after ALDEN's edition.

The value of the figures on which this diagram is based is reduced by the fact that strong as well as weak parallels are among those listed by both scholars, and that on some points their graphs differ in a conspicuous way. Yet on the whole ISAAC and DAVIS agree in

---

[8] The only point on which I agree with BALDWIN here is his observation that nos. L and LI may be imitated in the following sentence by Cornwallis: *I hate the dulnesse of my owne feet and my horses when I trauel, & cherish the nimblenesse of my thoughts which can flie ouer the world in an afternoone* (p. 255). This would place L and LI earlier than 1600, which there is no reason to doubt.

[9] *Die Sonett-Periode in Shakespeare's Leben*, SJ XIX, 1884, pp. 176 ff.

[1] Unpublished MS. notes in Stanford Univ. Library. Cf. ALDEN's edition, p. 447.

[2] *Op. cit., ibid.* FORT (*A Time Scheme for Shakespeare's Sonnets*, p. 18) also gives these tables.

[3] II, pp. 64 f.

[4] CHAMBERS's dates do not seem entirely satisfactory nowadays. It is probable that *Titus Andronicus* was written one or two years earlier than he thought. *Venus and Adonis* was probably composed in 1592, and *Lucrece* probably late in 1593. SCHRICKX's suggestion that *Love's Labour's Lost* was originally written in 1592 is naturally of a certain interest to the present author (cf. p. 115 above). It may be observed in this connection that allusions in the plays are for obvious reasons easier to identify than allusions in the *Sonnets*. — The date of *All's Well* is a problem. *Twelfth Night* may be somewhat later and *The Merry Wives* somewhat earlier than CHAMBERS proposed. On the whole, however, his dates may be acceptable in a rough survey.

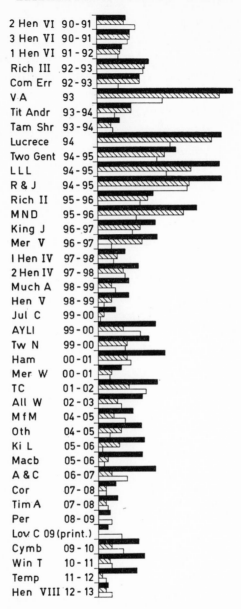

finding accumulations of parallels particularly in the early Shake-spearean works, and their figures yield some marked peaks, one for 1592—93 (if we date *VA* a little earlier than 1593), the others for 1594—95. Accumulation of parallels in works from these years is also found by other critics.[5] The following ones in particular stress the large number of parallels between the *Sonnets* and Shakespeare's first period: SARRAZIN, LEE, MC CLUMPHA, CHAMBERS, WIETFELD, ADAMS, FORT, BROOKE, and ST. CLAIR.[6] As mentioned before, BALDWIN also seems to accept the figures of ISAAC and DAVIS: "These statistics ... probably give some probability that the bulk of Shakspere's sonnets were early" (p. 342). This probability is supported by some observations of a psychological character that we might finally make on the basis of our previous findings.

We have pointed out that in grouping the sonnets there is a danger of jumping to conclusions and of mixing up sonnets on the same subject with sonnets written at the same time. Yet in the case of a number of sonnets it did not seem hazardous to suppose that they describe identical situations, fictitious or not (reunion after estrangement, friend's absence, 'triangle' etc.), while others are linked together by formal means. Now even if all the sonnets on erotic complications do not reflect identical situations in a narrow sense of the word, it is not going too far to say that they all deal with a coherent set of events, and that the drama they describe, whether a real one or not, must reasonably have been conceived — or enacted — during a fairly short period. This I think is tacitly assumed by most critics. Again, it is not hazardous to suppose that, if autobiographical, sonnets giving vent to suspicions and doubts, or describing the initial phase of an estrangement ('the clouding of friendship') are closely associated with the 'triangle' sonnets in that they immediately precede them. But this is not necessarily so if the sonnet story is fictitious. If this should be the case, we can only say that it is psychologically probable that all these sonnets on erotic complications are not too far apart in point of time. It would then follow that the second group of the sonnets surveyed on p. 188 above

---

[5] BEECHING dissented (ed., pp. xxiv ff.), arguing for later dates on the ground that there are parallels also with later plays (*Ham.*, *Oth.*). This is denied by nobody, but the cumulative evidence points to an earlier date. Cf. also ROLLINS II, p. 66. BEECHING's views seem shared by WALSH (ed., p. 30). FORT however rightly pointed out that parallels between the *Sonnets* and the early plays are "simple and direct", while parallels in the later plays are "very complicated phenomena" (*op. cit.*, p. 20).

[6] Cf. ROLLINS II, pp. 65 ff. ST. CLAIR's results, as yet unpublished, are given by ROLLINS on p. 69 ("the greatest number of the sonnets were written between 1591 and 1596"). ST. CLAIR has kindly informed me that he still regards these conclusions as valid, though he would prefer the year 1592 to 1591 if he were to set sharply defined limits.

would date from the same main period as those we have assigned to the time between 1591 and 1593.

As regards the poems belonging in the first group our situation is far more difficult. If we suppose that they are autobiographical, it could of course be argued that all these sonnets praising the friend's beauty, describing exchange of hearts, promising to immortalize the recipient, lamenting his absence and assuring him that he is always in the poet's thoughts, etc. were written during the happy period when no complications had as yet arisen. But the possibility cannot be excluded that this is a rash inference, and the texts — if we do not accept the Q order — do not allow our reading this into them. The happy state described in the sonnets may be one that prevailed *after* the dark lady affair, and may thus be the result of a reconciliation with the friend. Or these poems may be addressed to a different person than the rival friend, and some of them may be intended for a patron. Critics have too easily persuaded themselves that the recipient is all the time the same person. A study of Ronsard's, Tansillo's, or Tasso's poems should teach us to be careful. It is probable that, if autobiographical, most of the 'friend sonnets' have the same addressee, but it is not provable. It is simply impossible to say anything definite about these things, and unlike the sonnets in the second group, those in the first do not outline a sequence of events. Therefore we cannot group them chronologically with those on similar themes that we have earlier tried to date.

If again we suppose that the themes of this group of sonnets are wholly fictitious it is naturally even more difficult to suggest a probable period of composition. As pointed out above, these themes are more conventional than those of the second group, and may consequently be scattered over a longish period or written during a short one; it is impossible to say which. The point is that they do not describe certain definite situations likely to have been conceived and sketched in a short time, so the mechanism of composition cannot be reconstructed with any amount of probability. We must therefore resort to the overall distribution of parallels which indicates an early rather than a late date.

It is, if possible, even more hazardous to make suggestions in the case of the remaining sonnets. To the dating of the sonnet accompanying a gift and to that thanking the recipient for one, for example, we have not the slightest clue, any more than we have to the dating of the others. It is reasonable to hold that CLIII and CLIV are quite early, being strongly conventional and in the nature of exercises, just as the 'flower' sonnets, XCVIII and XCIX. But they may be later than we think and were perhaps written on request as variations on a given theme. Sonnets were often composed in this way. At any rate, just as some Shakespeare sonnets seem to have been written before the hey-day of sonneteering in England, so others may quite well have been composed after the fashion had passed, and some may be quite late. But this remains to be proved.

We have seen that parallels to Shakespeare's sonnets can be found not only in those of his works that date from 1591—1594, but also in later ones. Sonnets which offer resemblances to such later works, on the other hand, we have sometimes for various reasons proposed to date early. Therefore, if these datings are acceptable, it is in the sonnets that we not seldom find 'the germ' of an image, a figure, a motif, or a phrase. The sonnets — and perhaps actual experiences behind them — may long have continued to echo in the poet's mind.

A SELECT BIBLIOGRAPHY

TEXTS

Alexander, Sir William, *The Poetical Works* II (*Aurora*), edited by L. E. KASTNER and H. B. CHARLTON. The Scottish Text Society. Edinburgh and London, 1929.

Anthologia Graeca I—IV, ed. HERMANN BECKBY. München, 1957—58.

de Baïf, Ian Antoine, *Evvres en Rime* avec ... des Notes par Ch. MARTY-LAVEAUX I. Paris, 1881.

de Barbezieux, Rigaut, *Les Chansons* ... par JOSEPH ANGLADE. Revue des Langues Romanes 60, 1918, pp. 201 ff.

Barnfield, Richard, *The Poems*, edited by M. SUMMERS. London, 1936.

du Bellay, Joachim, *Oeuvres Poétiques* I. *Recueils de Sonnets* (*l'Olive*), édition critique publiée par H. CHAMARD. Paris, 1908.

Belleau, Remy, *Oeuvres Complètes* I—III, nouvelle édition publiée ... par A. GOUVERNEUR. Paris, 1867.

Bembo, Pietro, *Le Rime*. Venetia, 1561.

Caro, Annibal, *Rime* ... riviste ... par GIAMBATTISTA NOVELLI. Venezia, 1757.

Chariteo, *Le Rime* I—II a cura di E. PÈRCOPO. Napoli, 1892.

Constable, Henry, *The Poems*, edited by JOAN GRUNDY. Liverpool, 1960.

Daniel, Samuel, *The Complete Works* I—V, edited by A. B. GROSART. London, 1885—1896.
— *Poems and A Defence of Ryme*, edited by A. C. SPRAGUE. Cambridge, Mass., 1930.

Davies, Sir John, *The Complete Works* I—II, edited by A. B. GROSART. London, 1876.

Deloney, Thomas, *Works*, edited ... by F. O. MANN. Oxford, 1912.

Desportes, Philippe, *Les Amours de Diane* I—II, édition critique publiée ... par V. E. GRAHAM. Paris, 1959.

Drayton, Michael, *The Works* I—V, edited by W. HEBEL, K. TILLOTSON, G. H. NEWDIGATE. Oxford, 1931—41.

Drummond of Hawthornden, William, *The Poetical Works* I—II, edited by L. E. KASTNER. The Scottish Text Society. Edinburgh and London, 1913.

Elizabethan Sonnets, newly arranged and indexed ... by SIDNEY LEE. I (Syr Philip Sidney, *Astrophel and Stella, Sundry other rare Sonnets ..., Sonnets and Poetical Translations;* Thomas Watson, *The Tears of Fancie*, Barnabe Barnes, *Parthenophil and Parthenophe*, etc.). II (Thomas Lodge, *Phillis*, Giles Fletcher, *Licia*, Henry Constable and others, *Diana*, Samuel Daniel, *Delia*, William Percy, *Sonnets to the Fairest Coelia*, Anonymous, *Zepheria*, Michael Drayton, *Idea*, Edmund Spenser, *Amoretti and Epithalamion*, Bartholomew Griffin, *Fidessa*, Richard Linche, *Diella*, William Smith, *Chloris*, Robert Tofte, *Laura*). Westminster, 1904.

Emaricdulfe, edited by Ch. EDMONDS (*A Lamport Garland*). London, 1881.

England's Helicon I—II, edited by H. E. ROLLINS. Cambridge, Mass., 1935.

I Fiori delle Rime de Poeti illustrissimi, nuovamente raccolti ... da Girolamo Ruscelli. In Venetia, 1558.

Fowler, William, *The Works* I (*The Tarantula of Loue*), edited by H. W. MEIKLE. The Scottish Text Society. Edinburgh and London, 1914.

Gascoigne, George, *The Posies*, edited by J. W. CUNLIFFE. Cambridge, 1907.

Greville, Fulke, *Poems and Dramas* I (*Caelica*), edited by G. BULLOUGH. Edinburgh and London, 1939.

Guarini, Battista, *Rime*. In Amstelodamo, 1663.

Guidiccioni, Giovanni, *Le Rime* a cura di E. CHIORBOLI. Scrittori d'Italia 35. Bari, 1912.

Guittone d'Arezzo, *Le Rime* a cura di FRANCESCO EGIDI. Scrittori d'Italia 175. Bari, 1940.

Horatius Flaccus, Q, *Oden und Epoden*, erklärt von A. KIESSLING, siebente Auflage besorgt von R. HEINZE. Berlin, 1930.

Jamyn, Amadis, *Oeuvres Poétiques*, par G. COLLETET ... et Ch. BRUNET. Paris, 1879.

Jodelle, Étienne, *Oeuvres Poétiques* I—II, édition ... publiée par Ch. MARTY-LAVEAUX. Paris, 1870.

Labé, Louise, *Oeuvres publiées* ... par P. BLANCHEMAIN. Paris, 1875.

Lyly, John, *The Complete Works* I—III, edited by R. W. BOND. Oxford, 1902.

Magno, Celio, *Rime*. In Venetia, 1600.

de Magny, Olivier, *Les Souspirs* ... par E. COURBET. Paris, 1874.

Marlowe, Christopher, *The Poems*, edited by L. C. MARTIN. London, 1931.

Marot, Clément, *Oeuvres* IV (*Épigrammes*), édition GEORGES GUIFFREY ... par JEAN PLATTARD. Paris, 1929.

de' Medici, Lorenzo, *Opere* I—II a cura di A. SIMIONI. Scrittori d'Italia 54, 59. Bari, 1913—14.

Molza, Francesco Maria, *Poesie* ... da P. SERASSI. Milano, 1808.

Montemayor, Iorge, *Ocho Libros de la segunda parte de la Diana*. Burgos, 1564. (Perez's *Diana*).

Ovidius, *Amores* a cura di FRANCO MUNARI (Biblioteca di Studi Superiori XI). Firenze, 1951.

— *Die Metamorphosen* erklärt von M. HAUPT ... O. KORN, H. J. MÜLLER, R. EHWALD. Berlin, 1915—16.

Palingenius, Marcellus, *The Zodiake of Life translated by Barnabe Googe*. With an Introduction by ROSEMOND TUVE. New York, 1947.

Petrarca, Francesco, *Il Canzoniere*, con le note di G. RIGUTINI, rifuse ... da M. SCHERILLO. Milano, 1918.

— *Le Rime*, riscontrate ... d'ALESSANDRO TASSONI, di GIROLAMO MUZIO, e di LODOVICO ANTONIO MURATORI. In Modena, 1711.

Philoxeno, Marcello, *Sylve*. In Venetia, 1516.

The Phoenix Nest 1593, edited by H. E. ROLLINS. Cambridge, Mass., 1931.

Piccolomini, Alisandro, *Cento Sonetti*. Roma, 1549.

A Poetical Rhapsody 1602—1621 I—II, edited by E. H. ROLLINS. Cambridge, Mass., 1931—32.

Propertius, *The Elegies*, edited ... by H. E. BUTLER and E. A. BARBER. Oxford, 1933.

Puttenham, George, *The Arte of English Poesie*, edited by G. D. WILLCOCK and A. WALKER. Cambridge, 1936.

The Return from Parnassus, or the Scourge of Simony, edited by OLIPHANT SMEATON. London, 1905.

Rime diverse di Molti Eccellentissimi auttori ... I. In Vinetia, 1545.

— *di diversi nobili huomini et eccellenti poeti* ... II. In Vinetia, 1547.

— *di diversi nobilissimi et eccellentissimi autori* ... III. In Vinetia, 1550.

— *di Diversi eccellentissimi autori* ... IV. Bologna, 1551.

— *di diversi illustri signori napoletani* ... V. In Vinegia, 1552.

— *di Diversi eccellenti autori* ... VI. In Vinegia, 1553.

— *di diversi Signori Napolitani, ed altri* ... VII. In Vinegia, 1556.

— *di diversi autori eccellentissimi* ... IX. In Cremona, 1559.

— *di diversi nobili poeti Toscani* I—II, raccolte da M. Dionigi Atanagi. Venetia, 1565.

Ronsard, Pierre, *Oeuvres Complètes* I—VIII. Nouvelle édition publiée ... par P. BLANCHEMAIN. Paris, 1857—67.

— *Oeuvres Complètes* I—XVII. Édition critique ... par P. LAUMONIER. Paris, 1914—60.

Rota, Berardino, *Poesie* I—II. Napoli, 1726.

de Sainct-Gelays, Melin, *Oeuvres Complètes* I—III, édition ... par P. BLANCHEMAIN. Paris, 1873.

Sasso, Pamphilo, *Opera*. Venetiis, 1501.

da Sassoferato, Olympo, *Aurora*. In Venegia, 1539.

Scelta di Sonetti e Canzoni ..., terza edizione I—II. In Venezia, 1727.

Scève, Maurice, *Delie*. Édition critique ... par E. PARTURIER. Paris, 1916.

Secundus, Joannes, *Opera*. Parisiis, 1748.

Serafino de' Ciminelli dall' Aquila, *Le Rime* I a cura di M. MENGHINI. Bologna, 1894.

Shakespeare, William, *Love's Labour's Lost*, edited by R. DAVID (Arden edition). Fifth ed., London, 1956.

— *Love's Labour's Lost*. A New Variorum Edition, vol. XIV, edited by H. H. FURNESS. Philadelphia, 1904.

— *The Merchant of Venice*. A New Variorum Edition, vol. VII, edited by H. H. FURNESS. Philadelphia, 1888.

— *The Poems*, edited by C. K. POOLER (Arden edition). London, 1927.

— *The Poems*, edited by F. T. PRINCE (Arden edition). London, 1960.

— *The Poems*. A New Variorum Edition, edited by H. E. ROLLINS, Philadelphia, 1938.

— *The Poems*, edited by G. WYNDHAM. London, 1898.

— *The Sonnets* ... with variorum readings and commentary, edited by R.M. ALDEN. Boston and New York, 1916.

— *The Sonnets*, edited by H. C. BEECHING. Boston and London, 1904.

— *The Sonnets*, edited ... by TUCKER BROOKE. London and New York, 1936.

— *Vita e Arte* ... col testo dei sonetti riordinati e commentati di B. CELLINI. Roma, 1943.

— *The Sonnets*, edited by E. DOWDEN. London, 1881.

— *The Sonnets*, being a Reproduction in Facsimile of the First Edition 1609, with Introduction and Bibliography by SIDNEY LEE. Oxford, 1905.

— *Supplement to the Edition of Shakespeare's Plays* ... I—II, with notes by the editor [EDMUND MALONE] and others. London, 1780.

— *The Plays and Poems by W. Shakespeare* ... vol. X, with notes by ... EDMUND MALONE. London, 1790.

— *The Sonnets Never Before Interpreted*, by GERALD MASSEY. London, 1866.

— *The Sonnets*, edited by C. K. POOLER (Arden edition). London, 1931.

— *The Sonnets* ... edited by M. R. RIDLEY. London, 1934.

— *The Sonnets*, edited by W. J. ROLFE. New York, 1883.

— *The Sonnets*. A New Variorum Edition I—II, edited by H. E. ROLLINS. Philadelphia and London, 1944.

— *The Sonnets*, edited by T. G. TUCKER. Cambridge, 1924.

— *The Sonnets*, edited ... by THOMAS TYLER. London, 1890.

— *The Complete Sonnets*, edited by C. M. WALSH. London, 1908.

The Shakespeare Apocrypha, edited by TUCKER BROOKE. Oxford, 1918.

"Shakespeare's Ovid", being Arthur Golding's Translation of the Metamorphoses, edited by W. H. D. ROUSE. London, 1961.

Sidney, Sir Philip, *The Countesse of Pembrokes Arcadia*, edited by A. FEUILLERAT. Cambridge, 1912.

— *The Last Part of the Countesse of Pembrokes Arcadia, Astrophel & Stella and Other Poems* ... edited by A. FEUILLERAT. Cambridge, 1922.

Spenser, Edmund, *The Faerie Qveene* I—VI, edited by E. GREENLAW, Ch. G. OSGOOD, F. M. PADELFORD, R. HEFFNER. Baltimore, 1932—38.

— *Minor Poems* I—II, edited by E. GREENLAW, Ch. G. OSGOOD, F. M. PADELFORD, R. HEFFNER. Baltimore, 1943—47.

Surrey, Henry Howard, Earl of, *The Poems*, edited ... by F. M. PADELFORD. Seattle, Washington, 1928.

Tansillo, Luigi, *Poesie Liriche*, edite ed inedite, con ... note di F. FIORENTINO. Napoli, 1882.

Tasso, Torquato, *Poesie* a cura di F. FLORA. Milano e Napoli, 1952.

— *Le Rime* II—III, edizione critica ... a cura di A. SOLERTI. Bologna, 1898—1900.

Tebaldeo, Antonio, *Opere d'Amore*. In Vinegia, 1544.

BIBLIOGRAPHY

Tottel's Miscellany (1557—1587) I—II. Edited by H. E. ROLLINS. Cambridge, Mass., 1928—29.

de Tyard, Pontvs, *Les Oevvres Poetiques*, avec ... des Notes par Ch. MARTY-LAVEAUX. Paris, 1875.

Varchi, Benedetto, *Opere* I—II. Biblioteca Classica Italiana. Trieste, 1858—59.

Watson, Thomas, *Poems*, edited by E. ARBER. London, 1870.

Wilson, Thomas, *The Arte of Rhetorique 1560*, edited by G. H. MAIR. London, 1909.

Wyatt, Sir Thomas, *Collected Poems*, edited ... by K. MUIR. London, 1949.

CRITICAL DISCUSSIONS

ARMSTRONG, EDWARD A., *Shakespeare's Imagination*. London, 1946.

BALDWIN, T. W., *On the Literary Genetics of Shakspere's Poems & Sonnets*. Urbana, 1950.

— *William Shakspere's Small Latine and Lesse Greeke* I—II. Urbana, 1944.

BATESON, F. W., *Elementary, My Dear Hotson! A Caveat for Literary Detectives*. EC I, 1951, pp. 81 ff.

BRADY, G. K., *Samuel Daniel. A Critical Study*. Urbana, 1923.

BRAY, SIR DENIS, *The Original Order of Shakespeare's Sonnets*. London, 1925.

BULLOUGH, GEOFFREY, *Narrative and Dramatic Sources of Shakespeare* I. London and New York, 1957.

CLEMEN, WOLFGANG, *The Development of Shakespeare's Imagery*. London, 1951.

CROLL, MORRIS W., *The Works of Fulke Greville*. Philadelphia, 1903.

DAVENPORT, A., *The Seed of a Shakespeare Sonnet ?* NQ CLXXXII, 1942, pp. 242 ff.

— *Shakespeare's Sonnets*. NQ CXCVI, 1951, pp. 5 f.

EMERSON, O. F., *Shakespeare's Sonneteering*. SP XX, 1923, pp. 111 ff.

EWIG, WILHELM, *Shakespeare's 'Lucrece'. Eine litterarhistorische Untersuchung*. Anglia XXII, 1899, pp. 1 ff., 343 ff., 393 ff.

FLEAY, FREDERICK G., *A Biographical Chronicle of the English Drama 1559—1642* I—II. London, 1891.

FORT, J. A., *A Time Scheme for Shakespeare's Sonnets*. London, 1929.

— *The Two Dated Sonnets of Shakespeare*. Oxford, 1924.

FUCILLA, JOSEPH G., *A Rhetorical Pattern in Renaissance and Baroque Poetry*. Studies in the Renaissance III. New York, 1956, pp. 23 ff.

GITTINGS, ROBERT, *Shakespeare's Rival*. London, 1960.

GUGGENHEIM, JOSEF, *Quellenstudien zu Samuel Daniels Sonettencyklus "Delia"*. Berlin, 1898.

HANKINS, JOHN E., *Shakespeare's Derived Imagery*. Lawrence, 1953.

HARRISON, T. P., *Shakespeare and Montemayor's Diana*. Studies in English VI (University of Texas Bulletin), 1926, pp. 72 ff.

HART, ALFRED, *Shakespeare and the Homilies*. Melbourne, 1934.

HELTZEL, VIRGIL B., *Fair Rosamond. A Study of the Development of a Literary Theme*. Northwestern University Studies in the Humanities no. 16. Evanston, 1947.

HOTSON, LESLIE, *Shakespeare's Sonnets Dated and Other Essays*. London, 1949.

HUTTON, JAMES, *The Greek Anthology in France and in the Latin Writers of the Netherlands to the Year 1800*. Cornell Studies in Classical Philology XXVIII. Ithaca, New York, 1946.

— *The Greek Anthology in Italy to the Year 1800*. Cornell Studies in English XXIII. Ithaca, New York, 1935.

ISAAC, HERMANN, *Die Sonett-Periode in Shakespeare's Leben*. SJ XIX, 1884, pp. 176 ff.

— *Wie weit geht die Abhängigkeit Shakespeare's von Daniel als Lyriker?* SJ XVII, 1882, pp. 165 ff.

JOHN, LISLE CECIL, *The Elizabethan Sonnet Sequences*. New York, 1938.

KASTNER, L.E., *The Italian Sources of Daniel's 'Delia.'* MLR VII, 1912, pp. 153 ff.

LEE, SIR SIDNEY, *A Life of William Shakespeare*. London, 1898. Fourteenth edition, London, 1931.

LEISHMAN, J. B., *Themes and Variations in Shakespeare's Sonnets*. London, 1961.

LEVER, J. W., *The Elizabethan Love Sonnet*. London, 1956.

MCNEAL, T. H., '*Every Man Out of His Humour*' *and Shakespeare's* '*Sonnets*.' NQ CXCVII, 1952, p. 376.

MILLER, EDWARD H., *Samuel Daniel's Revisions in Delia*. JEGP LIII, 1954, pp. 58 ff.

MUIR, KENNETH, *A Reconsideration of Edward III*. SS 6, 1953, pp. 39 ff.

NOSWORTHY, J. M., *All Too Short A Date: Internal Evidence in Shakespeare's Sonnets*. EC II, 1952, pp. 311 ff.

ØSTERBERG, V., *The 'Countess Scenes' of 'Edward III'*. SJ LXV, 1929, pp. 49 ff.

OGLE, M. B., *The Classical Origin and Tradition of Literary Conceits*. AJPh XXXIV, 1913, pp. 125 ff.

PEARSON, LU EMILY, *Elizabethan Love Conventions*. Berkeley, Cal., 1933.

PLATT, ARTHUR, '*Edward III*' *and Shakespeare's Sonnets*. MLR VI, 1911, pp. 511 f.

REESE, M. M., *Shakespeare, His World and His Work*. London, 1953.

RIBNER, IRVING, *The English History Play in the Age of Shakespeare*. Princeton, 1957.

ROBERTSON, J. M., *An Introduction to the Study of the Shakespeare Canon*. London, 1924.

— *The Problems of the Shakespeare Sonnets*. London, 1926.

ST. CLAIR, F. Y., *Drayton's First Revision of His Sonnets*. SP XXXVI, 1939, pp. 40 ff.

SARRAZIN, GREGOR, *William Shakespeares Lehrjahre*. Weimar, 1897.

SCHAAR, CLAES, *An Elizabethan Sonnet Problem. Shakespeare's Sonnets, Daniel's Delia, and Their Literary Background*. Lund Studies in English XXVIII, 1960.

SCHMIDT, WOLFGANG, *Sinnesänderung und Bildvertiefung in Shakespeares Sonetten*. Anglia LXII, 1938, pp. 286 ff.

SCHRICKX, W., *Shakespeare's Early Contemporaries*. Antwerp, 1956.

SCOTT, JANET, *Les Sonnets Élizabéthains*. Bibliothèque de la revue de littérature comparée 60. Paris, 1929.

SIEGEL, PAUL N., *The Petrarchan Sonneteers and Neo-Platonic Love*. SP XLII, 1945, pp. 164 ff.

SMITH, ROBERT M., *Edward III*. JEGP X, 1911, pp. 90 ff.

SPURGEON, CAROLINE, *Shakespeare's Imagery*. Cambridge, 1958 (American edition).

STEADMAN, JOHN M., '*Like Two Spirits': Shakespeare and Ficino*. SQ X, 1959, pp. 244 ff.

STIRLING, BRENTS, *A Shakespeare Sonnet Group*. PMLA LXXV, 1960, pp. 340 ff.

WOLFF, MAX, *Petrarkismus und Antipetrarkismus in Shakespeares Sonetten*. Engl. Studien XLIX, 1915, pp. 161 ff.

ABBREVIATIONS

Abbreviations of titles of Shakespeare's works are self-explanatory. Abbreviations of magazines and periodicals are given below.

AJPh =The American Journal of Philology.
EC   =Essays in Criticism.
ES   =English Studies.
JEGP =Journal of English and Germanic Philology.
MLN =Modern Language Notes.
MLR =Modern Language Review.
MP   =Modern Philology.
NED =New English Dictionary.
NQ   =Notes and Queries.
PMLA=Publications of the Modern Language Association of America.
PQ   =Philological Quarterly.
SJ   =Shakespeare Jahrbuch.
SP   =Studies in Philology.
SQ   =Shakespeare Quarterly.
SS   =Shakespeare Survey.
TLS   =Times Literary Supplement.